MICHAEL A. SIMPSON
is a psychiatrist and physician
currently working in terminal care, suicidology,
and research on doctor-patient communication
at the Royal Free Hospital Medical School,
London University.

PRENTICE-HALL, INC.
Englewood Cliffs, N.J. 07632

A SPECTRUM BOOK

The
Facts

A COMPLETE GUIDE FOR BEING PREPARED

of
Death

MICHAEL A. SIMPSON

Library of Congress Cataloging in Publication Data

Simpson, Michael A
   The facts of death.

   (A Spectrum Book)
   Bibliography: p.
   Includes index.
   1. Death—Psychological aspects. I. Title.
[DNLM: 1. Death. 2. Attitude to death. BD444 S613r]
BF789.D4S56   155.9′37   79-104
ISBN 0–13–299636–7
ISBN 0–13–299628–6 pbk.

Editorial/production supervision by Norma Miller Karlin
Interior design by Fred Dahl and Norma Miller Karlin
Cover design by Muriel Nasser-Bernstein
Manufacturing buyer: Cathie Lenard

A SPECTRUM BOOK

10 9 8 7 6 5 4 3 2 1

PRENTICE-HALL INTERNATIONAL, INC., *London*
PRENTICE-HALL OF AUSTRALIA PTY. LIMITED, *Sydney*
PRENTICE-HALL OF CANADA, LTD., *Toronto*
PRENTICE-HALL OF INDIA PRIVATE LIMITED, *New Delhi*
PRENTICE-HALL OF JAPAN, INC., *Tokyo*
PRENTICE-HALL OF SOUTHEAST ASIA PTE. LTD., *Singapore*
WHITEHALL BOOKS LIMITED, *Wellington, New Zealand*

To my patients,
who teach me so much;
to Tom Bass and Richard Velandi,
Doreen, Graham, Joanna, Celine, Rikki,
and many others,
with gratitude and humility

Contents

PREFACE   ix

ACKNOWLEDGMENTS   xi

1

THE END: AN INTRODUCTION   1

2

DEATH IS A FOUR-LETTER WORD   9

3

WHAT IS IT LIKE TO DIE?   28

4

LIVING MORTAL   55

5

LIVING YOUR OWN DEATH   78

6

LIVING WITH THE DYING   101

7

PLANNING FOR DEATH   117

8

CHILDREN AND DEATH   170

9

EUTHANASIA AND THE "LIVING WILL"   186

10

SUICIDE   202

11

GRIEF, LOSS, AND BEREAVEMENT   222

12

LIFE AND LIVING   257

APPENDIX   261

INDEX   273

Preface

There are far too many books about death, of course, for death is the worst-kept secret around. Yet there are not enough books about death.

There are always new books being published about tennis, cooking, and sex. You'll never be a better player, cook, or lover just by reading about it; but you'd like to think it's possible, so there's always a good market for such books.

The literature on death has become a boom industry of late, yet there have been relatively few genuinely useful or conceptually new books, and a great many merely exploitative and imitative ones. But most of the literature, except for the frankly biographical or autobiographical, has been addressed to the professional reader, to the helper, rather than to those needing help; the books have been relatively inaccessible in style and with a heavy bias toward theoretical rather than practical issues, or toward rhetoric and polemic rather than reason. Making a distinction between professional and lay readers is traditional, but rather arbitrary. With the rapid expansion of interest in the subject of death and of demand for services related to death and dying, the traditional barriers are not feasible. The "professionals" (at least the honest ones, and those still capable of doing so) have had to learn from their patients. We need to learn from each other, and this book is, simply, for people.

This book is intended for the general reader and the professional alike; for both will meet death and grief in their personal life, and both will be called upon to help others. It aims both to raise many questions and challenges and to answer some of them, while providing practical advice on how one may approach some of the many problems with which death presents us.

The book deals with the nature of death and its characteristics, and with the relevance of the continuing problem of defining death and recognizing its arrival; with the existing evidence on what dying and death are like; with attitudes toward death and the fear of death, and how we may cope with it. It deals with how you can manage your own death, to share the responsibility for treatment, and to maintain your rights as a patient. It warns of the risks of exploitation and how to avoid the terminal rip-off. It discusses the problems arising from living with the dying and from explaining and discussing these issues with children. A Family Information Register and Planning Guide, included (at the end of Chapter 7) to assist in planning financial affairs and the funeral, will be a valuable resource when a death occurs. Another chapter considers the problems of euthanasia and the ways in which one might limit the extent of treatments that prolong dying without improving the quality of life. A discussion of the increasing problem of suicide suggests how one might seek to help a suicidal friend and how to review the situation if actively considering suicide oneself. Another chapter investigates the ordeal of grief and how one can cope with it. There is an Appendix listing the most valuable books and organizations to which one can turn for further help.

Maybe they told you about the Facts of Life. Here are the Facts of Death.

Michael A. Simpson

London, Pretoria, New York
1977–78

Acknowledgments

Special thanks are extended to the authors and publishers who gave permission to quote excerpts from their works, including those from

the "Living Will," reprinted by permission of Concern for Dying, 250 West 57th St., New York, New York 10019 (Suite 831)

"The Christian Affirmation of Life," reprinted by permission of the Catholic Hospital Association

"Standards of Care," reprinted by permission of the International Work Group on Death, Dying and Bereavement

"A Patient's Bill of Rights," reprinted by permission of the American Hospital Association

1

$$\boxed{\mathfrak{The\ End}}$$

An Introduction

Death is a dying art. There is probably no time in history when we have had so many different paraphernalia, professionals, and personnel, so many tricks and technologies, devoted to the seriously ill and potentially dying person. Yet, in general, the terminally ill patient receives less personal understanding and comfort now than at any other time. We have become pretty good at treating diseases, and little interested in treating people. The patient, more and more, becomes merely the ambulatory carrier of the interesting tumor or the cunning biochemical problem, and less and less the unique and responsible individual he used to be. Whether or not patients are still able to make decisions and control the content of their world and their destiny, they are treated as the passive and incompetent recipients of other people's intermittent attention. They are not allowed to derive much sense of personal meaning and significance at the end of life; futility and impotence are the predominant experiences. It may become a matter of pride to those responsible for patients' treatment that they should die with their blood chemistry as near normal as possible and perish with their

1

electrolytes in balance. But there will be little peace at the end. Such "medical care" may be "medical," but I'm not sure it's "care."

The patients are given little help in learning to live with their disease; they are merely left to die of it. Little is expected of the family save that they should be appropriately appreciative, not too demanding, and that they should as far as possible keep out of the way of the health care team so busily striving for pathological excellence.

The significance of death has changed in our society. Institutionalized medicine has become so adept at attracting funds and at impressing us with its marvelous achievements that we have almost come to assume that death is somehow avoidable—if you pay enough money and if the medical team works hard enough. Many people behave as if death is, accordingly, always someone's fault, always due to someone's act of omission or commission. But in Medicine, cure is still a rather rare event. Medicine is the science of prolonging disease—and, if we're lucky, also the art of improving the quality of life while it lasts.

Mass death, megadeath, has become an inescapable feature of modern life. Not only are there more people alive now than ever before, but in this century more people have been killed by other people than before, over the course of many centuries. There have been 110 million man-made deaths this century, give or take a few million. Perhaps 46 million were by gun or bomb or similar hardware; perhaps 2 million by chemicals, gas, and poisons; and over 60 million of privation and starvation, a rather more economical technique. In warfare, as in hospitals, death has become less of an interpersonal event, and is more commonly delivered at a distance. Whereas killing at least used to involve a modicum of personal exertion and direct involvement, and you couldn't get much farther away from your victim than the other end of a sword, now you can push a button and kill ten thousand men five thousand miles away, with little more effort than switching on an electric toothbrush. We have lost, to a significant extent, the sort of shared public beliefs that convinced generations that war could be a fine, noble, clean, and heroic enterprise that created a better world. Now its wastefulness and lack of demonstrable benefits impress more people. To "waste" a person has become acceptable military jargon, and just another item on the neatly tabulated "body counts."

It has become substantially less practical to live for a cause these days, though much easier to die for someone else's cause. It was once acceptable to ride out on your white horse and do battle for a principle you had chosen to fight for. It's quite another matter to be fragmented by a bomb while sipping your beer because a member of the IRA considers this will convince folk of the quality of his arguments; or to be exploded at the airport because some Palestinian philosopher calculates that this will provoke understanding of his people's needs. One thing you can say for modern democracy: it has brought the privilege of political assassination within reach of the man in the street.

Modern communications have added to the confusion. In earlier times, you could be aware of your community's losses and griefs, and might come to hear of more distant disasters occasionally and intermittently. Nowadays, it is commonplace to share your breakfast with the news of hurricanes in South America, famine in Pakistan, and disaster in Nigeria. We have become sated with the images of death throughout the media. A child may see 15,000 deaths before reaching puberty. Yet we are oddly unfamiliar with the facts of death, for we still avoid its realities. The Cowboys and the Indians, the Cops and the Robbers, can always pick themselves up, dust themselves off, and appear again in next week's episode. We may have finally gotten around to telling the children the facts of life, but we still hide from them the facts of death, and tell them the grim fairytales that obscure without comforting.

And we have learned to live with the Bomb, almost without noticing it. The potential destruction of each one of us has become so ordinary that it is seldom discussed or seriously contemplated. We are threatened with more complete extinction than ever before. There used to be at least the possibility of surviving in some way in your works, or your children, or in the memories of others. Now you can be more thoroughly dead, for the Bomb could wipe out all those works, those children, those memories. It could kill History.

Just as we have developed unnatural childbirth as a highly technologized event occurring in special places, conducted by special personnel, with the mother and child quite minor participants (she sometimes gets the feeling that if she doesn't cooperate, they'll just go ahead without her), so we have developed unnatural death, which also occurs in special institutions, attended by special professionals. Between such episodes, we are allowed out to live, as it were, only on probation.

Dying is largely done for us by the old, tucked away, out of sight; or by the young who die by suicide, in accidents, in war, or with drugs. People don't die at home, as they used to. Increasingly, they die in hospitals and institutions, and many of the rest simply die too quickly to reach the hospital.

Anyhow, people don't really *die*—they "expire," "pass away," "depart," "pass on," "go to their rest," or even just "go to sleep." The dead body or corpse becomes "the deceased," "the departed," "the remains of the loved one," or "a beautiful memory picture." We don't simply bury them, we arrange for "funeralization," from "removal" to "committal." We don't do anything so crude as to buy and sell a grave, though we may admit that "pre-need purchase of memorial property" is a "wise family investment." Oh, yes: guilt-edged investment.

But death, like sex before it, has been the Great Taboo, the Unmentionable Subject. Only comparatively recently have we laboriously made the same discovery about death that once we made about sex: we have found that everybody else does it, and worries about it, and that it can be both safe and helpful to talk about it. In the first half of the twentieth century, during a period of unprecedented carnage, man spent his spare time diligently overturning manifestations of the previous era's taboo regarding sex. In the latter part of the century, amid relatively unbridled expression of sex, he's been beginning to demystify and find ways of coming to terms with its twin, death. Now, dying is coming back into fashion, though people have been doing it for years. Various groups and agencies, teachers and authors, have been moving into death with all the grim zeal of a property developer who's just found a new slum. The trend is now well established in several countries, though especially prominent and organized in America. Where death was once an un-American activity (in one fell swoop it threatened the rights to life and liberty and interrupted the hectic pursuit of happiness), it has emerged as an industry.

Assuredly, we used to be a death-denying society. That must be so, for I have some 400 books on my shelves and some 2,000 articles on file on the subject of death, and most of them begin by announcing that we are a death-denying society, and then congratulate themselves on challenging that denial. Death has been a very badly kept secret. There's far more being written and published about death than anyone can read or keep up with. The growth of the death literature in recent years has been a remarkable cultural phenomenon. Courses on Death Lit. have begun. A Thanatology Book Service, a sort of Death-of-the-Month Club, has advertised. Often repetitious audiotapes and videotapes are widely marketed, and even an LP record. Just as the 1950s saw the production of the first Sexploitation films, so the late '60s and '70s have seen the Deathploitation movie, usually with some beautiful young person dying talkatively from a nondisfiguring illness and promoted as a superstar. Special materials for children are available, including a Deathword Puzzle! (*20 across.* Too great a dosage may cause death—abbr. *39 across.* May the Lord have ＿＿＿ on your soul. *43 across.* American Medical Association—abbr.) *The Death 'n' Dying Coloring Book* and an appropriate range of T-shirts can't be far ahead. Death kitsch is upon us.

The Death and Dying Course, or "D & D," has become an increasingly popular elective in colleges, universities, and even high schools. Some of the courses are undoubtedly valuable, and undertaken by sensitive, responsible, and talented teachers. Others are produced by self-seeking exhibitionists.

A whole new breed of researchers, philosophers, clinicians, and educators has emerged, dealing with matters relating to death. The leaders in the field include some of the most brilliant minds of our society. It has become a new specialty, which some call Thanatology. It is a paradoxical specialty, for many of its leaders do not wish to become peddlers of a new superspecialty or technology, but seek rather to make themselves redundant, when society can return to healthier approaches to death; rather than appropriating a natural part of life and creating an artificial need for new professionals, they seek to make death "all right" again, and to give it back to the people.

These "Deathniks," as they have been nicknamed, represent a fascinating new academic phenomenon and share several common features. They are highly intelligent and creative individuals, naturally interdisciplinary by inclination, often qualified and working in two or more disciplines or areas of activity. They mostly have a great ability for word play and a taste for the creative and exploratory use of words. They have an above-average familiarity with, and ability to accept, their own gut reactions to the people and the suffering they work with. They are friends with their own selves, sufficiently so to enable them to make close, but not superficial, relationships rapidly. They're somewhat less judgmental than other academic or clinical groups. They are enthusiastic about the quality of human experience they encounter in their work. They all talk about the patients they work with as extraordinary, remarkable people. Nobody ordinary ever dies, it seems, and nobody dies "ordinary." They are like Charon—they guide people right across the Styx, but the person they're with gets out at the other side, and they come back alone.

Most of the leaders of the movement have been relatively restrained in seeking to avoid the development of strong personality cults, though there are one or two pop gurus who work the tear-stained lecture circuit especially assiduously and attract the Death Groupies. Most like talking about their work, but avoid exposing their patients to public curiosity, feeling that much of what happens between patient and therapist is both privileged and intimate, and that a quasi-therapeutic performance before an audience is, like sex, perhaps feasible, but just not the real act.

This avoidance of exploitation of the patient is becoming increasingly important, for it is not an improvement to replace necrophobia with necrophilia. The dying have come out of the closet, along with homosexuals, blacks, women, the insane, and the old, to become fashionable exotics. Terminal Chic has replaced Radical Chic. For many people, this curiosity is not the brave confrontation they'd like to think, but merely a new means of denial. The gross interest in other people's deaths, an awe-full voyeurism, can still be used to evade the personal reality of one's own mortality: as if, as long as it's happening to thee and to thee, it's not happening to me. The dying are now trendy subjects of study like Tai Chi or macrobiotic diet. They have become a sort of local extension of the Third World, of those who we have long neglected, and can now get our kicks out of patronizing. They risk getting trampled by the earnest students and contemplators flocking to their bedsides, as Intrusive Care invades Intensive Care. We have become voyeurs of death, as if the dying can do it for us, if we watch them closely enough. It used to be said, wryly, that if the rich could pay people to do their dying for them, the poor could make a living. In this decade, that prophecy has almost come true.

Hegel defined *history* as "what man does with death." What, then, does this say about us? Why has a society that is so widely agreed to have been "death-denying" become so curiously noisy about it? Why has death become so difficult for us? As has already been said, the nature of the processes of death has been technologized and taken over by professionals. The body belongs to the doctors before the technical failure called death, and to the funeral director thereafter. The simple domestic skills of how to deal with a corpse or one's own grief have become lost folk arts, like grinding corn. We have lost our traditional mooring-places in shared beliefs and rituals, and have begun to seek satisfactory re-placements. We are passing through a period of great social disor-ganization with historical parallels to the last period of similarly great interest in death, centuries back, following the mass deaths of the plague of the Black Death and prolonged wars, and coinciding with the breakdown of feudalism at the early Renaissance.

Then, too, there was a genre of books about it, the *Ars Moriendi*, the books of the art and craft of dying. In this book we will seek a modern equivalent.

Death used to be a door, albeit one-way, leading to a fairly definitely agreed-upon further existence. As traditional beliefs have waned, it is for many people today more like running head-on into a solid wall.

Each death diminishes us more grossly. We used to have a large extended family, and lived embedded in an active and communicating community of grandparents, uncles, nieces, and others. There was more support available when a family member died, and the loss was partly diluted by being but one of many. Nowadays we've shrunk more often to the nuclear family—husband, wife, and children—and even this is often reduced to the postnuclear family, with more one-parent families, one-child or no-child families, and single people. Each death diminishes us by more. You can no longer say that "no man is an island." These days many men are indeed islands, and each of us belongs to a smaller archipelago.

Much of the current flood of interest in and talk about death is counterphobic, like whistling in the dark to keep our spirits up. By and large, we're no more accepting of death than we used to be—it's just much more difficult to hide from it than previously.

This book will attempt to look at many aspects of death as it affects us all; to consider the problems that arise and discuss ways in which you can prepare for them and cope with them when they occur; to make some of the content of the professional and technical literature available to the general reader; and to help you find the resources you will need. It includes a Family Information Register and Planning Guide and lists of organizations, agencies, books, and other resources in the Appendix.

I will not adopt clumsy circumlocutions to avoid the appearance of sexist bias to the unduly paranoid reader. If I call the corpse "he," it's not clear which sex I'd be favoring, and repetition of "he or she" or of innumerable "peoples" and "persons" gets very boring. It creates new depths of sexism where none previously existed, when we have quite enough of the real thing to be dealing with without sparring endlessly over innocent words. Thus "he" or "she" will be used equivalently and randomly in the generic sense, apart from specific uses. Eventually, after all, death completely fails to discriminate between the sexes, or indeed on any other prejudicial basis. Death is the ultimate democratic process. I will endeavor to follow that fine example.

2

Death Is a Four-Letter Word

One cannot look steadily at either the sun or death.
—La Rochefoucauld

LIFESPAN

What are the facts of death today? The nature and circumstances of our death have changed dramatically, especially over the last century. Indeed, historical and social changes have overtaken our ability to understand, conceptualize, or interpret what is happening to us. In the United States, the average life expectancy increased by 28 years during the first 75 years of the twentieth century. At the turn of the century, the average lifespan for both sexes was about 47 years, whereas today a Caucasian man can expect to live 72.5 years and a woman 75 years (Shneidman, 1976). This is part of a continuing pattern. According to some estimates, prehistoric man lived an average of 18 years, dying most commonly due to the violence of wild animals and other men. People in their 20s and 30s would have been wise elders, and survival beyond 40 was rare. Longevity increased only very gradually over the centuries. It is estimated that the average life expectancy was perhaps 20 in ancient Greece, 22 in Rome, 33 in England during the Middle Ages, and around 35 during the early colonization of North America. In nineteenth-century Britain it had reached 41, and a temporary peak of 54.5 by 1915. It dropped to below 40 with the 1918 influenza epidemic. There was an even more rapid increase between 1937 and 1945, but from 1946 to 1954 the rate of increase slowed down considerably. By 1954 the average lifespan was 69.6, and by 1967 it was 70.2 (ibid.). Interestingly, in the most technically advanced Western countries, we seem to be approaching a plateau with regard to our capacity to increase longevity, at around 70 years—the Bible's threescore years and ten.

The improvement has not been due to dramatic medical "cures," but mostly to simple improvements in public health measures, sanitation, and immunization. Many areas have practically eliminated diphtheria, scarlet fever, and typhoid as common causes of death; and mortality from other major infectious diseases, tuberculosis, poliomyelitis, influenza, pneumonia, gastrointestinal infections, and the other childhood illnesses has been greatly reduced.

CAUSES

The changing pattern of causes of death can be clearly seen by comparing the ten most common causes of death in the United States in 1900 and in the 1970s (see Table 2-1). The leading cause of death in 1900 was influenza/pneumonia, responsible for nearly 12 percent of all deaths that year. By the 1970s, this was only the fifth most common cause, affecting more exclusively the old and otherwise frail rather than younger age groups, and accounting for only about 3 percent of all deaths. The second and third most common causes in 1900, tuberculosis and gastroenteritis, didn't even appear on the 1972 chart. Diphtheria, tenth in 1900, killed more than 40 people out of every 100,000 in the population. By the 1970s there were fewer than 40 deaths in the entire United States from this cause—less than one person out of every 5 million of the population. By 1972, the tenth most common cause was bronchitis/emphysema/asthma, replacing suicide, which held that position in the 1966 listing, when it was responsible for 10.3 deaths per 100,000, 1.5 percent of the total.

TABLE 2-1. The ten major causes of death in the United States in 1900 and 1972
(representative data from the first and seventh decades of this century to illustrate changes
in predominant causes of death)

1900

Order	Cause of Death	Percentage of All Deaths	Deaths per 100,000 of the Population
	All causes	100.0%	1,719.1
1	Influenza, pneumonia	11.8%	202.2
2	Tuberculosis (all varieties)	11.3	194.4
3	Gastroenteritis	8.3	142.7
4	Heart disease	8.0	137.4
5	Strokes	6.2	106.9
6	Chronic nephritis	4.7	81.0
7	Accidents	4.2	72.3
8	Cancer	3.7	64.0
9	Infants' diseases	3.6	62.6
10	Diphtheria	2.3	40.3
	All others	35.9	615.3

1972

Order	Cause of Death	Percentage of All Deaths	Deaths per 100,000 of the Population
	All causes	100.0%	942.2
1	Heart disease	38.3%	361.3
2	Cancer	17.7	166.6
3	Strokes	10.7	100.9
4	Accidents	5.8	54.6
5	Influenza, pneumonia	3.1	29.4
6	Diabetes mellitus	2.0	18.8
7	Infants' diseases	1.7	16.4
8	Arteriosclerosis	1.7	15.8
9	Liver cirrhosis	1.7	15.7
10	Bronchitis, emphysema, asthma	1.5	13.8
	All others	15.8	148.9

Adapted from Monthly Vital Statistics Reports, 1976, U.S. Public Health Service Health Resources Administration (Washington, D.C., U.S. Government Printing Office); National Office of Vital Statistics Annual: Vital Statistics of the United States, U.S. Public Health Service (Washington, D.C., U.S. Government Printing Office).

The major communicable diseases have been replaced by the "degenerative" diseases—heart disease, cancer, stroke; by diseases of pollution and the results of drug and alcohol abuse, including bronchitis, emphysema, and cirrhosis; and by other problems of personal behavior, such as accidents and suicide.

With luck, further improvements in medical technology may delay the speed with which we wear out, so we could remain somewhat healthier for longer; and we may be able to learn to restrain environmental and personal pollution, and to restrain ourselves from killing ourselves and each other so readily. But it is rather unlikely that we will increase the average human lifespan very greatly in the foreseeable future, substantial effort adding perhaps 5 or 6 years to the present 72 to 75. The quest for a much longer life also overlooks the fact that we have a very long way to go before we can begin to make the customary 70 years consistently bearable, let alone enjoyable and fruitfully creative. Do we have any clear idea what on earth we would do with much extra time?

Some would prefer to think that we will somehow contrive to avoid the biological inevitability of death. Everything else dies— molds and algae and bacteria, trees and hippopotami, goldfish, beetles, and horses. In such splendid company, why should we seek special exemption? As Lewis Thomas points out in his essays, flies don't seem to develop a wide range of intricate diseases to lead them to death: they just age and die—like flies.

Our lifespan compares favorably with that of most other animals. Camels manage 25 to 45 years, the hippopotamus and rhinoceros, bear and horse, 40 to 50. The ostrich usually lives around 50 years; the elephant can achieve 70. We are consistently outlived only by such as the eagle (104 years is estimated) and the vulture (which can live 118 years) (Maguire, 1975).

AGE

The age distribution of our deaths has also changed since the turn of the century. We die older. In 1900, 53 percent of all the deaths recorded in America were of children under the age of 15; only 17 percent were of people over 65. The proportion of infants dying has fallen from 150 to 25 per 1,000 live births during this century. Probably one-quarter of all the human beings who have ever reached the age of 65 are alive today. By the late 1960s, 67 percent of all deaths were of people over 65—1.5 million out of the 2 million deaths in America annually. It is expected that the number of people over 65 will increase from the 18.5 million of 1966 to 24.5 million by 1980, when they will form one-eighth of the population (figures from Shneidman, 1976). And still, many old people "live in the past," because they have nowhere else to live, having been evicted from the present and the future.

SOCIAL CLASS

When you die and how you will die depend in part on your social class. The classic example of this occurred when the *Titanic* sank, on April 4, 1912. The official casualty lists show an interesting pattern of death rates. Of the 143 women passengers in First Class, only 4 died (and 3 of these had refused to leave the ship). Of the 93 women in Second Class, 15 drowned. Of the 179 women passengers in Third Class, 51 died. Thus, according to the class traveled, the mortality rate varied from 3 percent to nearly 30 percent.

The poor show higher infant, child, and young adult death rates and more severe childhood infections, gastroenteritis, and influenza/pneumonia death rates. By contrast, the death rate of the white-collar middle-class person rises in middle and later life, as a result of heart disease, cancer, stroke, and other so-called "diseases of affluence."

In 1961–63 the overall infant mortality rate in New York City was 26 out of every 1,000 live births. But in the sixteen areas identified as poverty areas by low income and high incidences of social problems, the rate was 35 out of every 1,000, and the maternal mortality rate in childbirth was two-and-a-half times higher than in the city as a whole. The infant mortality rate was four times greater in areas of low-quality housing than in areas of good housing (figures from Goldscheider, 1971).

Another study compared death rates among groups differing in family income and years of schooling. For example, among white males over 25 with no education beyond high school, mortality rates were about 10 percent higher than among the college-educated; among similar females, the mortality rate was 50 percent higher. For nonwhite men and women, the comparable handicaps were 31 and 70 percent. Similarly, white males with incomes below $2,000 per year showed mortality rates over 50 percent higher than men with incomes above $10,000.

BROUGHT IN DEAD

Should you ever collapse, suddenly and critically ill, somebody other than a doctor will most probably decide not only whether or not you are dead, but whether or not you will live. And the factors that will be very important in deciding your fate are likely to include your age, your social class and appearance, and your sobriety. David Sudnow and I have studied a neglected category of death, the BID ("Brought In Dead") or DOA ("Dead On Arrival") (Sudnow, 1967; Simpson, 1976). There are two main ways in which you could be brought into the hospital when moribund. Those who find you and pick you up may classify you as "Cardiac Arrest" or "Suspended Respiration" or some similar label implying the need for urgent medical attention. Resuscitation attempts will be begun in the ambulance en route to the hospital. The ambulance will approach the hospital with lights flashing and sirens wailing. Usually, the driver will radio ahead, so that the hospital will be warned to await its arrival. Thus, on arrival at the hospital, a resuscitation team will probably be waiting, ready to pounce on you as soon as you arrive.

On the other hand, you could be be classified as a BID or DOA. The passersby who find you may assume you to be dead; the ambulance men may agree. You could be driven to the hospital more slowly, sans lights, sans sirens. On arrival, the ambulance attendants may walk in and inform the receptionist that they've brought in a DOA. The doctor may finish his cup of coffee before strolling to the ambulance, and, after a cursory examination, pronounce you dead. It's often tidier for everyone to leave you in the ambulance, from which you can be transferred directly to the morgue, rather than bringing you into one of the emergency rooms, which would have to be tidied up afterward.

Of the chain of decisions that influence whether you will be resuscitated or not, none may be made by a doctor. His will be the final task—to make the final diagnosis and to legally pronounce you dead; but the decisions determining your condition will have been made by others, and even the doctor's actions and decisions will be unavoidably influenced by the frame of expectation that has been imposed by the time he arrives.

As a "Cardiac Arrest" you are perceived by all as a legitimate and deserving person, requiring the most urgent and skilled medical attention available. You are a valid person, with a medical and social history, expectations and rights. It's very different when you're "only a BID." Though your name may be required for the records and the unavoidable official documentation, you will have acquired an unalterable social anonymity. To many of those who will now deal with you, you will lack biography and history; you will be as nameless as the stillborn child whose wrist name-band reads only "Girl, Smith." You will have added little sense of occasion to the events of the evening, which will have become by morning "a quiet night, only a DOA."

There may not, in many instances, be a major difference in the initial clinical condition of the patients placed in either of the two categories, but there may be other noticeable distinctions. A child may be brought into the emergency room with no discernible heartbeat, pulse, or respiration—quite classically dead. But she is likely to receive definitive and prolonged attempts at resuscitation. An aged woman with precisely the same clinical condition is unlikely to receive the same attention. However carefully phrased the definitions of death may be, they are not carefully applied in many instances, especially late at night.

There seems to be a strong relationship between the age, social class, background, and apparent moral character of patients and the amount of effort put into attempts to revive them. While working in a large inner-city emergency room in London, I discussed these findings with a group of ambulance men. "No, no," protested the senior driver, "we're trained that you must always pick 'em all up and treat 'em all the same." There was a pause. "Mind you," he added, "after you've been on the job a month or two, you learn how to do it *properly*." Our studies show what "properly" consists of. Generally the older a patient is, the more likely his tentative death will be accepted as fact. Over 50, certainly over 60, the likelihood of energetic resuscitation drops dramatically. No differences have been noted between the treatment of men and women, or between different racial or ethnic groups. Age also seems to determine how long resuscitation attempts, if begun at all, will be continued, and how much time and care will be spent on establishing that death has, beyond doubt, taken place.

Social class and perceived moral character also influence the outcome. If the patient on arrival smells of alcohol, especially if he is shabbily dressed or unwashed, he can be classified as "drunk" or "alcoholic," and more languid attempts at revival are often felt to be justified. The lower the apparent social class, the less energetic the resuscitation is likely to be. Other people can be at similar risk if their way of life is similarly perceived by the staff as morally reprehensible: the drug addict, the well-known prostitute, the vagrant and homeless, the sexually deviant (as long as your deviancy isn't one enjoyed by the doctor, it's deviant enough to be risky), the violent aggressor, the suicide, and those patients known to be rude, noncompliant, or particularly ungrateful.

The reverse will be the case if you are well known in a socially acceptable context. Famous people die as readily as the rest of us, but often take significantly longer to be declared dead, and may attract the most vigorous and persistent attempts at resuscitation. A prime and bizarre example was the treatment of General Franco of Spain, whose dying was greatly and unpleasantly prolonged. Ironically, the great and powerful may be denied the possibility of an unharassed death, which a tramp can at least be guaranteed.

Thus it appears that if you want to maximize your chances of being rescued from catastrophic illness—perhaps a sudden heart attack—you should strive to look as young as you can, dress well and traditionally, disguise your deviancies, and keep your breath fresh.

PLACE

There have also been dramatic changes with regard to *where* we die. At the turn of the century some 80 percent of deaths took place at home. By 1949, 50 percent of deaths occurred in a hospital; by 1958 the figure was over 60 percent. The present situation in both America and Britain is that 60 to 75 percent of deaths occur in a hospital, and the proportion is slowly rising (Shneidman, 1976; Lerner, 1970). The proportion of people dying at home has been falling, and the percentage dying in public places has stayed fairly constant. Most of those dying outside simply don't have time to get to a hospital, collapsing with coronaries or strokes or dying in accidents.

DEFINITIONS OF DEATH

But what actually is death? How do we define it, and how do we recognize it? The signs which the earliest medical-legal texts listed differ little from those generally recognized today. Breathing and heartbeat stop; the eyes no longer respond to light; there are no responses to stimuli (sound, touch, pain); there is pallor, and gradual color change in the skin; and eventually rigor mortis, a phase of muscle stiffening, sets in.

　　It was eventually recognized that these signs—as well as checking for breath with a mirror or a feather—were unreliable. There was especially great awareness in the nineteenth century of the danger of premature burial, especially during epidemics, when there were occasional documented cases of moribund persons being mistaken for dead and then buried, only to revive later—and too late. People used to order in their wills that before burial their death should be proved by surgical incision, or by application of boiling liquids or red-hot irons to the skin. Or they insisted that they should be "killed" once they had been pronounced dead—by stabbing, bleeding, or even decapitation. The idea isn't obsolete. A well-known celebrity confessed to me during an interview that he had a profound fear of premature burial and had left instructions that a "strong poison" be injected into him after his death had been certified. Many ingenious gadgets were devised allowing one to signal from within one's coffin if one revived, by ringing a bell or setting off an alarm. It was agreed that the only unchallengeable sign of death was the onset of putrefaction, and one of the functions of a delay between death and burial was to ensure that one only buried the thoroughly dead. In France at one stage, burial could not officially take place until twenty-four hours after the death certificate was signed. In some other countries, the body had to be left in a mortuary with an experienced inspector until unequivocal signs of decomposition had begun.

In fact, you die many deaths. There is the point at which your personality, your Self, is extinct, probably synonymous with *brain death*. *Somatic death* is the point where all the body's vital functions (heartbeat, respiration) cease. Later still comes *cellular* or *molecular death*, and all your cells die at different rates. Muscle cells, for example, will still be able to respond to electrical stimuli for some two hours after somatic death. Metabolism within the cells continues for a time, and in fact is necessary to produce rigor mortis—the well-known stiffening of the muscles following death. The more highly specialized the organ, the more rapidly its cells die after somatic death; the brain is especially vulnerable to lack of oxygen and nutrients.

A traditional American legal definition of death, written in 1890, is "the cessation of life; the ceasing to exist defined by physicians as a total stoppage of the circulation of the blood, and a cessation of the animal and vital functions consequent thereon, such as respiration, pulsation," and so on. This is clearly inadequate, and has been for some time, at least since we learned how to resuscitate people whose heartbeat and respiration have ceased. After hanging or decapitation, the heartbeat or breathing may continue for seconds or minutes. Is the beheaded man alive or dead?

In an attempt to improve and clarify this definition, Kansas and Maryland have recently passed laws embodying new definitions. The Kansas law (Kansas Statutes Annotated 77–202 [Supp. 1971]) states:

> A person will be considered medically and legally dead if in the opinion of a physician based on ordinary standards of medical practice, there is the absence of spontaneous respiratory and cardiac function and, because of the disease or condition which caused, directly or indirectly, these functions to cease or because of the passage of time since these functions ceased, attempts at resuscitation are considered hopeless; and in this event, death will have occurred at the time these functions ceased; or [a] person will be considered ... dead if ... there is the absence of spontaneous brain function; and if based on ordinary standards of medical practice, during reasonable attempts to either maintain or restore spontaneous circulatory or respiratory function in the absence of aforesaid brain function, it appears that further attempts at resuscitation or supportive maintenance will not succeed, death will have occurred at the time when these conditions first coincide. Death is to be pronounced before artificial means of supporting respiratory and circulatory function are terminated and before any vital organ is removed for the purposes of transplantation.

The law in Maryland (Maryland Sessions Law, Ch. 693. [1972]) is substantially the same, omitting the phrase "in the opinion of a physician." These are better definitions, but still inadequate.

Some patients who are rescued from impending death after cardiac and respiratory arrest are left with a dead brain, artificial ventilation by machine, and a beating heart—biological and technical artifacts. Since the cardinal features of respiration and circulation have become artificially maintainable, the important question has arisen of when, if ever, it is permissible to switch off machines serving no intelligence, when there is no possible chance of recovery. The Maryland and Kansas statutes lean heavily on the physician's opinion and the "ordinary standards of medical practice," without defining those standards.

Death of a cell is easier to be sure about. It is an irreversible state of absence of any chemical, physical, or electrical activity necessary for function and response to the environment. But, as we have seen, your cells die at differing rates. Brain tissue is especially vulnerable. Within seconds, certainly within minutes after circulation has stopped, brain cells will die and will never regain their functions, because such tissue cannot regenerate. The more developmentally primitive parts of the brain, those dealing with the control of breathing and heartbeat rather than thinking, are tougher and can put up with rather more deprivation. Thus you can lose all the brain with which you think, love, quarrel, and otherwise consciously exist, but continue breathing, as a "vegetable." Hair and nails, by comparison, may continue to grow for a couple of days after burial.

Brain Death

With the increasing ability and desire of medical technology to intervene in these processes, there has been a growing desire to recognize the person as dead before total death of every single body cell has occurred. This can lead us to ask: What is so significant to a person that its loss constitutes such definitive change in his moral and legal status? When the soul leaves the body? Well, we can't tell when that occurs. There is growing agreement that the significant point of transition is brain death—the irreversible loss of consciousness, of the ability to think, reason, dream, feel, experience, interact, and deliberately control one's actions.

There have been progressive developments and improvements in the shaping of definitions of brain death, by such groups as the Council for the International Organization of Medical Science and a Harvard ad hoc committee. The most recent version, prepared by leading British medical authorities, has been unanimously endorsed by the Conference of the Royal Colleges and Faculties of the United Kingdom and, in 1977, issued to doctors as an advisory document by the British Department of Health and Social Security.

The Royal Colleges propose the following criteria for distinguishing between those patients who "retain the functional capacity to have a chance of even partial recovery" and those for whom no such possibility exists:

The Diagnosis of Brain Death should be considered under the following conditions:

The patient is deeply comatose.
There should be no suspicion that this state is due to depressant drugs, such as narcotics, hypnotics, and tranquillizers, or to hypothermia [very low body temperature]. Metabolic, chemical and hormonal factors which could be contributing to the persisting coma should be excluded.

The patient is being kept on a mechanical ventilator because spontaneous breathing had previously become inadequate or altogether stopped. Drugs such as muscle relaxants must be ruled out as a cause for this state of affairs.

There should be no doubt that the patient's condition is due to irremediable structural brain damage. The diagnosis of a disorder which can lead to brain death should have been fully established. This may be easily and early established in such cases as severe head injury, brain haemorrhage, or after brain surgery. After cardiac arrest, lack of oxygen or severe circulation problems, and in other circumstances, it may take longer to be sure of the diagnosis and the prognosis.

Diagnostic Tests to Confirm Brain Death:

All brainstem reflexes are absent—for example, the pupils are fixed in size and don't respond to light, there's no blink when the surface of the eye is touched, and other relevant movements, reflexes, and responses to stimuli are absent. No movements of breathing occur when the patient is disconnected from the mechanical ventilator for long enough for the rising level of carbon dioxide in the bloodstream to stimulate breathing, if the brain can still respond.

The testing may be repeated if the results are equivocal. It is now established that electroencephalography [recording the electrical brain-waves] to demonstrate the absence of brain-waves is *not* required to diagnose brain death; though clear criteria are available for the use of this technique, it is more useful earlier, when the diagnosis is in doubt.

When all the above criteria are fulfilled, the decision to withdraw artificial support can be made by the doctor in charge of the case and one other doctor.

There are other patients in persistent vegetative states in which the cerebral cortex (the seat of thinking and the personality) is dead, but the lower parts of the brain survive, allowing the patient to breathe without artificial assistance. In this situation they can no longer function as human beings, but physical life can continue for months or years. They are not covered by the existing criteria for brain death which are beginning to gain legal recognition. They pose major problems with regard to ethics and the use of scarce and valuable resources, and some experts would prefer us to refine the criteria for brain death to include simply cerebral (higher-brain-function) death, irrespective of whether spontaneous breathing or a heartbeat remains. While this would most accurately represent the death of the person rather than death of the body, it would still present substantial ethical and logistic problems.

The definitions of death we have considered so far do not take into account organ transplantation, for the circumstance of brain death is common, while transplants are still relatively rare. It is thus essential that the clinical decision about death should be made on objective criteria, free from pressure from potential transplanters or recipients. The doctor's loyalties must be clearly, even conspicuously, undivided. One survey of public attitudes toward kidney transplants showed that over 80 percent of the people questioned had no objection to them, but many said that the reason they did not carry an organ-donor card was fear that organs might be taken from them before they were "really" dead and fear that people might not try so hard to keep them alive (Kastenbaum & Aisenberg, 1972). Wider adoption of objective criteria should ease these worries as well as enabling more useful transplants to take place. In general, as in British law, a person is considered dead when a doctor says so: the law does not usually specify exactly how he should arrive at that decision.

CRYONICS AND FANTASIES OF ESCAPE
FROM DEATH

Misunderstanding the nature of death has led to some desperate attempts to avoid mortality. We have seen the advent of groups like the Committee for the Elimination of Death (P.O. Box 696, San Marcos, California 92069), dedicated to "the conquest of 'the last enemy,' " and offering an "I Am an Immortalist" lapel button. "Death is an imposition on the human race and no longer acceptable," thunder the Immortalists. "We will continue to de-animalize our bodies," they tell us, "creating new durable attractive physiologies." "If dying is natural, then to hell with the tyranny of nature."

Similarly improbable has been the freeze-you-now, cure-you-later Cryonics movement. It is based on the proposition that people with fatal illnesses (who can afford the large costs involved) can be cooled to a state of "suspended animation"—after the certification of death, but perhaps hopefully before complete cellular death has occurred. Their blood might be drained and replaced with a special antifreeze solution (of "cryoprotective agents" like DMSO or glycerol) while, wrapped in aluminum foil like frozen food, they are first cooled to the temperature of solid carbon dioxide. This procedure currently costs around $3,000. Later, the corpse (often now called the "donor" or the "patient") is transferred to a storage capsule cooled with liquid nitrogen to several hundred degrees below zero, this procedure costing about a further $5,000. Annual storage costs are then around $2,000. Supposedly, at some indefinite time in the distant future, when the cure for the "patient's" terminal illness has been discovered, he could be thawed, revived, and cured.

Only to a very limited extent is the proposition plausible. The adult arctic beetle reportedly has been revived after freezing to temperatures as low as $-86°C$ for five hours. Some individual animal organs have been preserved and cooled for short periods, then returned to partial functioning. Some human parts such as skin, corneas, blood constituents, sperm, and bone have been stored at low temperature and been viable for later use.

In many other ways, the practice of Cryonics is extremely naïve. There is absolutely no evidence that the human corpse, even if stored indefinitely at a sufficiently low temperature, can ever be revived and resume any variety of normal function. To assert otherwise is pseudoscientific fantasy and wish-fulfillment.

Should this become possible at some time in the future, it is not especially likely that the corpses frozen now, before we learned the proper technique, could be revived. Even the experimental animal material so far preserved has not died of any terminal illness. This is significant, because the process of dying, especially when lengthy, leads to cumulative damage to many body systems (dying is damaging to your health). Also, the animal material has not been frozen for comparatively long periods. It is still likely that the formation of ice crystals within especially vulnerable cells would damage them, perhaps irreparably. But even if tissue revival were generally possible, there would be the problem that to have any real chance of success, the dying person should be deep-frozen *before* he is dead. Not only would this be illegal in most if not all circumstances, amounting to murder, but I can trace no one who has had sufficient faith in the process to volunteer to be frozen alive. If you are frozen after death has occurred—after brain death—then by definition your brain, your "you," will never under any circumstances recover. The prospect that for $50,000 or more one can look forward to a day, far in the future, when one's muscles might twitch again if subjected to suitable electric shocks, though one will never be aware of that dim pleasure, is a pretty pathetic and highly resistable vision of the future.

Attendant legal problems have never been clarified. What of the widower who remarries while his wife is frozen—is this bigamy? What happens when she's restored? What litigation will be necessary for her to regain her former property and rights? What of her will and the estate taxes—does she get a refund? There are other practical problems. If you suffered accidental nitrogen "boil-off" or other causes of raised temperature, your body would continue its routine (even if delayed) decomposition and would no longer be worth refreezing. If the payments are not kept up, you will, like some of the early "Cryonauts," be defrosted and buried.

Despite all the publicity Cryonics has received over recent years, little has been achieved. Almost all the early nonprofit societies have folded up, and the few surviving societies have grown far more slowly than they had expected. Interest in Cryonics may be cooling off, because not many people seem keen to join the self-selected few of this expensive and chilly elite, these cuckoo eggs in the nest of the future. It is very difficult to get reliable figures for those who have joined God's Frozen People. There are perhaps six corpses in storage in California; the brain of a 15-year-old girl is apparently also in "suspension," and at least sixty people have enrolled for freezing when they die. Of the earliest frozen "patients," few had made the necessary legal and financial arrangements in advance, and there were no sources of adequate funds to maintain them, so they are now buried in a more orthodox fashion.

Life Extension Magazine is published bimonthly by the Society for Life Extension, Inc. (663 West Barry, Chicago, Illinois 60657), and there are several groups actively promoting the development of the practice. The Cryonics Association (24041 Stratford, Oak Park, Michigan 48237; phone 313–398–5524), one of the oldest, publishes *The Immortalist* and has its own mobile suspension unit. Hartman Help, Inc. (Stuart, Iowa 50250; phone 515–279–6649) provides a Cryonics suspension service, as does Trans Time, Inc. (1122 Spruce, Berkeley, California 94707; phone 415–525–7114), which has five "donors" already in suspension; and there is also the Bay Area Cryonics Society (7710 Huntridge Lane, Cupertino, California 95014; phone 415–763–6642). Full membership and provision for freezing will cost at least $50,000, often through life insurance or investment trusts. Two payment plans are available: $1,000 the first year plus $70 per year thereafter, or $300 the first year plus $250 per year thereafter.

Other organizations in the field are: the ALCOR Society for Solid State Hypothermia (Box 282, Verdugo City, California 91046; phone 213–768–0414), the Manrise Corporation (Box 731, La Canada, California 91011), and the Cryonics Society of San Diego (4791 50th Street, San Diego, California 92115).

The other question that is usually ignored by proponents of Cryonics is whether you think it likely that at any time in the future anyone would want to unfreeze you and cure you and would actually bother to do so. Would anyone be anxious to uncan and unfreeze a 1970 vintage professor, or a 1980 model executive? We have never yet managed to provide really good medical care for a majority of the population of any country, and for the foreseeable future all the fruits of medical technology are not likely to be available to all of us. Is it justifiable to waste scarce resources on reviving people who usually have already had a full life? Many of the people who have been frozen or are likely to be are getting on in years when they die. They would continue to age after revival. What would we do when they die a second time, of their next terminal illness—freeze them yet again? Or do we store them all in the freezer until immortality has been achieved, aging conquered, and all diseases are curable? If so, it'll be a long, cold wait. Any future society, it is clear from present economic and ecological trends, will be fully occupied trying to care for its existing citizens and will hardly be able to afford to revive and care for a population of freeloaders from the past.

A much more practical concept, but one less likely to have general appeal, is the potential cultivation and harvesting of the dead. After brain death, the body could be maintained with persistent basic functions. One would have a cadaver, fully legally, personally, and spiritually dead, and with a dead nervous system—but warm, breathing, and with heart beating (with mechanical assistance), excreting, and requiring feeding, nursing, and haircuts. Dr. Willard Gaylin of the Institute of Society, Ethics, and the Life Sciences in Hastings-on-Hudson, New York, has explored the possibilities (1974). Such newly dead functioning cadavers, which he calls *neomorts*, could be maintained in body banks or what he calls *bioemporiums*. Medical students and young doctors could practice physical examinations, technical procedures, and operations on neomorts rather than on live patients. Experimental surgery techniques could be performed, and new drugs and vaccines tested very reliably and without risk to the living. Diseases could be induced to allow comparisons between different treatments. Organs would be available for transplant after careful testing of compatibilities. The neomorts could supply blood for transfusion ("like a saw-mill produces sawdust," in Gaylin's words), as well as several rarer blood constituents. Antitoxins and antibodies could also be produced by them.

Whereas "Cryonics" is psychologically attractive to some but at present technically impossible, the bioemporium is technically possible but psychologically repugnant. That the value of such a system would be far greater and of benefit to far more members of society is undeniable. It would be far less selfish than the Cryogenics fantasy. We have come to accept progressively more major varieties of donation, from blood transfusion through artificial insemination, through tissue and organ donation, to donation of the body for dissection. The concept of farming the recently dead is a logical step along that progression, yet one that seems more outrageous, more disturbing. Are our emotional reactions merely resistance to new and far-reaching possibilities, or will we have lost something valuable when we lose our revulsion against such technological proposals? Does our response stem, as Gaylin suggests, from "one of those components of humanness that barely sustains us at the limited level of civility and decency that now exists"? In our overzealous pursuit of existence at any cost, we can reduce those very qualities that make something worth sustaining at all.

REFERENCES

GAYLIN, WILLARD, *Harvesting the Dead*. New York: Harper's, 1974, pp. 22, 23–28.

GOLDSCHEIDER, CALVIN, *Population, Modernization, and Social Structure*. Boston: Little, Brown & Co., 1971, pp. 259–65.

KASTENBAUM, R., and R. AISENBERG, *The Psychology of Death*. New York: Springer Publishing Co., 1972.

LERNER, MONROE, "When, Why, and Where People Die," in *The Dying Patient*, ed. Orville Bruin, Howard Freeman, Sol Levine, and Norman Scotch. New York: Russell Sage Foundation, 1970.

MAGUIRE, DANIEL C., *Death By Choice*. New York: Schocken Books, 1975, p. 19.

SNEIDMAN, E. S., ed., *Death: Current Perspectives*. Palo Alto, Calif.: Mayfield Publishing Co., 1976, Chap. 3.

SIMPSON, MICHAEL, "Brought In Dead," *Omega*, vol. 7, no. 3 (1976), 243–48.

SUDNOW, DAVID, *Passing On*. Englewood Cliffs, N.J.: Prentice-Hall, Inc., 1976, pp. 95–107.

3

What Is It Like to Die?

Dying is like—nothing on earth.

Dying is like—the first day at school. It offers the unknown, the unexpected, a challenge, the next stage in growing up. We fear that we might not measure up to it, but we have to go through with it. People who aren't doing it themselves assure dying people that it will be all right, and we can see that many people have made the transition before us, and there are no sounds of moaning from the other side of the wall. We are very aware of what we are leaving behind, what we are losing, for we can see that clearly. We regret the loss even of people and things that were very ordinary, even those we never valued before now: we are not sure what, if anything, will replace them. We can bring nothing with us from the old school, except what we are and what we have learned, what memories we have built and what skills we may have. People who are close to us can come with us, but only as far as the gate—then we have to leave them behind and go on alone. All of which may make us feel pretty inadequate in the face of what may lie ahead.

Dying? It's the last thing I'd do.

Freud said that we are unable to imagine our own death, and

that even when we attempt to do so, we imagine ourselves surviving as spectators. "At the bottom, no one believes in his own death" he declared. ". . . In the unconscious, every one of us is convinced of his own immortality" (in Jones, 1959). He was wrong, but then he was himself particularly afraid of death. Certainly it is difficult to picture our own death and to believe firmly and steadily that it will happen. Similarly, it is not easy to believe that we will be senile, or that we were ever helpless infants. It is hard to imagine any state we have not known, so it must be hard to imagine the unknowable. Our consciousness and our memory are heavily invested in *Being*. We may lack models with which to imagine a state of personal non-Being, but that is because the concept is itself contradictory. Non-being is wholly impersonal—"I" cannot imagine "me" not existing, because the "me" or "I" we speak of here will not exist. It's like the old question which asks whether a tree falling in the forest with no one around to hear it makes a noise. The only "true" answer is that I don't know, because I'm not there. Maybe "no one" hears it. We could only experience death by being alive to experience it—so of course it must be, in that sense, unknowable.

Admittedly, the nature of death is uncertain, for, by definition, the dead do not return to tell us what it is like. One's view of what happens after death must be a matter either of belief (an intellectual assent to accept a particular account of what follows) or of faith (a trusting and hopeful relationship with the Deity or the universe, which need not be very specific), or a decision that one cannot decide, like a verdict of "Not Proven." But while we cannot readily experiment with death, we can learn a great deal about dying if we are humble and honest enough to learn from the dying.

EXPERIENCES OF DEATH

One's experience of death can vary according to one's relationship to it. It may be as Robert Neale (1973) and others have pointed out, (1) near and certain—any hour now, as for the seriously ill and incurable patient; (2) near and uncertain—very likely at any time, but it might not happen yet, as for the person who has had a heart attack or someone with a very dangerous occupation; (3) near and certain but averted—as for the survivor of an illness, accident, or other threat; (4) distant and certain—as for all of us not already in the first three categories; or (5) distant and uncertain—as for those who manage to convince themselves "maybe it won't happen to me." We would call these categories, for short: (1) doomed, (2) in peril, (3) saved, (4) mortal, and (5) denied.

Some of us have had personal experiences that teach us something of the nature of dying. I was reminded of this by one of my dying patients some years ago. When I returned to work after a severe viral illness, lips still cracked and bleeding, voice hoarse, and feeling very weak and rather brave for venturing out at all, I went to see Rosie, with advanced breast cancer. She roared with laughter when she saw me, then exclaimed: "So, Doctor! Now you've been doing some *practical* research on death and dying!" I realized that I had, indeed, and I have continued these studies. In our seminars, many students deny that they have ever been in peril, but after one or two of us have shared such experiences, many remember genuine occasions when they approached death. I have been trapped under fire in Beirut during the Lebanese Civil War (a very uncivil war, actually), and was once in a plane that was expected to crash. On both occasions, death was near though uncertain. The warfare was sufficiently interesting for me to be distracted from attending fully to how much danger I was in, and sufficiently long-lasting for me to organize some efficient denial. The plane couldn't get its wheels down, and we had to circle to use up fuel before attempting a crash landing. For an hour we sat quietly, flying quite low over the city. Looking out the window, I could see people going to the supermarket, catching buses—near, but too far away for me to be sure I would ever reach them. As we came in to land, I remember feeling cool and solemnly counting my pulse rate, thinking that it would be interesting to know what happens to the pulse during a plane crash. That meant I faced up to the fact that we would probably crash, but assumed that I would survive it, for otherwise neither I nor anyone else would ever find out what happened to my pulse rate. Denial is not an all-or-nothing phenemenon; in fact, one may even find it easier to turn away from some unpleasant aspects of the situation, by facing another part of it.

My closest approach to death, perhaps, was when I was attacked by a highly disturbed patient who tried to strangle me. He grabbed me efficiently from behind, and because I knew him to be a judo, jiu-jitsu, karate, and aikido enthusiast, I knew I had little chance of releasing myself by physical force. As he increased the pressure, my consciousness began to fade. There was a rushing noise in my ears, but I felt very alive, clearheaded, and alert. I seemed to be out of my own body, somewhere behind both of us, watching. I revolved between three mainstreams of thought. One, with a mixture of sadness, annoyance, and anger, was concerned with how much the patient would lose. His situation was desperate, but I had not yet begun working with him, and I was sure he could achieve a great deal. "But if he kills a doctor," I thought, "he's had it!" I conveniently overlooked the fact that I would also have "had it." The second line of thinking was a great swell of humor. Knowing how much I enjoy talking, it seemed a splendid irony that I should have to die speechless. "Damn it, Simpson!" I thought, "you'll get no famous last words!" The third stream of thought was a quiet mulling over of the question of whether there was, in fact, anything whatsoever I could do to save myself. It seemed very unlikely—he was strong, frenzied, and not thinking clearly. Any attempt at force on my part led him to grip harder still, and I had little consciousness left. I wanted to get through to him with something unexpected but nonthreatening, something that might just indicate that I meant him no harm. So, as I began to fade out, feeling as if I were falling headlong down a narrow grey tunnel, I stroked his arm very, very gently. (He said, afterward, that it puzzled him, and he let go to think about it. He was sure that a violent response from me would have let him finish the job promptly.) I recovered quite rapidly, and we later became firm friends.

THE LAZARUS SYNDROME

We are beginning to learn something of what the experience of death may be like from similar accounts from people who have approached it—especially from the increasing number of patients with heart disease who have suffered cardiac arrest and have been successfully resuscitated, the successors to Lazarus. Some such experiences are occasionally recalled by people who have undergone anesthesia.

In recent years certain collections of such anecdotes have been widely read, greatly overpraised, and misrepresented in their promotional material and reviews. They have been described as "exciting evidence of the survival of the human spirit beyond death," for example. They are definitely not that. Only a deliberate use of obsolete definitions of death could allow one to claim that anyone has ever returned to tell us what lies beyond death—by definition, death is just beyond the point from which anyone can return and tell us anything. But there is indeed a range of interesting similarities among the accounts of their experiences given by victims of accidents, falls, severe allergic reactions, drowning, suicide attempts, and cardiac and respiratory arrest. Those who have good experiences to report often describe several of the elements of the following composite account:

> I knew I'd died—my heart flopped in an odd way, and I knew this was the end. For a short while, I felt anxious and bitter. I could hear my own grunts as my chest was massaged, and the noise of people shouting and dropping things. I could feel myself being squeezed and handled and injected, but without physical pain. I heard them say "He's gone!" and wasn't able to struggle. I was no longer afraid. At the same time, I felt I floated out of my own physical body—as if I could watch, like a spectator, from above, while they worked over my body. I felt ambivalent—in a way I was scared they'd stop too soon; in another way I wanted to be able to tell them not to bother. I heard a loud, vibrating, echoing, buzzing noise, and felt as if I were moving very rapidly down a long passage or pathway. As I moved on, there seemed to be people who came to meet me and help me. I could recognize relatives and friends who had already died. There

was a tremendous sense of peace and love. I saw a sort of instant, vivid, brilliantly colored flashback of the major and most pleasant scenes of my life; time seemed to have stretched out so that a great deal could happen in an instant. There was beautiful music. I sensed that I was reaching some sort of border or frontier. Somehow, I was not allowed across; I had to go back. I didn't really want to return— the situation was so lovely I didn't want to give it up, and I felt irritated at having to leave it. But suddenly I found myself back in my physical body and regaining consciousness.

After such experiences, patients may say that they will "never fear dying again." These experiences seem to occur most fully, and in most detail, in situations where the person is convinced that his death is imminent. But when escape appears possible, then more of the phenomena are missing, much energy is devoted to mastering the situation and seeking escape, and there is far more fear. When the position is perceived as hopeless, the feeling of letting go, of passive surrender and acceptance, is usually experienced as pleasant or even joyful. The playback of previous experiences through life is combined with a sense of panoramic perspective, enabling one to review and comprehend one's life as now complete and meaningful, as if the question "What am I?" or "Who am I?" were finally answered. Time becomes greatly expanded, thinking quick and clear. There can be a sense of transcendence, of intuitive knowledge of the structure of the universe and of unification with it.

The similarities are challenging, though providing no evidence of the quality of life after death, and reassuring in their agreement about the general pleasantness of many encounters with death. Such accounts are not new or a recent discovery, but a recurring feature of scientific reports including those of Heim (1892), who collected the stories of men who had survived Alpine climbing accidents and falls; he stressed the calm acceptance, painlessness, time expansion, review of the past, impressive music, and brightly colored visions. Jung (1961) brilliantly described such an experience after his heart attack.

Of the various explanations that have been offered for these recurring features, purely physical causes are not fully convincing, because there can be significant differences in the physical and chemical states of the people concerned. It is, however, likely that many of the states share a tendency toward delirium, a state in which the brain and mind are temporarily out of contact with reality and more disposed to perceive images whose content is determined by one's psychological condition. There are indeed more convincing psychological reasons to account for these experiences, with a strong component of romantic wish-fulfillment; a variety of well-recognized psychological defense mechanisms would produce similar phenomena. It is intriguing that the experiences seem to depend more on how serious and hopeless the dying people perceive their condition to be than on any objective assessment of their peril. Better studies, with more careful and less biased collection and interpretation of the information (without the interviewer behaving in such a way as to suggest the type of responses he expects) and with cross-cultural comparisons, are needed to improve our understanding of these events.

The situation nonetheless is certainly not always so blissful for survivors as the recently popular accounts offering the "Joy of Death" might suggest, as has been clearly shown in several careful clinical studies. Some patients remain very quiet and passive, though cooperative, after resuscitation. For days or even longer, they calmly claim "I am dead." There is now no need to fear further pain or dying—for they are dead already. One patient explained that the flowers in his room meant that it was a wake and the visitors had come to view the body. Other patients reveal vivid hallucinations and delusions. During the time he was in an intensive-care ward, one man was convinced that he was in fact in another unit waiting for some routine investigations. Another stated that he'd seen his wife lying beside him, so he'd concluded that he was at home. Such delusions serve the function of allowing the patient to see himself as well or greatly improved, removed from the position of very real danger. Patients who have been in a coronary-care unit, surrounded by crises and the deaths of others, may insist that there have been no deaths and no emergencies in the ward. Some survivors describe an odd and unpleasant lingering sense of being "special," since their revival, and unlike other people.

One should avoid uncritically accepting at face value what people say about such feelings and experiences. Detailed psychological testing of patients who were recovering from coronary thromboses showed a major discrepancy between what the tests revealed the patient to be experiencing and what he said about himself (Cleveland & Johnson, 1962). Even though they might maintain an unperturbed front, they appeared to have intense and disturbing unconscious fantasies concerning death. Another study of male survivors of cardiac arrest describing themselves as tranquil showed that eight out of ten had dreams of violence, death, and aggression—for example, trying to defend oneself against a murderer, falling out of a wheelchair and being run over by it, automobile crashes, concentration camps, and shooting one's way out of the hospital only to be captured and killed by an evil nurse (Druss & Kornfield, 1967). Patients who had had coronaries without cardiac arrest did not describe similar dreams.

It seems, then, that the experience of death may not be uniformly rapturous; or at least that while the terminal phase of dying may be calm, pain-free, and even pleasant, surviving it is a profoundly disturbing experience.

THE STAGES OF DYING: FIVE OR FIVE HUNDRED?

Some years ago, Dr. Elisabeth Kübler-Ross (1969), a small, intense, and charismatic Swiss-American lady who had interviewed over 200 terminally ill patients, proposed a model that described five stages through which people pass in discovering and coming to terms with their death: Denial and Isolation, Anger, Bargaining, Depression, and Acceptance. The model became very widely accepted and used, often in ways that Dr. Ross cannot have intended. As a way of helping one to understand what may be happening with the dying person, it is useful. It has certainly been invaluable in encouraging people to seek to understand the patient, at least, and to realize that the situation isn't as simple as they previously preferred to think. Dr. Kübler-Ross stressed that it was a model for understanding, not a set of rules—that while most patients move through the stages in about that order, others omit stages, or move back and forth. But the stages came to be misused. They sounded definite, and nurses could memorize them. Offering the sound of security in such difficult circumstances, they were used with far greater rigidity than ever intended. Instead of being used as a guide to comprehending how the dying person feels and thinks, they came to be thought of by some as telling us what that dying person *should* feel and think.

Denial

Most people react to the first awareness of terminal illness as they respond to most bad news, with some variation of "No—not me! It can't be true—there's been some mistake, this can't be happening!" This could be a brief reaction, or it could last for months, involving much shopping around for second and third opinions, new tests and treatments, and poring over what everyone has said about the condition, scanning for clues that can be interpreted as meaning that it is not serious. It is usually a temporary defense or moratorium, but it can become elaborated into a complex system of evasion of reality. It is a defense that we may turn back to many times during the illness when we are faced with new aspects of the loss and when we need a rest from reality.

Denial may manifest itself in many different ways. The patient may deny that she is ill at all, or use curious euphemisms that avoid the point of the threat but stay close to it: "They brought me in because I needed a rest; I've been overdoing things" or "They just want to make sure that I don't have anything serious." Denial isn't an all-or-nothing phenomenon. One may accept the basic fact of being ill, but deny that one is seriously ill. One may accept that it is serious, but deny the diagnosis. One may accept the diagnosis, but deny that the condition is fatal. Even if one accepts that, one may deny that it bothers one at all, or ignore its implications and consequences.

Denial is often used as a general term to cover any sort of behavior that allows a person to avoid facing reality, to evade a painful perception or to keep separate from it, or to escape confronting anything unpleasant. Denial is an interpersonal as well as an intrapersonal act. Denial lies in the eye of the beholder. It may be found because the doctor is looking for it and expects it, rather than because the patient is truly denying. It is not a formless foam emitted by some psychic fire extinguisher, but a many-layered and complex mechanism. There may be, at some level, a *recognition* of the reality, followed by a *rejection* of the threatening part of it and its *replacement* by some more comfortable interpretation.

Dr. Avery Weisman (1972), who has contributed more to our understanding of denial than anyone else, speaks of *middle knowledge*—something between open acknowledgment of reality and utter repudiation of it—territory that many patients inhabit for varying periods of time. People may seize on pieces of ambiguous evidence that can be interpreted in ways that serve denial, but can subsequently be reinterpreted more realistically. "Well, I think if you don't get radiotherapy, it's not cancer. I hope that's right. I know you can get radiotherapy for cancer, so it's probably a good sign if you're not getting it," said one patient with cancer. Another, with a similar condition, but receiving radiotherapy, interpreted it differently: "I'm in for radiotherapy now. It's not cancer, it's a benign sort of thing that fortunately succumbs to radiotherapy." One patient felt sure that his very prompt hospital admission was "because they found it early, so they could get rid of it and cure me"; another felt relieved that he had not been speedily admitted: "If it was malignant they'd have had to get me in sooner, so it can't really be cancer."

The patient's denial can be puzzling for friends and relatives, who aren't sure how best to respond. The patient may begin to make quite unrealistic plans for a future he will never have, or express overoptimistic opinions about how successful therapy will be. At times, it may be dangerous, because he may ignore doctor's orders or refuse to accept treatments and take precautions that are necessary for his own good. Even when they have been clearly and explicitly told their diagnosis, surveys show that some 20 percent of patients who've had a heart attack or cancer deny the diagnosis and may even deny having been told anything (Bennett, 1976; Aitken-Swan & Easson, 1959). The process of selective inattention and selective perception can be unpredictable in its pattern. Denial isn't usually a permanent or steady state, and tends to fluctuate from day to day. So a person who can talk to you very realistically about her illness on one day may seem to know nothing whatsoever about it the next day. Doris, a Cockney taxi driver, spoke to me very clearly and movingly about her bone cancer and how it had spread to her brain, how bitter she felt toward her family who refused to admit that she was seriously ill, and how she wished people would talk more openly about it all. She asked if she could take part in one of my seminars, to get this message across to other people. She asserted that she would wear no makeup and, although her hair was temporarily falling out due to her therapy, refused to wear a wig. "Let them see me as I really am!" she insisted, "I'm not afraid of it—let them see that!" Because this seemed so important to her, I agreed that she should join our seminar. Two hours later she arrived. Her wig was wrapped with a smart silk scarf, and her makeup was impeccable. She launched into a glowing account of how she had been cured of cancer and how important it was for people to go for treatment early, so they too could be cured. She insisted that she was now entirely well.

It is not only the threat of death and extinction that drives us into denial but also the threat of helplessness, of humiliation, of the loss of whatever qualities we use to define our identity. It is used not just to avoid facing the disease, but to evade the loss of significant relationships. Thus the degree of denial doesn't fluctuate randomly over the course of time or according to how the patient perceives the information reaching him. Patients tend to deny more to some people than to others, according to the nature of their relationship and to how they expect each person will respond to what they say. When I went to see a 32-year-old woman whose doctors assured me that she didn't suspect she had leukemia, her first sentence to me, after I had asked her how I might help her, was: "I'm not so much afraid of dying, for myself, but I'm terrified about what it'll do to my children."

Patients may indeed ask nothing of some people, often including doctors and nurses, if they have reason to expect they won't get the response they need. These same professionals will then tell us that "patients never want to know." Recently, for example, a sociologist published a study of communication in a cancer ward (McIntosh, 1977); his need to deny the patient's illness was so strong that he convinced himself that most patients didn't know what was happening and didn't want to know, even though the conversations with them which he recorded and published indicate the exact opposite. Similarly, much of the routine, unsolicited "reassurance" most doctors hand out is for their own benefit, serving their own denial, rather than really for the patient's sake. Patients may often entrust their fears to someone unexpected—a medical student, a ward receptionist or aide, another patient, or a porter, choosing someone who may know what is going on, and is perhaps more likely to understand their concerns.

Since the different types of emotional reaction to the knowledge of one's impending death (especially denial) have been more widely recognized, there has been a great tendency to assume that denial must be a bad thing, and something we must change or treat. In fact, denial is a normal and an *essential* defense mechanism—one that enables us to turn our attention from the frightening, gloomy, and miserable aspects of our life to focus on the more constructive aspects of everyday living.

When it enables a person to live his life with the maximum available freedom and enjoyment, then the denial is healthy and should not be disturbed by amateur meddling (not even by professionals!). When, as can happen, denial is so exaggerated as to isolate the patient from his family and friends, then it may need to be modified to allow him to enjoy his relationships. Here, as in all aspects of terminal care, we must pay attention to what the person himself wants, rather than try to prod him into conforming to our own ideals or expectations.

Remember that the whole range of emotional responses to dying occurs among family, doctors, and other staff as well. I have seen far more instances of maladaptive and troublesome denial among doctors and nurses than I have ever seen among patients. If, considering any model of the stages of death, the medical team and family are out of phase with one another and with the patient, as is often the case, problems unavoidably arise. Care taken to coordinate our responses can be most valuable. All responses are contagious in a way. The patient is very likely to recognize and respond to your gut reactions to the situation, and if you are denying or hiding from reality, he or she will often join you in your hiding place.

Anger

When a person moves beyond denial, it can be replaced by feelings of anger, envy, and resentment. "My God, this *is* happening to me. But *why me?* It's so damn unfair! What have I done to deserve this? I can look out the window and see a dozen other people who merit it more than I do. Why not him? Nobody needs him! Why me?"

Such anger can be very hard for family and for doctors and nurses to deal with, because it is projected outward at any suitable target. The amount of bitterness may be great, but for the person to consciously link it to the illness itself could be too close to accepting the facts rather than rebelling against them. So it is rather less likely that one will hear someone complain directly and only about the illness, but more likely that he will direct the resentment onto the people and conditions around him. He may seem impossible to please—you are neglecting him, or visiting too often; the hospital food is terrible, the nurses rude, the doctors unavailable and incapable, and he's just not being properly treated. Some of these complaints become self-fulfilling prophecies, for people tend to turn away from the angry, ungrateful, dissatisfied patient. The nurses may become hard to get hold of, take longer to respond when the bell is rung; the doctors may become still more unavailable; the family may sharply reduce their visiting, dreading the inevitable scenes. Responding to this sort of anger by getting angry ourselves, by withdrawing, or by punishing the patient directly or indirectly is understandable but singularly unhelpful.

How can you best deal with the angry patient? Treat her with respect and with patience, control your own feelings, and hear her out. You don't need to agree with everything she says, but let her pour it out, because this helps to relieve her feelings. Some of the anger may be an exaggerated response to a perfectly legitimate complaint which you may be able to alleviate. Don't patronize her, and don't keep telling her to control herself and stop being angry. You may well agree that you yourself would feel angry in her position. You may become upset at how unfair it is for her to be angry at you—you, who are trying so hard to help her. What a perfect reflection of her own resentment! You may be serving as a lightning rod, attracting and collecting all the fury generated by many other incidents, great and small, But like a lightning rod, you may help to draw it away to earth and reduce the charge.

The most common type of anger response is that shown by Tom. Aged 31, with liver cancer, he had three small children, the youngest only three. He was not fearful of his own death, but furious that he should be prevented from looking after his children and his wife. "Why me? There are so many men out there that nobody needs—that nobody has ever needed—why not them?" he asked. We were soon able to work through this, and when he died two weeks later, it was with great calm and dignity. The night before, we talked for a while, exchanged a couple of wry jokes about the ward, and said goodbye.

Occasionally, the anger can be all-consuming. Joan was urgently referred from the radiotherapy clinic. She had breast cancer, and stormed into my room incandescent with rage. Her husband, whom she'd bitten several times, was reduced to holding his hands out to me saying, "Look what she's done!" I was assured by all who accompanied her that she'd kill herself or him before the night was out. But after I'd listened calmly for a while, she stopped and smiled: "Do you know? I've got that bastard scared of me for the first time in his little life!" She explained that she knew well that cancer was caused by stress, and her husband had caused her stress, so she blamed him for her cancer. It took more than a month before she was able to get beyond her anger.

Bargaining

Less frequently seen in a clear and obvious form, but poignant at times, is the phase of bargaining. It's rather like saying, "OK, so it is happening to me. But can't we be reasonable about this? Let's sit down and talk about it—surely if I'm a good husband/wife/Christian/patient, you can let me go? I'll be good." Or a patient says: "Yes but ... I'll go, of course, but first let me just finish what I'm doing. Just one more time." Rich, 19 and suffering from the same variety of leukemia that had killed his mother six years earlier, talked readily about his disease and the results of his blood tests, then said: 'I was so stupid to leave school early. *My* kids are going to go to the university." He doesn't have any children, and isn't likely to, but he'd like to be able to do something about that before he goes. It is a phase of negotiating with reality, exploring to see if one can improve the terms and conditions of the contract. Many of the contracts are made with God or with "fate" and are not revealed to anyone else. It is a process also related to deciding what one values in one's life, as one prepares to leave—but not just yet.

Depression

A phase of depression and sadness is very understandable and natural. When you consider how you feel when you lose a loved one, you can perhaps understand how the dying person feels, when preparing to lose everyone she ever loved, to lose all her possessions, and her future, and all that she had ever hoped to do and to be. Though it is an undeniably sad situation, and the person may initially seem inconsolable, we may help again by allowing her to express her feelings freely, to weep when she wishes, and simply to reflect our understanding (or our attempts to understand) and our compassion. This is another phase which the family and medical attendants may find upsetting. Yet if they withdraw, the conclusion that "no one understands and no one cares" may be inescapable. There are so many losses to try to accept—loss of prospects, of functions, of body parts, of appearance; and the depression is a preparatory grief, accommodating to all the loss, present and to come.

As Weisman has said: "People die to many things before they die, at last, from a disease" (1972). Guilt is also common, and self-blame. One study found that 93 percent of patients with cancer felt guilt—"It's all my fault!" They tended to attribute the cause of their illness to their own sins (sexual or aggressive, real or exaggerated), or to accidents and falls.

The phase of "normal depression" doesn't need treatment with antidepressant drugs. One shouldn't overlook the fact that dying people, especially those who have had emotional illnesses in the past, may indeed have typical depressive illness and anxiety states as well as their major disease, and such depressions and anxieties can respond well to appropriate treatment in their own right. Some of the depression takes the form of sadness and withdrawal, and may be more readily comforted with silent companionship—the holding of a hand—than by conversation.

Acceptance

If there is enough time and especially if there has been suitable help available, a stage of calm acceptance can be reached which is beyond anger, envy, and sorrow. The patient can then contemplate his imminent end quietly and peacefully, not with bitter resignation, but accepting what will happen. It is not necessarily happy, either, and may be relatively free of strong feelings. The separation from the rest of us is almost complete. "When Death comes," said one patient, "I'll just say, 'What kept you so long?' I'm ready to go."

One can be perfectly willing to die without explicitly hoping or wanting to die, and this is an important distinction to recognize. Too often it is assumed that one must be suicidal or "mad" to be willing to die. Once again, Weisman has phrased it especially well when he says: "Only someone who is extremely apprehensive himself would fail to see that many dying patients accept death with equanimity" (1972). Stewart Alsop, the journalist who wrote about his own experiences with leukemia (1973), said: "A dying man needs to die, as a sleepy man needs to sleep, and there comes a time when it is wrong, as well as useless, to resist."

THE FIVE HUNDRED STAGES OF DYING

It is essential to realize what one can and can't do with the "five stages." They are by no means as clear-cut or as universal as they are too often assumed to be. Kübler-Ross' model describes five perfectly normal and relatively common types of response to any significant loss. While they quite often occur in more or less the sequence described, they can occur in any order, disappear and recur even in the course of one conversation, and may at times even seem to be present simultaneously. There are not five stages—there are three, fifteen, ninety-two, and five hundred. Though often seen, they are not—except probably for some variety of denial—*necessary* stages. They are very complex patterns of states of knowing and of emotional response, varying in whether they last moments or weeks and firmly embedded in the person's personality and his approach to life. The movement doesn't flow in one irresistible stream toward acceptance. There is often marked fluctuation, especially with retreats to denial. The patient can rivet you with absolutely open and clear acknowledgment of the nearness of death, and the next day talk about totally unrealistic and impossible plans for the future. The variance is merely the surface sign of deeper debate within, of the shifting balances between knowing and needing not to know.

Overriding any model is the person's tendency to die in style—with the personal style typical of his way of life. He may die angrily, or noisily, or melodramatically, or spitefully, if he will. Those who have rarely expressed their emotions can die taciturn. Maureen, an actress—expressive and flamboyant—did it her own way. She treated Death like an impatient and unreasonable agent whose contract had no escape clause. Accordingly, she'd go if he insisted, but was damned if she'd abandon her usual style. She greeted me each ward round with "Darling! *Do* have a whisky! Why ever not?" She prepared for her new role with panache. ("You may not think it's much of a part, darling," I assured her, "but it'll run for *ages!*") She was the center of attention when she died, dead drunk, after a cheerful and amusing afternoon, scandalizing some other people's visitors. It was unexpected in its timing—she could never quite resist jumping her cue if it would steal the scene. A sudden exit, Stage Left.

We must not seek to compel people to conform to our norms and die a quiet, tidy death for our sake. At long last there is a slow reversal in the process poet Rainer Maria Rilke noticed earlier in this century, declaring that the desire for a death of one's own was growing increasingly rare, as was the freedom to live a life of one's own. "We die as best we can; we die the death that belongs to the disease from which we suffer," he complained. In hospitals, people "die from one of the deaths assigned to the institution: that is regarded very favourably."

Even here, we must avoid oversimplifying. People don't really die as they live, for they may live on a plateau of triviality. Their behavior during dying is more likely to resemble their behavior during previous periods of threat, crisis, and failure.

THE QUALITY OF LIFE BEFORE DEATH

While most unpleasant symptoms accompanying terminal illness can be controlled by skilled medical care, they are usually not dealt with properly, because most doctors and nurses have never learned how to do so. Physical symptoms are inadequately treated. In several studies of terminal illness (Hinton, 1963; Rees, 1972; Simpson, 1976), it has been found that over 50 percent of patients had unrelieved pain, some 26 percent were in severe or very severe pain, and 16 percent were in continuous distress. This is unnecessary, for the pain could be controlled in almost every case by the proper use of drugs and techniques available for some years.

The sociologist Ann Cartwright and her colleagues made a detailed study of life before death (Cartwright et al., 1973). They found that many people suffered symptoms for which they did not seek advice or help. Over half of those with loss of bladder control or an unpleasant smell, two-fifths of those with depression, and a quarter of those with loss of bowel control didn't seek help. They either felt too embarrassed to do so or were sure that there was nothing that could be done about it. The old were especially likely to give up.

Three-quarters of those who stayed out of the hospital needed help at home during their last year. There were inadequate community services to provide help and poor coordination of such services as did exist. Most of the nursing, night and social care, and housework had to be dealt with by relatives—the spouse, the children, the sisters of the unmarried. Once a relative had begun to look after someone, he or she did not seem to get relieved, or to get any further help from other relatives or friends, however long the need for care persisted.

Untreated Symptoms

Of those with distressing symptoms during the last year of life (69 percent of them, overall, regarded as being *very* distressing), 66 percent suffered pain, 49 percent sleeplessness, 32 percent loss of bladder control, 28 percent loss of bowel control, 15 percent unpleasant smell, 30 percent nausea and vomiting, 48 percent loss of appetite, 28 percent constipation, 16 percent bedsores, 36 percent mental confusion, 45 percent trouble with breathing, and 36 percent depression (Ibid.).

The reasons for this sad state of affairs lie partly in the fact that the professional staff have not received proper training in symptom control. Wise use of drugs can control most of these symptoms. Too often management of the symptom is not attempted; if it is, problems may arise because a too-short-acting drug is used, or it is used too seldom, or in too small a dose. Staff may be afraid the patient will become "addicted" to powerful pain-killers. So what? It wouldn't matter in the least if he did, though in fact he need not become addicted. True addiction needs a certain type of personality using the drug under certain circumstances for certain reasons. Some patients may become very insistent, demanding their injections—when they are being given too little analgesic too seldom. Craving for relief of pain is not addiction. Such analgesic drugs are often prescribed "p.r.n." or "s.o.s.," technically allowing the nurses to give the drug as often as it is needed up to a certain stated maximum dose. This is disastrous, usually meaning patients can have a dose every time they can catch the nurse's attention and convince her that they are suffering "enough." Patients will often be asked how bad their pain is. That's very hard to answer—how does one measure pain? How bad is it "supposed" to be? For some reason, people often suggest that the patient should try to bear his or her pain and to use as little analgesia as possible. Rubbish! Such beliefs are pure and unjustifiable cruelty. Or nurses may try to argue that because the patient has had the usual or standard dose of pain-killer, he or she has had "enough." They may even try to argue with patients to convince them that they are not in pain. Pain is what you have when you say you are in pain, and it should be relieved. The only "right" dose of pain-killer is enough to abolish the pain. Patients should never have to accept less-than-adequate pain control. Unrelieved pain damages every other aspect of life and relationships; pain is useless once the patient's diagnosis and condition are known.

Analgesic drugs should be given in adequate and regular doses, such as every four hours, in amounts sufficient to get rid of the pain and keep it away, till the patient has lost both the pain and the fear and memory of it. All other symptoms, including hiccoughs, dry mouth, diarrhea, and itch, should be properly treated. Technical details are readily available to any doctor who tries to find them. Most of these symptoms can be well controlled if only doctors would pride themselves as much on achieving this as they already pride themselves on the pursuit of elusive cures. The old idea of the "death agony" is generally very inaccurate. Suffering can be eliminated in practically every case, and reduced in all. Many people lapse into coma before they die, and so really do "die in their sleep." As their various organs and body systems begin to fail, toxic substances that would ordinarily be metabolized or excreted build up and lead into coma.

Some years ago, after an English poet laureate died at the home of friends, one of them was quoted as saying: "We wanted him to die in peace, not in hospital." Those don't have to be alternatives.

GETTING RID OF THE BODY

Death is a social disease, like VD. It is not polite, not well-mannered. When a death occurs in a public institution like a hospital, one of the problems that arises is how to dispose of the body in a seemly and proper fashion. This provides a very clear illustration of the extent to which death, and the body, are an embarrassment and a threat to hospital and medical staff. Ostensibly, great care is taken to avoid upsetting the other patients and relatives, but they are often familiar with the true facts and upset by the subterfuge that is designed to avoid upsetting the medical and nursing staff.

Let us examine a typical occasion. Mrs. D. was ill for some months, and her condition rapidly deteriorated in the last week before she died. She was barely conscious for the last thirty-six hours. The curtains had been kept closed about her bed during most of this time, and the moment of her death was not witnessed. After it had been noticed and the intern had arrived and confirmed it, the nurses dealt with the preparation and laying out of the body. When they were ready to have the body removed, they called the mortuary porters and began to prepare the ward. They pulled the curtains around every other bed in the open ward. The doors to all single rooms were closed. This is the only occasion on which this happens, and after a short while on the ward most patients know just what it means. Patients were asked to stay at their beds. A nurse checked in the bathrooms and lounge to be sure no one might walk in at the wrong moment. The ward on the opposite side of the corridor was warned—and its nurses put a screen across the entrance to their ward and made sure that no one left the ward until the removal was completed.

Finally, two porters arrived with the mortuary trolley. Sometimes, especially very late at night when no onlookers are expected, the porters may use an ordinary trolley and sheet, or one of the older "concealment" models, with a hooped metal and canvas top to hide its occupant, often called the "covered wagon." In some pediatric departments, a child's body may be removed in a laundry cart. But modern technology has provided a more sophisticated vehicle, the *concealment trolley*. The porters pushed in what

looked like an ordinary trolley. However, when they reached the
bedside, they removed the blanket and pillow—and the whole top
of the trolley swiveled over to reveal a narrow stretcher down
between the wheels. Mrs. D. was placed on the stretcher, the top
swung back, and the blanket and pillows were replaced. The lady
had vanished. An "empty" trolley was ready to leave the ward,
which could then return to its normal activity—with an empty bed.
Most ward inhabitants would realize that a death had taken place,
for it was made quite obvious. But they would also have received a
clear message that no death had occurred, that nothing at all had
happened. The implied message is that death is too horrible for
them to be able to see, that it must be covered and secret and they
must not talk about it. Death has been made socially invisible and
psychologically obscene.

JOANNA

In the early 1970s I made a BBC television program which discussed the way the dying are treated and how the situation could
be improved. It was a sign of the times that the TV authorities
anticipated complaints for having discussed such a subject, and
they had their switchboard specifically staffed to handle calls of
complaint. None were received, but among the letters we received
was one from a lady doctor dying of severe heart disease in the
north of Scotland. We began a correspondence in which she shared
her thoughts and feelings with me and expressed the hope that I
could use them in my teaching. It was a painful effort for Joanna to
write at all; some days the effort was too great, on other days she
wrote several pages. Periodically, I received a small bundle in the
mail, with her notes written over the course of some months.
Then, with no warning, a continued silence, and her death. What
follows are extracts from the correspondence, for she was anxious
to share her beliefs and experiences with us. They are a painfully
honest account of what dying, too often, may be like—an experience that could have been very different.

There are so many things for the doctor to learn: How to keep hopelessness at bay, when there is no hope; how to keep the silent courage alive, to make it fly the flag of acceptance with a kind of pride that will allow self-respect and dignity (all that is left); to make it simple—truth, sincerity, no drama, no false cheerfulness, but equally important, no overplayed sympathy.

During the years since I could be called "doctor," I have learned many things. I have learned most from being a patient. If I could think that I could add one grain to your knowledge to pass on to others, my uselessness now would be that bit easier to cope with.

I have no fear of Death itself, but how long can I bear the dying? To be useless, and lonely to the point of agony, that's the fear. I know I'm going down and there is no return. But before this time, I was never bitter. Due to my illness, I have, perforce, to spend my time alone, as I can't go out alone; and the loneliness is devastating. I know that my face has turned to the wall; my uselessness is cruel. I loved my work, and being no longer of any use to anyone is bitter, above all.

Physically, I suffer badly: even turning over in bed makes me struggle for breath. The change in my appearance offends me. I know, though, that if I am presented with a mental challenge, I will for a time put aside the physical effects I know to be irreversible. I will pay dearly for that mental effort later, but for that little while I am nearly *alive* again; that's why writing to you helps.

The loneliness is still the worst thing to bear, so far. Total isolation, cold, still, far away from the world now, and encompassed in this silence. I am looking back to that world I used to live in, and observing everything going on normally out there. There is no emotion in that silent steady drop of ice. But where am I? Where am I going? I don't know, I hardly even care.

My idea of an after-life is perfectly simple. Something of myself may go on in the children I have worked with and for; if I have furthered learning in any way, in any sphere, that small crumb may go forward. That's all.

But I had hoped that pre-death would be short. That would be in character, the quick coronary disaster and immediate death—that would be correct. I was always "quick," in all ways. It is very *out of character* for me to take so long, to wait for an indefinite period, a burden to all—that's what I resent and regret most. Justice? I become angry when I hear of a young wife killed in an accident or a young mother dying in childbirth. And I, useless and having had a life, continue to use up precious oxygen. Were this an industry, my opinion of the Manager would be low indeed.

My loneliness may be hard to bear, but who would want to visit such a misery? Those who are well can only enjoy *fun*, it seems. Visits impelled by a sense of duty have now dwindled away. Gregarious by nature, it was usually I who was the visitor to cheer up an invalid. They're busy; maybe they want to come, but they can't find the time. I don't blame them for that—life must go on, and each must find his own priorities. I wouldn't have believed it, but this time I am bitter, quite against my own nature. I feel deserted, grumbling and resentful over being so useless.

My new General Practitioner doesn't help. How dangerous the inexperience of a young doctor is—book perfect, he has no clinical sense. I am in continuing pain, but I am non-curable, and so of no interest to him. He comes every 13 weeks, as he needs to sign my certificates then. I don't see him between times.

The mornings are terrible; my spirits are at lowest ebb then. For the first half-hour, I have to hold on hard to myself, and try not to pray, yet, for death. I am easily irritated. I can be snarly and unkind, and then I break my heart with regret over having been so. I am different now. I know and hate the sight of myself now. And I do not want my friends to see me. But yet I long to see them.

I am very misleading. I phone people from my bed and chat in a strong voice. I write to people only when I'm feeling most cheerful. How can anybody know how I feel, when I so deliberately choose my timing? I can hardly bear my loneliness, but I know it will only increase if I let it be known. I try to mislead you, too. I decide not to write when I'm feeling too bad, because it would sound so depressing, yet that's what I should share with you.

They have told me that the only possible treatment for my heart would be a cardiac transplant, but my general condition would not allow me to survive the operation. I would gladly take the risk, but I accept their decision.

I get no comfort, no peace in the thought of the God my mother trusted so implicitly. In all her suffering, He never failed her, and she found comfort and sustenance in that belief. I envy that. But I regret deeply, actively, the cruelty of the God who's supposed to be kind. I rail at the unfairness of what's been done to me! Why cut me off, at a time when I am at my most useful and when good doctors are scarce? Why *nearly*, so very nearly dead, but not quite? But not alive either. I resent my uselessness so much. I seem to be wrestling with "why?" all the time. It doesn't make any sense. I think I resent waste. Waste of time; and there never was enough. If I could find a reason, or a purpose, I'd be less of a bother. I don't accept easily what I can't understand. And I'm stuck this time. I must find the courage, for as long as I breathe, to stand the lonely desolation within me, and which cannot, it seems, be understood by anyone who has not passed this way yet. How long? Death will come as a friend; but I dread, more than fear, the time I must wait.

I have just lived too long; I have been discarded. I'm not good company, so why should they come? Yet I sit and brood. I didn't think so-and-so would desert me like this. . . . I'd be grateful even for crumbs. Just five minutes of their time, just one phone-call I didn't make myself. And often I'm hoping that this experience will happen to them, in all its misery, its pettiness, its "spoilt-child"-ishness.

Oh yes, I am just the old, hopeless case in the corner bed, forgotten. If I cry out, no one will hear me. I don't expect to be found. Nobody will look for me: nobody knows I'm lost. Were I a dog, I could crawl into a corner and die in peace. I would know that my mistress would not allow me to suffer so, and I could trust her to let me sleep, for she would love me that much.

I believe that the fear could be eliminated, if the doctor would only talk it over with us. Little by gentle little we could lose the fear of the unknown, and could work *with* him, to face the end. Just commonsense talk about my needs. Have some regard for my occupation, my life, my activities. I have rarely met a patient who did not want to speak about his ailment. *Use* that. Ask my opinion, my views; and let me talk about my death when I want to.

Be gentle, without being maudlin; care, and do so truly. At this stage, there is an uncanny clarity of true and false. Lack of sincerity is so obvious, it is cruel. So, while we must not wallow in grief, we must be genuinely kind and show that we care. Use and support whatever strengths we have. The fear can only be removed by truth.

I can tell when people are being false, and you can never trust them after that. We must be able to have someone we can trust completely—a relative, a friend, you. And that trust must not fail. We need encouragement, and a cheerful, gentle, few minutes. Not hurried, not protracted. Don't make us feel we're just a bother, taking up time that could be put to better use. There's time for a "Hi there, Mr. Smith, I'll be along later, I've got something to ask you"; but that promise must be kept. Make me feel useful, ask my advice, my opinion. Use "Mr." or "Mrs.," unless you know I want you to use my first name. Self-respect must be maintained, and my name may be all I have left, so don't let it be "Mrs. . . . Umm . . ."

It is so important that we should be able to rely on any promise, and visitors should realize this, too. If there has to be a change in plan, knowing the reason won't distress us; but your failure to come, will. It's not much we need. A little company, kindness, any indication that one is not forgotten. And useful. It's so easy to give the love that lessens pain and helps us all to endure.

Heart break is much harder than heart failure.

REFERENCES

AITKEN-SWAN, J., and E. C. EASSON, "Reactions of Cancer Patients on Being Told Their Diagnosis," *British Medical Journal*, 1 (1959), 779–83.

ALSOP, STEWART, *Stay of Execution*. New York: Lippincott, 1973.

BENNETT, A. E., ed., *Communication Between Doctors and Patients*. London: Oxford University Press, 1976.

CARTWRIGHT, A., L. HOCKEY, and J. ANDERSON, *Life Before Death*. London: Routledge & Kegan Paul, 1973.

CLEVELAND, S. E., and D. C. JOHNSON, "Personality Patterns in Young Males with Coronary Disease," *Psychosomatic Medicine*, 24 (1962), 600–10.

DRUSS, R. G., and D. S. KORNFELD, "The Survivors of Cardiac Arrest," *Journal of the American Medical Association*, 10, no. 5 (1967), 75–80.

FREUD, SIGMUND. "Thoughts for the Time on War and Death," in *Collected Papers of Sigmund Freud*, The International Psycho-Analytical Library, vol. 4, ed. E. Jones. New York: Basic Books, Inc., 1959.

HEIM, A., "Notizen über den Tod durch Absturz," *Jahrbuch des Schweizes Alpenklub*, 27 (1892), 327.

HINTON, J. M., "The Physical and Mental Distress of the Dying," *Quarterly Journal of Medicine*, 5 (1963), 1–21.

JUNG, C. G., *Memories, Dreams, Reflections*. New York: Pantheon, 1961.

KÜBLER-ROSS, E., *On Death and Dying*. New York: Macmillan, 1969.

MCINTOSH, J., *Communication and Awareness in a Cancer Ward*. London: Croom Helm, 1977.

NEALE, ROBERT E., *The Art of Dying*. New York: Harper & Row, 1973.

REES, W. D., "The Distress of Dying," *Nursing Times*, 68 (1972), 1479–80.

SIMPSON, M. A., "Planning for Terminal Care," *Lancet*, 1 (1976), 192–93.

WEISMAN, A., *On Dying and Denying*. New York: Behavioral Publications, 1972.

Living Mortal

Dying, like living, is simple—but not easy. The principal difficulty lies in the fear of death and of dying. We need some sort of strategy for handling these matters, and humankind has tried many methods over the ages. The Hedonist approach was to concentrate on enjoying life as much as possible before we lost it. It literally encouraged us to "eat, drink, and be merry—for tomorrow we die." The Pessimists, on the other hand, decided that life was so awful that death was bound to be at least the lesser of the two evils. Others denied that the problem had any relevance. Euripides, for instance, argued simply: "Where I am, Death is not; and where Death is, I am not; therefore, there is no reason to worry about death."

From the most primitive of times there have been beliefs that the future life could be assured by supplying the corpse with food, drink, and equipment. While we may not fully share such views today, the modern American cadaver will be surrounded by quilted satin, polished wood, and bronze handles, which would be considerably less helpful in any future existence. Maybe you can't take it with you, but you can wrap it around you as you go. Other ancients believed that by preserving the body from its natural decay, one somehow aided the preservation of the life force that had inhabited it, so embalming developed. The only established beneficiaries of the Egyptian style of death were the embalmers, the grave robbers, and the archaeologists. Modern funeral practice can allow every man to be his own Pharaoh.

In India, there has been the great aim to get in touch with Ultimate Reality and to merge with it. Several Eastern schools have believed that all sentient beings will go through a cycle of deaths and rebirths that will continue indefinitely, until in one of these lives the person manages to bring the series to an end. The rebirth is often seen as a greater evil than death, and the hope is to avoid rebirth, not to avoid death, often by lengthy and arduous spiritual work.

IMMORTALITY

The concept of an afterlife seems always to have been with us. It's an especially appealing concept for the underdog, encouraging him to believe that somewhere there will be a final judgment of absolute justice. It provides a neat safety valve for the existential failures of life, but it ought not to excuse us from expecting justice now. We complain of death coming too soon, as if we'd naturally be happier if we lived longer. Already, we live about twice as long as our ancestors—are we twice as happy? They also wanted a longer life. We've got it, but we want more. There is no clear, unequivocal evidence that anyone has ever been in communication with a literally disembodied human spirit. We may believe in the personal immortality of the human soul, but find it difficult to describe the state of existence of these souls that is not analogous to the life on earth we already know. There are several versions of the splendid home for the souls of those who have lived appropriately in this life—the Kingdom of Heaven, the Scandinavian Valhalla, the Greek Elysium, the Egyptian Kingdom of the West. There may be an alternative Hell for the bad souls—like Hades or Sheol. This, then, needs a belief in the judgment and partitioning of souls after death. The combination of the idea of a personal and specific immortality and a judgment or sorting after death, awarding bliss or torment, heaven or hell, offers the possibility of personal continuance at the cost of anxiety in life—like any other entrance examination.

One should also recognize the political functions of immortality. It is clearly easier to maintain a social and political system that provides poverty and promises when there is a shared public belief in an afterlife of infinite reward for those who humbly accept their lot. It might not be unduly cynical to suggest that such beliefs have always been especially useful to oppressors—keep the workers believing in the big bonus scheme in the sky. While the fear of death has the biologically useful function of persuading people to invest in their present existence, belief in a paradise is a useful supplement to natural aggression and patriotic zeal in encouraging the troops. It greatly assists the recruiting officer to enlist young men for war, when the army can offer a sort of heavenly reunion in the Ultimate Officer's Club.

There are also intense personal reasons for fiercely desiring immortality, and for the wistful wish to have hard evidence on the issue. The Spanish philosopher Unamuno (1950) explained that the arguments designed to demonstrate the absurdity of belief in immortality failed to impress him, however reasonable they were, for the heart is not appeased with reasons. "I do not want to die—no; I neither *want* to die nor do I *want to want* to die; I want to live for ever and ever and ever. I want this 'I' to live." Thus, the struggle for personal immortality, for the continued existence of this conscious *me*, continues. It is a stubborn habit of mind. I might, daydreaming, fantasize having a new and more beautiful body, with nicer habits and greater skills, perhaps—but I'd assume that the same *me* would inhabit it.

MEANINGS OF LIFE

We are more or less used to recognizing basic drives and needs like hunger and thirst, but we tend to overlook the primary hunger for existence—and for meaningful existence, at that. We can lose the appetite for enjoying food at times; similarly, we may temporarily lose the appetite for existing. But even the suicide may be seeking for escape from a way of life that has become unbearable rather than authentically seeking oblivion. He may wish to escape from a lifestyle that has come to be experienced as living death, as meaningless life. Viktor Frankl (1964, 1971, e.g.) has eloquently described the need not just to be, but to be *someone*; the drive for meaning. As Nietzsche said, "He who has a *why* to live for can bear almost any *how*."

Frankl has also emphasized that even at the very end of life, however much it may have been wasted, life can gain meaning by the way in which one faces the inevitable; one can retroactively flood one's life with meaning by a final phase of growth. Similarly, the meaningfulness of life is not threatened merely by its ending—either it has meaning, however short it may be, or it has no meaning, and will gain none by having more meaningless years added to it.

Death is existentially purposeful, adding a spice, a tension, to life. A pleasure that does not end is tedious, even painful. It must not outstay its welcome. Everything that is worthwhile has a worth and a while. The duration, which must be finite, is an essential part of its value.

IS THERE LIFE BEFORE DEATH?

Active fear of death, or a continuing need to deny its reality, is a real limitation on the extent to which we can fully invest in life itself. What I would propose is not a permanent living-with-death in the sense of a permanent fearful awareness of it, but simply living with the fact that we are finite. It is *not* impossible to comprehend our own eventual demise, though that is a popular claim among the most fearful philosophers.

We do not need to live by the dream of direct and literal personal immortality, or as if the insurance companies' actuarial tables guaranteed us any specific lifespan. However many techniques are available to us to shorten it, we have little genuine capacity to extend our lifespan. We can simply refrain from short-ening it. It is remarkable that even those simple things that can help to achieve this—like better diet and exercise, following com-petent medical advice, and avoiding alcohol, narcotic, and tobacco addictions—are actions we so often neglect.

If our basic hunger is for a particular quality of life, not its quantity, then excess concern over future nonbeing can lose us the art of being *now*. As Seneca said: "Expectancy is the greatest im-pediment to living. In anticipation of tomorrow, it loses today." For the man who avoids the present, the future is a hoax.

Living with the need for immortality allows us to continually mortgage the reality of our present existence for the fantasy of a future. Rather than really live in the present moment, we can keep on postponing matters. I'll spend time with my children—next year. My husband and I can have that special holiday together—the year after that. I'll tell her I love her—some day. We'll settle our personal business—eventually. I'll decide about what I really want out of life—one day.

You can become so involved in earning and accumulating material wealth and possessions, getting and spending, that you automatically postpone the actual enjoyment of your possessions, your people, and your relationships until an indefinite future.

Living mortal is not the same as living with a constant fear of death. It is not the same as bitterly waiting to lose everything you have; it is fully enjoying what you have. The fact that you will die does not make existence futile. In a very real sense the opposite is true. It is the fact that you are a temporary phenomenon, but one with the opportunity of meaningful existence, that is most impor-tant. One of the things that is wrong with a plastic rose is its permanence, its incapacity to change, to alter, to die. Few of us grow attached to modern buildings, but ruins can be charming.

Does life really need to be infinite to have meaning? Are we really seeking to bargain with God or Existence, and saying: "If I live for a hundred years or a thousand years, then life really means something. However, should I live to be only 78 or 45, then it is meaningless"? It is the same with the challenge of suffering. Belief in the value of life, like belief in God, is unconditional or it is not belief. We don't say: "Today my tight shoes hurt me—life is pointless." Why, then, should the greatest suffering remove life's point? At what stage on the continuum of human suffering does life lose meaning? The suffering during the World Wars was grim, and a terrifying reminder of the evils of which humankind is capable. It is easy when confronted by the obscenities of war and violence to say: "There can be no God, no goodness, if 6 million can die." But we don't say: "If Mrs. Cohen dies, then there is no God, no goodness." At what point does the transition occur? Are we saying: "Even though 4 million die I'll still believe in you, God. But 5 million, and you no longer exist"?

We are permanently in transit, always going somewhere, never arrived. This inability to live in the present is almost a defining characteristic of the modern person. It is as if he is living in an apartment—but continues to pay last year's rent, and the years' before; and pays next year's rent, and the years' after. He lives in the past with its regrets and grievances and "might-have-been's," and in the future with its hopes, fears, and "must-be's." Existence has been postponed, due to lack of interest in the present.

Maybe what you are now is all you will ever be. Maybe this is the last book you will ever read. If that is so, how important are your current problems? Some may still seem significant, but some at least must surely pale into insignificance. How important are your present quarrels and arguments? Does it matter very much what you eat for lunch, or who won the game?

"Live each moment as if it were your last" is an old saying and a much-neglected one. It does not mean retiring to sleep in one's coffin, clad in a shroud. But it does mean not wasting your energy or time in conflicts about essentially meaningless trivia. It makes it much more difficult to hate consistently, to scheme for revenge or for special personal advantage. It makes self-deceit and the deceit of others seem even more pointless. Yes, you are ephemeral and vulnerable and fragile and finite. So what? You always have been thus, and will remain so. Only your impermanence is permanent. You cannot by any means available to you substantially extend your life in regard to its length—but you can extend it in breadth and depth, the very dimensions most people neglect.

Before asking, "Is there life after death?" ask the more important question, "Is there life before death?"

FEAR OF DEATH

The prospect of death, of ourselves or of others, arouses a wide range of emotions, including sorrow, despair, resentment, anxiety, anger, defiance, pity, resignation, helplessness, curiosity, hopelessness, and fear. The major trio of responses are fear, sorrow, and anger. It is both normal and of positive biological value that we should not look on death with complete equanimity. There may indeed be a component of our fear of death that is genetically determined and instinctive. But a good deal of the fearfulness of death is learned, and although no one may set out deliberately and consciously to teach us this specific lesson, it is well learned. Certainly society would find it far more difficult to control us if it could not assume that we feared death—what would the death penalty achieve if it were not fearful?

The price we pay, inevitably, for leaving death entirely to other people is that when it eventually comes to us, it will take us by surprise, and find us shocked and unprepared. We will then, unavoidably, face it with bewilderment, anguish, and whatever denial we can muster.

There have been many attempts by psychologists to measure the fear of death among us. The scales they have produced are often just naïve attempts to find fifteen ways of asking us, "Are you scared of death?" and the more often you answer yes, the more scared they assume you are. Other experiments are rather more imaginative. When over 550 people were asked to rank seven statements regarding death in the order of their importance to them (Diggory & Rothman, 1961), the statement that ranked first was "My death would cause grief to my friends and relatives"; second was "All my plans and projects would come to an end"; and third was "The process of dying might be painful." Among fifty possible events, college students listed the loss of a family member as the most potentially upsetting and feared, ranking even their own death lower (Means, 1936). In other, related studies, the death of a spouse was found to be the most significant and stressful life event (see, e.g., Kastenbaum & Aisenberg, 1972).

Even supposedly well-informed people have a very unrealistic concept of their own death. In some of my own research, I have given students (of various ages and disciplines) taking part in my courses on death and dying one session in which they learn the facts about death in their society—who dies, when, and from what cause, including statistical estimates of their own likely morbidity and mortality. They were then asked to open a personally addressed envelope they had been given when they arrived. It contained a genuine death certificate bearing their own name. They were asked to complete it as they expected their own eventual certificate would one day be completed. Analysis of the results showed that their perceptions of their own death were very unrealistic—they expected to die far older and more suddenly than was likely (the certificate didn't allow them to deny death, but they could and did deny dying—by making it instantaneous and unexpected, whenever possible). Very few anticipated cancer or suicide, though these were likely causes in such a group. The older the students, the younger they expected to die; the youngest students saw themselves living to a great age.

IMMORTALITY AND ATTITUDES TOWARD LIFE AND DEATH

Other aspects of immortality and human concepts of immortality influence attitudes toward death and the fearfulness with which one may approach it. In the seventeenth century, Blaise Pascal, the French philosopher, proposed that the situation regarding belief in an afterlife is a wager. If there is no afterlife and you have believed that there was, you have lost nothing. If there is an afterlife, and you fail to gain admission because you don't believe, then you have lost everything. Thus, he argued, since you have everything to gain by believing and nothing to lose by believing, you should make the wager, and decide to believe in an afterlife.

Consider the symbolic possibilities of immortality open to you, quite apart from a personal continuance:

There is *biological* or *biosocial immortality*, obviously. You live on through your children, and their children. You may extend the concept to draw comfort from the continuance of your tribe, people, nation, or even species.

There is *creative immortality*—living through your works—in which by making things (art or craft), building, repairing, teaching, writing, inventing, healing, producing lasting influences on others, you leave a cultural trace.

There is *theological/religious immortality*. Historically, many churches and beliefs have promised varieties of afterlife, of rebirth, or reincarnation. Often, they have lost their symbolic quality and function and have been interpreted absolutely literally, as if people don't actually die at all, as if there is a physical-chemical reality in the structure of heaven.

There is *natural immortality* available through your continuity with nature, dust to dust, rejoining the chemicals you ultimately came from, recycling your ingredients, even if your particular bag of ego won't recur.

And finally, there is *experiential transcendence*—a psychological state, attaining rapture and trance, going beyond the boundaries of ordinary day-to-day life. Reached through music, contemplation and meditation, battle, art, athletics, dance, creation, sex, friendship, and so on, it can provide a sense of psychological unity with the world and its contents, intense sensual awareness, and ineffable, inexpressible insight.

Every variety of immortality open to us has been altered since we entered the nuclear age. Biosocial continuance is obviously threatened—you may have no descendants after the Bomb, or they could be so genetically altered, so mutated, as to be no representatives of you. Your tribe, your people, your nation could be wiped out. Your works could be destroyed, and there would be none to remember you. The religious imagery seems to hold less, if any comfort, for many people now. Now that we can kill History, what continuance seems likely? Even nature itself doesn't seem so permanent—it may be polluted out of all recognition. One might gain some small satisfaction in the prospect of participating in the fertilization of next year's crops. But in the absence of crops, what joy is there in the possibility of being just another isotope, calmly decaying amid the nuclear waste, swapping your life for a nuclear half-life?

Experiential transcendence, available in the here and now, has become much more popular and more earnestly sought after; and its techniques have included more clearly than previously an experimentation with the risk of death. It'll come anyway, so why not enjoy the brinksmanship and teeter on the edge of death? Play with danger, seeking intense, sudden bursts of experience, toying with meaninglessness. "Give it to me *now*," is the cry; "I may not be here tomorrow."

There are many fears that can be part of the fear of death: fear of finitude, and of impermanence; fear of time itself; fear of growing old; fear of decay; fear of irreversibility; fear of losing—possessions, people, relationships, sensations; fear of loss of Self.

It has been argued that fear of death is the primary source of the vigor and energy of our culture and of our creativity; that everything human beings do, build, or create is primarily intended, consciously or unconsciously, to soothe their fear of oblivion. Ernest Becker (1973) has been especially associated with this point of view, which seems to see life as essentially meaningless while you live it, only gradually accumulating meaning, like guano deposited on a rock by visiting birds, by whatever creations or constructions of yours outlive you. A curious point of view. Only to perpetuate your name do you struggle to succeed, to get ahead, make money, make children, build your monuments in physical structures and in other people's memories. It is as if no one alive today is important enough for you, and only posterity must hear you and appreciate you. What has posterity ever done for you that you should be so worried about its welfare and its opinion? From the old wooden cross to the World Trade Center, we are struggling to remind the future of the past.

But this is an unnecessarily gloomy, pessimistic, and fear-ridden view of humankind. We can also, if we choose, interpret the same data very differently. We can see human beings as essentially exploratory, self-affirming creatures who create in spite of their fear of death, perhaps to spite their fear of death, but essentially because in creating objects and relationships lies the truest and most exuberant expression of Being. Creativity is the most competent way of Being, of expressing and enjoying life. And one's creations need not endure in order to give pleasure and satisfaction. Some necessarily brief relationships can give real gratification. Making love is delightful though even the most arduous lovers don't continue indefinitely. Part of the joy of orgasm lies in its short duration. If it lasted half an hour it would probably be both boring and painful.

CONTINUANCE

If we find continuance appealing, rather than insisting upon immortality for our particular ego, we can rely, at least until the process is disturbed by holocaust, on the continuity of our genetic material. The gene is the true and the only ultimately triumphant imperialist, and most of our behavior can be understood as destined to serve the best interests of promoting the survival of the genes. We now know the answer to the old riddle concerning the chicken or the egg. The chicken is just the egg's most efficient way of making another egg. Similarly, in the strictly genetic sense, you are no more than the current production of the repertory company of your genes. And your ego and sense of self are simply ingeniously competent creations of these genes to oversee their protection and their efficient transmission.

Alan Watts (1972) has written especially effectively about our shared delusion of being a lonely, alien "I myself" temporarily visiting this universe and separate from it, rather than a true part of it. We don't "come into this world" from somewhere else—we come out of it, emerging as a temporary, unique, and integral arrangement of its parts, like a wave on the surface of the sea. We tend to see ourselves, in Watts' phrase, as "isolated 'Egos' inside bags of skin." To consider the alternative is in no way a necessary challenge to establish faiths—faith is an open act of trust in what goes beyond what we know, in God or, in Paul Tillich's term, in the Ultimate Ground of Being. Death is when we take the mask off and rejoin. As Watts describes it, "the death of the individual is not disconnection but simply withdrawal. The corpse is like a footprint or an echo—the dissolving trace of something which the Self has ceased to do."

THE AFTER-DEATH AND THE BEFORE-LIFE

It is a persistent feature of Western culture that we find the question "What happens to me after I die?" to be relevant, logical, sensible, and troubling. "What happened to me before I was born?" is often felt to be a pointless, silly, irrelevant, or vexatious question. Yet it is of precisely the same logical structure. Both imply the more important and more frightening (and therefore the more studiously avoided) question: "Who am I?" They are concerned with the question of the continuing existence of the bag of ego I currently recognize as myself. If there is indeed any sort of continuity of the existence of my consciousness or any part of it, then it is by no means logical to insist that the stream of existence may continue into the future but that it must have begun with my contemporarily recorded birth. That is a very uneconomical explanation. If there is continuity beyond presently accessible consciousness, there is no reason to believe that it does not extend in both directions. Why is it frightening to contemplate the prospect that we may cease to be when we calmly accept that at an earlier stage we never were?

TIME

A related illusion is the spectre of time. "Modern man is concerned more with saving time than his soul," wrote David Cole Gordon (1972). Our tenacious Western image of time is conditioned by our way of measuring it. It moves; it flows; it runs away from us like sand pouring through an hourglass. It ticks *away* (it doesn't tick toward us). It flows away. We are navigating by looking out of the back window of the automobile. But you can't "save time" by catching it in a bucket as it pours away, or by tucking some away in a piggybank or safe. So you have to work faster, to cram more activity into it as it flows past, like throwing stones onto a passing train. "Don't waste time!" they cry, just as during the drought we were urged, "Don't waste water!" Time, presumably, is a commodity in similarly limited and finite supply, which must be used properly and not wasted. The work ethic has hooked us into the belief that living for yourself, pleasuring yourself, is never entirely justifiable and never so at all until all the work has been done and one has paid for it fully. The unspoken motto for many people is that if you're not making money out of it, you probably shouldn't be doing it at all—and you're wasting time.

But part of the tyranny of time as we create it (and it does not exist except at our insistence) lies in the fact that we imagine for ourselves a finite length of time (perhaps the threescore years and ten, perhaps as long as our parents lived). We see the time *until then* ticking away like an oven timer, so we must accomplish everything before the bell rings. After surviving a serious threat to our life, or on living unusually long, we are said to be living "on borrowed time." From whom have we borrowed it, and how do we repay it?

Obviously you haven't read the small print in the contract of life. You're not guaranteed any particular period of time at all. You could last till you are 98 or cease tomorrow. No matter how hard you work at it, you won't get it all done "in time." Only by living in the moment can you get close to having lived properly until then. Finally, only the love you have given and received will really count. If you have lived well and lovingly, life will have been well worth it, whenever death comes. If you have not, death will always come too soon and be more terrible to face.

We are now very conscious of time because we have collectively chosen it as the arbitrary convention by which to measure out our life. Suppose, instead, that someone had calculated the average number of breaths we took during a lifetime. It could be of the order of 394,200,000. Of course this is only an average, but just as "of course" is "70 years." We'd be inclined to focus on that number, and to feel somehow entitled to at least that many. When someone died prematurely, we'd say: "What a waste—only 127,563,854 breaths, poor fellow." You'd think a lot more about drawing each breath. "Don't waste your breath!" would be a more common and more menacing comment than it is now. Is each breath really necessary? Should you try to draw them out a little, to make them last longer? A watch would be less relevant, but a breath counter would help you keep check on something really important. If you exceeded 400 million breaths, you'd know that you were "living on borrowed breath." The passage of time wouldn't worry you much, but you'd be a lot more aware of your breathing. Already, even this preposterous analogy may have made you breathless, and you've probably been more conscious of your breathing during the last couple of minutes than you have been for a long time.

We don't have to let ourselves remain victims of our arbitrary creations.

THE LITTLE DEATH

Another important component for most of us (who have been able to realize it as a potential) is the capacity for being a free-moving, free-acting, unique individual, not merely a nonentity or nobody (interesting words!), having meaning and purpose, being involved in something one regards as having value beyond oneself, something self-transcendent. Some people clearly find the peak experience of being unified with the world in death-risking activities— mountain climbing, car racing, hang gliding, drug abuse. It is possible to see death as the ultimate peak experience. Wilhelm Reich (1942) described the culmination of sexual excitement in orgasm as a way of getting out of and beyond ourselves into the universe. For most people it is a unique experience of this "letting go," giving, risking, melting, surrendering, and touching a sense of unity. It is not altogether forcing or straining the simile to suggest that dying can share some of those features. This does not necessarily imply that death is orgasmic, though the reverse simile is commonplace—calling orgasm "la petite mort," the little death. It certainly does suggest that we don't have to fear an ultimate letting go. Orgasm involves giving in to what is happening to you, loss of awareness of bodily boundaries, of the limit between you and the rest of it; and it is not unusual for an individual to feel that he would like to keep going and not come back. But when the opportunity presents itself to do just that, must we pull back in alarm and reject it?

Dying can represent a new way of Being in the world. Yes, it involves facing the unknown—but we live with that all the time, for however predictable it may seem, even the next moment is unknown to us. Sadly, we have become so used to a society so controlled, so air-conditioned and preshrunk, a world that has been "sanitized for your protection"—that unknown experiences are always seen as fearful, as unwelcome. Yet we need to seek new experiences. Minds are like noses—they should be blown regularly, and for very similar reasons. In a society that has eliminated adventure, leaving it may be the final and truest adventure.

FEAR OF DYING

More prominent than the fear of death can be the fear of dying, which may include fear of pain, of indignity, of loss of control, of bedpans, smells, disfigurement, being a burden. The fear of indignity can be exaggerated. Too often we treat all illness as something shameful, needing to be hidden; to be apologized for when it becomes noticeable; a personal weakness or indulgence, almost immoral. One's life can become excessively concentrated on the avoidance of shame and indignity, beyond pride, to the point of vanity. It can be awful to be a burden, but this too can become an inordinate concern in those who have never learned to accept gifts with grace. It may be more blessed to give than to receive, but it is also blessed to receive. We may be too preoccupied with evading situations in which we will need help from others, or struggling to pay it back as soon as possible. We must be able to accept our interdependence. We cannot proceed in life if we regard our debt to our parents, for example, as something to be closely itemized and accounted for, and narrowly repaid. We are born dependent, and we may well die dependent.

Excessive need for control also makes it more difficult to deal with terminal illness. Some people are deeply concerned about self-control and fear losing it. "I may lose control—then anything might happen." They fight losing consciousness, hate going to sleep, hate taking drugs, and see death as the ultimate loss of control. Those who care more intensely about controlling others also suffer death as a great defeat. They may find some comfort in preplanning their funerals and, through their wills, extending their control beyond the grave. They may favor voluntary euthanasia, so that they may regulate even their end. Frustration at the incompleteness of life is natural, especially in the young. It can also be acute for the persistent failures in life, the people who never finished or really achieved anything. They may hope that "next time" everything will work out at last, and feel cheated at losing the chance of "one more time." Many people see themselves as failures not because they have truly done nothing of any real value, but because they have set excessively high standards which they shift so as to always keep the standards well ahead of whatever they achieve.

How man confronts the realities of life may create nobility. There is real meaning in the way one faces the inevitable, including unavoidable suffering. It is important not to mistake this point of view with a masochistic acceptance of unnecessary suffering. Such avoidable suffering does not ennoble, but demeans people. In reacting against the gratuitous ugliness that society and institutions have imposed upon dying, some authors have exaggerated the sweetness and light of a "dignified death." The sick person can also be selfish, petulant, childish, petty, and ungrateful—and so he should. Although much can be done to improve the quality of dying, we must not expect transcendent spirituality and grandeur from the dying, at least not consistently. However much we might like to end with truly memorable last words, we seldom do. ("This *is* the way the world ends / Not with a bang but a whimper.") But that is all right.

ETHNIC INFLUENCES ON ATTITUDES
ABOUT DEATH

In contemporary society, cultural and ethnic factors influence our experiences of death and our attitudes toward it. A recent major study by Drs. Richard Kalish and David Reynolds (1976), for instance, studied Anglos, blacks, Japanese-Americans, and Mexican-Americans and demonstrated a variety of cultural differences. Death had affected most lives—over two out of every three adults had attended at least one funeral within the previous two years, and over 25 percent had been to three or more. Most adults had been friendly with at least two people who had died; one in four had known five or more dying friends.

Anglos were likely to have had the least contact with the dying and the dead and more likely to have avoided funerals. Anglos and black Americans were much more likely to believe that patients should be told when they are dying (71 and 60 percent, respectively) compared with Japanese- and Mexican-Americans (49 and 37 percent). A high proportion wanted to be informed when they were mortally ill (77, 71, and 77 percent, with only 60 percent of Mexican-Americans wishing to know). Three-quarters of the Anglos, blacks, and Japanese-Americans (but less than two-thirds of the Mexican-Americans) would try very hard, when someone close died, to control the way they showed their emotions in public, though private expression of grief was widely agreed to be appropriate. Anglos were considerably more likely to consider slow death more tragic than sudden death, and to see a child's death as the most tragic. Blacks and Mexican-Americans were more likely to see a woman's death as more tragic than a man's.

Asked whether they had experienced or felt the presence of someone who had died, 55 percent of blacks and 54 percent of Mexican-Americans said that they had, while only 29 percent of Japanese-Americans and 38 percent of Anglos reported similar experiences.

Black Attitudes About Death and Dying

During my work in Africa, I have been able to discuss black attitudes toward death with authorities such as Father S. K. Nkoane, Anglican Dean of Johannesburg. In African terms, misfortunes, illness, and death are not just things that happen at random: they always have a cause. They may result from transgression against a taboo, or witchcraft, or a manifestation of the displeasure of ancestors, or an indication of dislocation of the patient's personal relationships. Seeing the cancer cells under a microscope does not settle the matter, but leads to the question: "Who sent these cells to destroy this person?"

Death is always seen in the context of the family, and your father's sister, your mother's brother, your grandmother—all are involved in the resolution of such a crisis. Man is seen as having a solid relationship with nature which can provide medicines to strengthen him or protect him; he also has a very intimate and profound relationship with his kith and kin, especially his forbears—the family is extended in time. Father Nkoane quotes a traditional verse:

> The dead have never gone away,
> They are at the breast of the wife,
> They are in the child's cry of dismay
> And the firebrand bursting into life.
> The dead are not under the ground,
> They are in the fire that burns low . . .
> The dead are never dead.

When one of the Mpondo was asked where the dead lived, he waved his hand around his home, saying: "They are here—all round."

It is ironic that Western scientific medicine has only more recently returned to realize the importance of the family network in the management of illness, and of psychological factors in the causation of serious illness.

Death is a vital presence throughout the rich literature and music of black Americans. Death, often sudden and violent, has been a familiar accompaniment of racial strife and ghetto life. Yet death has been almost ignored in formal and academic studies of the black experience. The Kalish and Reynolds study cited above provides some of the best available data on the subject. Compared to other ethnic groups, they found, black Americans as a whole wanted to and expected to live longest, though this was in marked conflict with the mortality statistics. Far more black men and women *expected* to be alive around or beyond 100 years of age than any other group (22 and 33 percent compared with 9 and 14 percent for Anglos); a still greater proportion *wanted* to live beyond 98 (52 and 39 percent, compared with 16 and 16 percent).

In the face of discrimination and undoubted stress, this fierce desire for a long life despite the statistical improbability is curious. Kastenbaum, who has spoken with many elderly black men and women, has described their uncommon high regard for living, as if maintaining existence so far has needed such resourcefulness, energy, and endurance that they are not likely to consider letting go merely because of further difficulties in life (Kastenbaum & Aisenberg, 1972). Swanson and Harter (1971), after interviewing a similar group, found that "they have never considered that life might not be worth living, nor can they conceive of a situation or problem with which they, themselves, or with the help of the Lord, cannot cope." Pain and suffering are not seen as justifying giving up and dying. Compared with whites, more black Americans had been in contact with the dying, one in four having eight or more friends who had died in the preceding two years. They had also had significantly more contact with victims of accidents, homicide, and war death. Yet they showed less overt fear of death than other groups, especially among elderly men.

Black Americans were less likely to encourage family members to spend time with them during a terminal illness, and were no more likely to depend on the family for support than other groups. They were more likely than other groups to feel that it was unimportant to wait after a family member's death before returning to work, wear signs of mourning, date, or remarry. Well over half of the black Americans believed in some form of life after death, and in a hell, but far fewer of those who did believed that "those in heaven watch over those on earth" (39 percent as compared with 83 percent of Anglos and 100 percent of Japanese-Americans). This is a very dramatic difference from the prevailing beliefs of black Africans.

PSYCHOLOGICAL FACTORS AND
THE CAUSES OF DEATH

Psychological factors can have some intriguing influences on death, particularly among the elderly. One research project (Fischer & Dlin, 1972), for example, showed that old people are less likely to die in the months preceding their birthdays than in the months that follow. Though the findings were based on only a small proportion of deaths, it does seem to confirm the clinical impression that some people seem to be able to influence when they die. One old lady, for instance, made a bet with her priest that, contradicting her doctor's prediction, she would survive until Christmas. She won the bet and demanded payment cheerfully on Christmas Day—then died peacefully.

Mortality rates increase sharply among elderly people forced to move from familiar surroundings to strange ones, as when they are transferred from one institution to another. When such a move seems unavoidable, the effect is probably considerably lessened if they can make preparatory visits to their new home rather than seeing it only once or not at all before the move. (In a study done by Aldrich and Mendloff [1973], 52 percent of those who had made few or no visits to their new home died within one year; only 27 percent of those who had made several visits died during that year.) It also appears that those who had to move more than 45 miles had a higher mortality rate than those who moved a shorter distance. And fewer of those who either definitely accepted or rejected the move died than those who didn't seem to care.

Other researchers compared cancer patients who had survived longer than had been expected statistically with those who died sooner than predicted (Kastenbaum & Aisenberg, 1972). They found that motivation to survive, expressed as a positive attitude toward treatment and a "rising resentment" against the illness as it progressed, was associated with longer survival. Another study (Schmale & Iker, 1966) involved women hospitalized for a biopsy to investigate the possibility of having cancer of the cervix. Interviewers looked for two factors: whether the women had suffered a serious break in significant social relationships, and if so, whether they had reacted to it with feelings of hopelessness and depression. If both factors were present, the researchers predicted that the hospitalized woman would be likely to have cancer. They were correct in 60 to 75 percent of the predictions, both positive and negative.

Others have confirmed that it is not just stress that seems dangerous to individuals with any biological predisposition to illness, but stress in combination with a hopeless/helpless response, a perception of oneself as unable to cope with the stress in any way, and giving up. Drop a wild rat into a tank of warm water and it will be likely to swim for about sixty hours before it becomes exhausted and drowns. Take another, and hold it in your hands so that it cannot escape, until it stops struggling. Drop it into the tank, and after splashing around for a few minutes it will stop and sink passively to the bottom (Seligman, 1975). This pattern of a giving-up, helpless response seems associated with the onset of a whole variety of serious diseases. Collecting details of 170 cases of sudden death not expected for medical reasons, Dr. George Engel of Rochester found that the common element in all cases was a tremendously intense emotion combined with feelings of helplessness (1971).

Hope

Thus it seems that although we may hope to achieve a calm acceptance of the ultimate inevitable when it truly is inevitable, an approach to life that leads one to helpless surrender in the face of all difficulties is risky; hope is truly therapeutic.

To Emily Dickinson, hope was "the thing with feathers" that "perches in the soul." It remains there, however close we come to death, though its point of focus may alter, so long as we perceive the possibility of influencing what happens and how we respond. It may become smaller and more specific, but remain sturdy. One may cease hoping for eternal life, or for fifty years' more life, but still hope for tomorrow, hope for a small meal, hope for peace. *Hope is a way of being*, and not a matter of cool, rational, mathematically predicted expectations. Thus there is no necessity to lose it. One may remain open to the possibility of improbable improvement without being dishonest or greatly unrealistic.

Hope, in order to exist, doesn't need us to be in complete control of our situation or our destiny—or none of us would ever be hopeful. Probably one of the main components of hope is the continuing belief that survival is still desirable and worthwhile; survival need not be sure or even likely. Certainty of survival can be associated with lack of hope, as many a depressed patient can testify. Hope incorporates, perhaps, a good image of oneself and positive regard for oneself, and the ability to affect one's world. It has to do with the authenticity and genuineness of our existence, not its length. (As the old tailor said of the cloth he sold, "Never mind the width, feel the quality!") Finite does not mean futile.

Jean Cocteau has referred to the beauty of failure as the only lasting beauty. Certainly, failure is not without its quality of fulfillment. Failure can only come after and because we have tried, and as an indicator of both the limits and the extent of our power. Everything ends, and rarely at times we choose. By choosing how we will face finitude and failure, we bring cessation within our area of influence and choice. That is what we can master: not our fate, but the style with which we meet it.

REFERENCES

ALDRICH, C., and E. MENDLOFF, "Relocation of the Aged and Disabled: A Mortality Study," *Journal of the American Geriatrics Society*, 11 (1963), 185–94.

BECKER, E., *The Denial of Death*. New York: Free Press, 1973.

DIGGORY, J. C., and D. Z. ROTHMAN, "Values Destroyed by Death," *Journal of Abnormal and Social Psychology*, 63 (1961), 205–10.

ENGEL, G. L., "Sudden and Rapid Death During Psychological Stress," *Annals of Internal Medicine*, 74 (1971), 771–82.

FISCHER, H. K., and B. M. DLIN, "Psychogenic Determination of Time of Illness on Death by Anniversary Reactions and Emotional Deadlines," *Psychosomatics*, 13 (1972), 170–72.

FRANKL, V. E., *Man's Search for Meaning: An Introduction to Logotherapy*. Boston: Beacon Press, 1959.

————, *The Will to Meaning: Foundations and Applications of Logotherapy*. London: Souvenir Press, 1971.

GORDON, D. C., *Overcoming the Fear of Death*. Baltimore & London: Pelican, 1972.

KALISH, R., and D. REYNOLDS, *Death and Ethnicity: A Psycho-Cultural Study*. Los Angeles: University of Southern California Press, 1976.

KASTENBAUM, R., and R. AISENBERG, *The Psychology of Death*. New York: Springer Publishing Co., 1972.

MEANS, M. H., "Fears of One Thousand College Women," *Journal of Abnormal and Social Psychology*, 31 (1936), 291–311.

REICH, WILHELM, *The Function of the Orgasm*. New York: Noonday Press, 1942.

SCHMALE, A. H., and H. P. IKER, "The Affect of Hopelessness and the Development of Cancer," *Psychosomatic Medicine*, 28 (1966), 714.

SELIGMAN, M., *Helplessness: On Depression, Development, and Death*. San Francisco: W. H. Freeman, 1975.

SWANSON, W. C., and C. L. HARTER, "How Do Elderly Blacks Cope in New Orleans?" *Aging and Human Development*, 2, (1971), 210–16.

UNAMUNO, MIGUEL DE, *The Tragic Sense of Life* (translation). New York: Dover Publications, 1954.

WATTS, ALLAN, *The Book: On the Taboo Against Knowing Who You Are*. New York: Vintage Books, 1972.

5

Living
Your Own Death

SO, YOU'RE DYING

How one spends one's remaining time is more important than how long that time may be. There are some advantages to living with death. Neither you nor your friends need to get so tied up in the trivialities and petty games of life. There is often a greater intensity and sincerity in relationships, and a keener appreciation of things one normally takes for granted. You can begin to enjoy the simple luxuries of life while they last, tasting them the more acutely because they will not last—the pleasures of walking, of eating, of resting, of watching children play. You can cease the pointless postponing of important messages. Do all the things you always wanted to do but never got around to because of lack of time—the vacation, the hobbies, more time with friends and family. You can settle old quarrels and disagreements, tell people you love them, and deliver whatever you have often promised but always put off till later. "Later" has arrived.

Telling other people about your illness will be a gradual and sometimes an uncomfortable process. You will obviously choose whom you want to share such information with from among your family, friends, and business associates. With some people you may want to share all the information you have; others may need to know that you are ill, perhaps seriously ill, but they may not need the details or particulars. You may well find that, at first, you are more active in comforting others than they are in comforting you. Their reactions will usually be sympathetic and understanding—one problem you will have to face early on will be to learn to accept sympathy. We tend too often to demean sympathy and to think of accepting it in terms of begging and receiving grudging charity, of emotional blackmail, of pity, of "just feeling sorry for" someone, or even oneself. Yet it is an entirely natural response, and to angrily reject the sympathy of others is as selfish and unkind as to spurn a gift. You may fear that your relationships with others will come to amount to nothing but sympathy or pity, but this is very unlikely. To the extent that you remain a real and genuine person (which is in no way dependent on health or physical strength) people will be able to relate to you as that person. Sympathy will probably be a part of that relationship, just as you may feel sympathy for some aspects of their predicament; but it won't be the whole of that relationship. In fact, your capacity to accept the sympathy and go beyond that to the other parts of your relationship will, in a way, itself minimize the sympathy. If people don't feel able to express this very natural part of their feelings for you, it may be difficult for them to think of, or express, much else.

Some patients have described a feeling of glee, of almost enjoying breaking the news to friends, phoning round to say, "Guess what I've got!" For a time, they wanted to excite the pity and bask in the affection and sympathy they stirred up.

CURE AND CONTROL

One often pins all one's hopes on *cure*, yet this is inappropriate for many types of illness. We often seem to assume that medicine generally cures people, with a few unfortunate exceptions. But in fact, cure—returning someone to a state of health identical to his state before the onset of the illness—is rather a rare event. Some fractured bones may heal very well and return to their previous state. Some acute infections may clear up completely, leaving the person undamaged. Basically, though, medicine is truly the science of prolonging disease, and its art lies in improving the quality of life during the illness.

We can often *control* a disease. Diabetes or epilepsy, for example, are never cured, but may be very well controlled, allowing the individual to live a normal or near-normal life. Control of your illness, to a greater or lesser extent, perhaps for many years, perhaps for months, is a far more realistic expectation. Even in the absence of cure, *care* is always possible, and can greatly ameliorate the unpleasantness of an illness.

Contact with other patients in the ward, the clinic, and the waiting room may worry you. Some may look very much sicker than you are, and may remind you of gloomy possibilities. There is much you can learn from each other about ways of dealing with the illness and its various effects, and there's much useful support and help you can give each other. On the other hand, remember that not only will other patients often have conditions different from your own but also, apart from the general similarities, the results of the interaction between each individual and his illness may be quite different.

SEX AND DYING

Sex may be a valuable comforter, and just as children and adults may often healthily masturbate to help them relax when they are worried or scared, so a couple may seek solace in sexual activity. Occasionally, though, one spouse may be horrified to find that his or her partner "can think of sex at a time like this." One should rather see it as a natural comforter.

Until quite recently, physicians have tended to ignore the sexual problems of patients with serious illnesses. All parties involved were generally too embarrassed to talk about them, so they tacitly pretended they just didn't exist. But we have begun not only to realize that such problems exist, but to learn how people can adapt to phsyical incapacities and maintain pleasing sexual relationships despite major physical illness or handicap.

During the acute stage of any illness, lack of any substantial desire for sexual activity is common; lack of desire matches physical incapacity, because one is preoccupied with the symptoms of the illness. For some people this stage is long-lasting—their total energy, interest, and attention become occupied with their pain and debilitation. The patient's ignorance about his condition, his embarrassment, guilt, and naïveté, may be matched only by the professional's ignorance, embarrassment, guilt, and naïveté, so that little help may be sought or given. But gradually, more experienced counselors are becoming available, and more can be done to help than was previously considered possible.

In the context of a warm human relationship and with the relief of the initial symptoms of the illness, the primary phase of sexual disinterest can pass. Further problems may still arise. The effects of the illness may make familiar sexual behaviors unusually uncomfortable, and although experimentation with new or modified positions and varieties of activity may alleviate this, many people are hesitant to experiment. Even apparently major crippling conditions such as paraplegia do not cause insuperable difficulties. Long before doctors and physiotherapists had begun to realize that this was an important and remediable problem, patients themselves had devised techniques to help themselves, and professionals have been able, in turn, to learn from them.

Something that is particularly disturbing to most people is the change in body image that illness may bring—scarring or skin lesions, maybe a mastectomy, or amputation, or a colostomy. In such cases more difficulty is often caused by patients' distaste for their altered self, leading them to feel ashamed to be seen or touched, than by their partner's objections. A revision of one's customary esthetic judgments may be necessary, but is achievable.

In other circumstances, such as after a severe coronary thrombosis or a stroke, or during the course of a relapsing illness, either or both partners may be fearful that sexual activity may aggravate the condition or bring about another attack. Even during a lengthy remission from the illness itself, the fear may persist. A relationship can be greatly strained by this situation, especially where the healthy partner feels that to request sex might amount to homicide and the ill partner fears that to allow sexual arousal might be suicidal. Either or both are likely to become frustrated and irritable, and feel guilty, and may even consider separating. The well spouse may seek sexual activity outside the marriage, while feeling a mixture of defiance, resentment, and guilt, and usually a lowered self-esteem. Doctors very often add to the problem by masking their ignorance of what best to advise by announcing with dogmatic vagueness, "You're medically quite fit now—but take it easy." Quite what that means, or what you're supposed to do about it, is far from clear.

Sometimes the physical illness or incapacity may be used as a smokescreen for more basic sexual problems which existed long before the illness started. A person who has had difficulty coping with sexual feelings may find the illness a very useful justification for sexual failure and for evading the relationship. Help from a competent and properly trained sex therapist would be appropriate.

Mastectomy not only may leave a woman with real anxieties about cancer and the extent to which her life may be threatened by the disease but also may lead to worries about her image as a woman and her ability to maintain her normal sex life. The husband should be involved actively in helping his wife to deal with this and reassure her not only that he still loves her, but that she is still feminine and attractive to him. He may be able to play a part in helping her recover from the operation—assisting her in changing the dressings and massaging her arm, which may be uncomfortable for a while. Sexual activity should be resumed as soon as the woman wants it and, with due concern for her comfort, need not be restricted in any way.

Colostomy and ileostomy may be lifesaving in the treatment of bowel cancer, and are at any rate likely to relieve disabling symptoms. However, they are operations that produce a major change in body image, and may cause genuine physical difficulties, especially at first. Good management of the 'ostomy should be a high priority of the whole treatment team, and should result in a more predictable, comfortable stoma, with fewer problems from odor or increased intestinal activity. In many areas there are now " 'Ostomy clubs" which can be most helpful.

The majority of people can resume their normal sexual activity after a heart attack; the cardiologist should be able to advise on how soon and how often. Sexual intercourse does place some strain on the heart, because it is associated with an increased pulse rate and faster respiration. But severe family anxieties and arguments can be even more stressful, and considerably less enjoyable. Abstaining from sex, and the results of doing so, are unlikely to be of any benefit to the heart, while regular and pleasurable sexual activity can form an excellent part of a recuperative exercise plan (and the part of the exercise program that people are rather less likely to skip). The cardiac patient is not likely to die because of sexual activity. Studies indicate that less than 1 percent of heart patients seem to die as a result of having intercourse (Lief, 1975; Trumble, 1970; Koller et al., 1972). Not only are those that do quite likely to have died at some other moment of exertion, but many who die during intercourse seem to have been engaged in an extramarital affair, which tends to be more stressful. This might not be regarded as just retribution, perhaps, but it serves to illustrate further the point that psychological tensions may be far more lethal than simple physical sex.

As has been mentioned, some variation in techniques and positions may be helpful. For example, the woman-on-top position may be less exerting for the man. In one case, a man of 38 described losing consciousness for a few seconds at a time during intercourse quite unrelated to orgasm. Sometime earlier, he had had an artificial heart valve inserted. This device worked excellently if his pulse rate stayed below 160 per minute. Vigorous coitus in the traditional "missionary position" pushed his pulse rate above this level, his heart valve worked less efficiently, the blood flow to his brain was slightly but significantly reduced, and he lost consciousness. Changing to the woman-superior position kept his heart rate below 160 per minute, and the distressing symptoms disappeared.

To summarize, then, sex is usually therapeutic. If you have any doubts about your health in this respect, ask your doctor for advice.

ON ADMISSION TO THE HOSPITAL

Though many hospitals try to make the admission process easier these days, it can be both a confusing and an upsetting experience. There are forms to fill in and varieties of personnel in different uniforms to deal with, many of whom seem too busy to stop. You lose your familiar home environment, your usual clothes and possessions, and you may feel anonymous, less sure of your usual identity. Most hospitals now provide some sort of information leaflet explaining the uniforms, rules, and procedures. If yours doesn't, ask one of the nurses to spend a few minutes explaining.

Planning for your admission will make it easier for you. Pack a small case with a dressing gown and pajamas you like and feel comfortable in; slippers and toilet items you enjoy using; writing materials and stamps, photographs of family, books and magazines. When you must be in bed for days on end, unorganized time can become monotonous. Time becomes a problem when there seems to be nothing to do. You can plan your day once you know the ward routine and the timing of ward rounds, medications, and other regular procedures. You can plan time for reading the newspaper, writing, reading books, particular radio and television programs. Keep note of the questions you want to ask your doctor and things you want to tell him about your condition. It is too easy to forget these when he does visit you.

Most hospitals now have reasonably generous visiting times, but it is important to remember that you do not *have* to have visitors. Sometimes you will not feel like having visitors—it can be tiring to be the center of attention for long. Perhaps you can advise your friends to phone your spouse or the ward before visiting, to check whether you are feeling like having visitors. Some people feel embarrassed to leave too early—and the longer visiting times may now leave you and your friends with no outside signal for ending the visit. Feel quite free to let them know when you have enjoyed the visit but feel too tired to continue conversation.

When you are feeling tired and sick, it is easy to get angry about little things, but this usually passes soon. If, however, you have real complaints or suggestions about the way the hospital is run, by all means offer your constructive criticism to the hospital administration. Discuss the problems you encounter with a member of the staff, and if there is no simple explanation, write a letter to the hospital's director or administrator.

For some illnesses and problems there are associations or groups of patients, ex-patients, and/or people interested in the condition and in raising funds for research in the area. Such groups often publish helpful literature. For example:

Helping Words for the Laryngectomee, published by the International Association of Laryngectomees (219 East 42nd Street, New York, New York 10017); and *Your New Voice,* by William Waldrop and Marie Gould, from the American Cancer Society, Inc., at the same address. Local groups of the ACS run self-help groups for patients, such as Help Yourself to Recovery in New York and the Cancervive Project in Los Angeles County.

Ostomy Quarterly is published by the United Ostomy Association, Inc. (1111 Wilshire Boulevard, Los Angeles, California 90017).

SHARING RESPONSIBILITY FOR TREATMENT

You, the patient, should know what medicine you are getting and why, and what it is doing for you (if it isn't doing anything for you, you shouldn't be taking it at all). This can make side effects less alarming and cooperation easier. The doctor's responsibility is to explain to you, in a manner you can understand, the various courses of action or different treatments available, the results that are to be expected from each, and the problems, risks, and inconveniences associated with each. When you know what the doctor is trying to do and why, you are able to give properly informed consent to treatment, and can join in the monitoring of your progress.

The following are some of the questions you may want to ask the doctor about your treatment. Some doctors may take offense if you don't ask these tactfully, and sound as if you are doubting the correctness of this advice. Make it clear that you want to understand so you can cooperate more effectively with therapy.

1. *Why and how?*
   What kind of medicines are these and how should they help? How and when should I take them? Will I be able to tell if they're working properly? If I accidentally miss a dose, what should I do? How do they work?

2. *How important?*
   How important is it for me to take these medicines? What is the most important thing for me to remember about them? What is likely to happen if I don't take them?

3. *Side effects?*
   Does the drug have any other effects I should watch out for? Do they ever cause any problems? Are they all right to take with any other medicines I might need? Is it all right for me to drive while I'm taking them? Is it all right for me to drink alcohol while I'm taking them?

4. *For how long?*
   How long will I need to continue taking the medicines? What should I do with any that are left over? When will I need to see you again, and what should I be able to tell you then?

PATIENTS' RIGHTS

Be sure your doctor satisfies you. You have a clear right to ask questions about things that trouble you and to expect answers you can understand. If, at times, the doctor is too busy to spend enough time with you (business can also be an excuse to avoid what he might find to be an uncomfortable encounter—check with his secretary to find some free time), he should direct you to someone who has more time. Besides, here as elsewhere, it's not the amount of time the doctor can spend with you that matters as much as the quality of the relationship and the use you make of whatever time he gives you. Be frank with the doctor—by lying, equivocating, or avoiding, the only person you cheat is yourself. Expect the doctor to be at least as frank as you are.

The doctor should pay attention to your total comfort. Small but cumulative complaints (constipation, cramps, cracked lips, itching) can needlessly add a great deal to the misery of serious illness. Don't hesitate to mention such matters to your doctors and nurses.

As a patient, you can greatly help in the training of young doctors and medical students by allowing them to learn about your illness, how it affects you, and how you deal with it. You can be a valuable teacher. On the other hand, you also have the right to refuse to take part in teaching. If you find that you are treated without consideration or respect in such circumstances, you should make it clear what has upset you, and be prepared to refuse to cooperate unless you are properly treated.

Your doctor will probably be doing his very best to help you. If you are dissatisfied with the treatment you receive, you have the right to seek another doctor. But be sure that you do this only with good reason. Be sure that your goals are realistic. It is too easy to blame the doctor or the hospital for not curing what cannot be cured, and some people shorten their life and increase their misery by restlessly shopping around among different doctors and hospitals, seeking magic cures.

There have been numerous attempts to state clearly what the rights of patients are and what they should be.

In 1973, the American Hospital Association published a series of statements of these rights:*

1. The patient has the right to considerate and respectful care.

2. The patient has the right to obtain from his physician complete current information concerning his diagnosis, treatment, and prognosis in terms the patient can be reasonably expected to under-

*Reprinted, with permission, from "A Patient's Bill of Rights," published by the American Hospital Association.

stand. When it is not medically advisable to give such information to the patient, the information should be made available to an appropriate person in his behalf. He has the right to know, by name, the physician responsible for coordinating his care.

3. The patient has the right to obtain from his physician information necessary to give informed consent prior to the start of any procedure and/or treatment. Except in emergencies, such information for informed consent should include but not necessarily be limited to the specific procedure and/or treatment, the medically significant risks involved, and the probable duration of incapacitation. Where medically significant alternatives for care or treatment exist, or when the patient requests information concerning medical alternatives, the patient has the right to such information. The patient also has the right to know the name of the person responsible for the procedures and/or treatment.

4. The patient has the right to refuse treatment to the extent permitted by law and to be informed of the medical consequences of his action.

5. The patient has the right to every consideration of his privacy concerning his own medical care program. Case discussion, consultation, examination, and treatment are confidential and should be conducted discreetly. Those not directly involved in his care must have the permission of the patient to be present.

6. The patient has the right to expect that all communications and records pertaining to his care should be treated as confidential.

7. The patient has the right to expect that within its capacity a hospital must make reasonable response to the request of a patient for services. The hospital must provide evaluation, service, and/or referral as indicated by the urgency of the case. When medically permissible, a patient may be transferred to another facility only after he has received complete information and explanation concerning the needs for and alternatives to such a transfer. The institution to which the patient is to be transferred must first have accepted the patient for transfer.

8. The patient has the right to obtain information as to any relationship of his hospital to other health care and educational institutions insofar as his care is concerned. The patient has the right to obtain information as to the existence of any professional relationships among individuals, by name, who are treating him.

9. The patient has the right to be advised if the hospital proposes to engage in or perform human experimentation affecting his care or treatment. The patient has the right to refuse to participate in such research projects.

10. The patient has the right to expect reasonable continuity of care. He has the right to know in advance what appointment times and physicians are available and where. The patient has the right to expect that the hospital will provide a mechanism whereby he is informed by his physician or a delegate of the physician of the patient's continuing health care requirements following discharge.

11. The patient has the right to examine and receive an explanation of his bill regardless of source of payment.

12. The patient has the right to know what hospital rules and regulations apply to his conduct as a patient.

Beth Israel Hospital in Boston gives its patients a pamphlet, *Your Rights as a Patient*, which includes further important points. You have the right to be treated respectfully by others, to be addressed by your proper name and without undue familiarity, to be listened to when you have a question or want more information, and to receive an appropriate and helpful response. Your right to privacy includes the right to talk with your doctor or nurse in private, the information not to be overheard or given to others without your permission. You have the right to receive adequate instruction in self-care, prevention of disability, and maintenance of health.

Remember also your responsibilities as a patient. Keep appointments, or phone when you can't; bring all possibly relevant information about past illnesses, hospitalizations, and treatment. Let professionals know when you can't understand them.

Recently, at meetings of the International Work Group on Death, Dying, and Bereavement, attended by the world's leading experts in this area, there has evolved a series of standards for the proper care of the dying patient. In one version, these recommendations are as follows:*

---

*"Standards of Care," used by permission of the International Work Group on Death, Dying, and Bereavement.

The wishes, attitudes, and needs of the professional staff need to be taken into account, but we must evolve primarily patient-oriented standards, not only in theory and declaration, but in practice. The terminally ill patient's own preferences and beliefs, life-style, and philosophy must be understood and taken into account. This means that we cannot lay down rigid rules and standards, though this would be far easier for medical staff and administrators. A terminal-care plan should be devised for each dying patient, and reviewed and modified in the course of the illness. This plan would include what should and should not be done during the last stages of life, and in the period immediately after death—who should be there and how it should be managed. The plan should be an expression of the patient's wishes, even though we may not be able to meet them all. The patient himself should be consulted early and as often as necessary, in planning for this part of his life.

Extension of life, where possible and desirable, will continue to be a goal of treatment during any severe illness, but it will not always be the only or over-riding goal. Remission of symptoms will also be a major aim. Functional capacities (such as nutrition, ambulation, and excretion) will be maintained or restored where practical; and distress, whether from pain, anxiety or fear, or breathlessness, will be reduced or relieved by all available means. Pain control is first priority, for uncontrolled pain can be wholly demoralizing and can disrupt interpersonal and spiritual relationships, adding to the distress of the physical pain itself.

It should be clear to the patient that his opinion matters; that his care-givers will not lose interest in him; and that he is not a heavy burden on his family or the staff. Patients should be enabled to return home to die there, if they so wish; and help from the hospital and local social services should be available to make this possible. When the patient is to die in a hospital or institution, such modification and personalizing of the surroundings as can accommodate the patient's values and wishes should be undertaken where practical. While precise prognoses are rarely possible, the patient should be given such information about his likely prognosis as he wishes, to allow him to bring his personal affairs to order, and to take leave of family and friends, staff, and other patients in the manner he desires. Visiting hours should be flexible, and all participants in the process should be given the opportunity to discuss their problems relating to the death with someone competent to do so. After the death, effective help for the survivors should be available.

We should be prepared to modify usual hospital and medical practices to enable patients to spend their last days in a way that has real meaning for them. This may especially include the opportunity to be in the arms of a spouse, parent, or child. No one should have to be alone when they die unless, uncommonly, this is what they want. If they so wish, they should be able to keep some personal possessions, and their own clothes, to maintain some continuity with their life-style.

When re-admitted in the course of a terminal illness, the patient should be in the same ward or unit as previously (if they prefer this) to allow for continuity of relationships. The hospital must keep in contact with the family doctor and community services so that care is continuous, whether at home or in hospital.

We have to avoid oversimplification and stereotypes. When I began to work in this area, it was shocking to medical people when I said, "Patients can die at home," or "The family is also important," or "Take love into account, as well as biochemistry." Now I have also to say that some patients don't want to die at home, that some families don't care at all, and that hate exists as well as love. The fact that the dying person is so often refused the opportunity of talking frankly about his or her situation has led us at times to exaggerate this need, and to deny the patient the right to denial. He or she may wish to avoid the topic. As always, it is the patient's wish that we should seek to respect, rather than requiring him or her to conform to our wishes or to meet our needs.

ON DEATH AND LYING—
KNOWING AND TELLING

We are all dying, only some of us will get there a little earlier than others. But we avoid commenting on it. When one of us is seriously ill, people don't know what to say. We have what Richard Kalish (1977) has called the "horse on the dining-room table" syndrome.

At a pleasant dinner party, a horse is sitting in the middle of the table. But we all talk as if the horse weren't there, for it would embarrass the host if the guests mentioned it at all, and the host doesn't refer to the horse lest it upset the guests. Though it is ignored in conversation by us all, the horse sits there still, in the very center of everyone's thoughts all night.

The evidence shows that most people want to be able to know about their illness and its seriousness, and that most doctors prefer not to tell them. If the question is posed in a general theoretical way, some 80 to 90 percent of people state that they would want to know if they had cancer or a similar serious illness (Gilbertsen & Wangensteen, 1962). It has been argued that this is only because they are in a secure state of health when they are answering, and that the situation would be different if there were a real and present possibility that they had a fatal illness. But the wish to know does not change. When 560 patients attending a tumor clinic were asked whether or not they wanted to know of a potentially fatal diagnosis, 80 percent said that they did want to know, 12 percent said they did not, and 8 percent were unsure (Hinton, 1966). Another study (Aitken-Swan & Easson, 1959) compared 100 patients with cancer and 100 other patients; 89 percent of the cancer patients wanted to be informed if they had inoperable malignancies, while 82 percent of the other patients said that they wished to know if they developed a fatal illness. Of people with a treatable cancer who had been told their diagnosis, two-thirds were glad to have been told and only 7 percent weren't. Nineteen percent denied that they had been told, reminding us that one does not necessarily remember or even hear what one doesn't wish to know. On another ward where it was the usual practice not to tell patients, 86 percent of patients with advanced cancer knew their diagnosis, and many of the rest had suspected and asked about it but had been given vague and evasive answers. Some four-fifths of these very ill patients felt that cancer patients should be told the truth, because it helped them to understand what was happening to them, allowing them to plan and settle their affairs and giving them peace of mind (Aitken-Swan & Easson, 1959; see also Kelly & Friesen, 1950; Kline & Sobin, 1951).

No competent study has produced any valid evidence to the contrary.

Generally, doctors don't believe in telling the patient the truth. In most surveys, some 80 to 90 percent have indicated that they never or very seldom do so (Oken, 1961; Mount et al., 1974). They may protest that "of course" they make exceptions according to the individual circumstances of each patient. But they do not do so in practice. Several observational studies have shown that doctors use a completely stereotyped response. Such statements as "Well, your ulcer shows a little bit of activity about it, so we've decided to remove it before it becomes troublesome" and "There were some suspicious cells which were going malignant—the little growth might have turned into a cancer if it had been left" have been recorded, even in response to a patient's direct question, "Is it cancer?" Otherwise one may hear no more than "We operated to make sure that you wouldn't have any more trouble. Those X rays are just a routine that we do to all patients." (These are direct quotations from doctors' conversations.)

Yet some 80 percent of doctors indicate that they themselves would want to be told if they were similarly ill (Oken, 1961). Such double standards are surely not justifiable. Similarly, if one observes which patients are the exceptions—those who do get straight answers—they are usually mature, of relatively high social class, wealthy and with considerable business and financial affairs to settle, and may show striking similarities to the doctor concerned, who finds that he can readily identify with them.

It appears that doctors and nurses may be more frightened of death than the general public—and indeed, one of their motivations for entering the healing professions may be to seek to control these fears by conquering death. Certainly the inability to face some of the needs of the dying patient and the refusal to speak frankly is as much or more due to the doctor's difficulties as to those of the patient, just as some of the empty "reassurance" is for his own benefit rather than that of the patient. It is not uncommon for a doctor or nurse to give the patient extra analgesia or sedation because the doctor or nurse cannot bear the encounter. The patient gets the morphine because the nurse and doctor are in pain;

the patient gets the tranquilizer, and the doctors and nurses get the tranquillity.

In fact, the question isn't whether to tell or not to tell—these are false alternatives. Too often it is assumed that the alternatives are crudely forcing the most unpleasant news upon a patient willy-nilly versus keeping him or her in happy ignorance of the disease and its likely outcome. In practice, total refusal to disclose the relevant information is not possible. It is like refusing to tell a pregnant woman that she is pregnant and refusing to discuss childbirth. She is bound to find out sometime; the actual choice involves not whether she will know or not, but whether and how the doctor can help her to know what will be helpful. The terminal patient is pregnant with death, and will just as unfailingly discover what the doctor wishes to keep secret.

The commonest questions I am asked about terminal care are probably "Do you believe in telling the patient?" and "What do you tell the patient?" In fact, the patient usually tells me, if we can talk about the illness in a way that conveys that we can be honest with each other and that I don't need to deny the reality of the situation. The real question is how freely should we talk about it on any particular occasion? How should one encourage the patient when he begins to talk in such a way as to lead to talk about dying? When should we change the subject, and when would it be wrong to do so? How do we deal with the patient's suspicions? There is no question that we should talk about them, but how shall we best do so? In my regular practice I talk openly with my patients about their illness and their worries about it. When they are ready to face the fact that their illness is probably going to be fatal and want to discuss that, we talk about that.

In most cases it is impossible *not* to tell the patient about the gravity of his or her illness. Not saying anything about it says a lot. When a patient feels awful, spends a good deal of time in the hospital, receives multiple investigations and various treatments, and fails to get better, then the fact that nobody gives a convincing explanation of what is happening says a great deal about the seriousness of the situation. People correctly assume that they will hear the good news. You can't help someone cope with "it" when you've got to pretend that "it" isn't happening at all. In fact, what the patient fears may be very much worse than the reality—but you can't relieve the fears unless you can talk about them frankly.

Whatever they are told, patients eventually find out about their illness in various ways. When you are ill, you naturally want to find out what's happening and what the likely outcome will be. If you are given no direct information, you can become very sensitive at picking up indirect information. You may notice that you're moved into the "Death Bed"—one of the high-dependency beds near the nurses' station, usually reserved for the seriously ill and moribund. You may be sent to the radiotherapy department and know or find out what that means. You may notice the decreasing interest of the staff once it has been decided that "there's nothing more that can be done." As a patient once said to me: "I feel like a railway station that's been closed—the ward round doesn't stop here anymore."

You notice that the little lady with the same condition, whom you used to meet every time you came to the clinic, doesn't come any more—and she didn't get better. You sneak a look at your chart or medical records. (Isn't it interesting that you are almost always the very last person to be allowed to see your own records? The doctor talks about "*your* diagnosis"—but he behaves as if it belonged to *him*.) You read medical textbooks in public libraries or bookstores. You learn from your visitors, who are usually bad actors, and whose red-rimmed eyes and stuffy noses say more than their would-be encouraging words. Treatment that doesn't work, symptoms that stay, and slippery, evasive conversations tell a lot.

One fear that both doctors and relatives have is that if they should begin to speak honestly about the patient's illness and fears, he "won't be able to take it" and might "break down" or "go crazy" or commit suicide. Some researchers (Aitken-Swan & Easson, 1959; Kelly & Friesen, 1950; Kline & Sobin, 1951) have compared patients with an incurable illness who had been told about it with others who had not been told. In the great majority of cases, people maintained their emotional balance and were glad they had been told. Some patients were initially upset, but gained composure later. Only a small group never achieved serenity, and they were found among both those who had been told and those who had not. None of those told with care reacted badly or dramatically. Those who had been told showed improved family relationships and less tension and upset in response to the progressive deterioration in their physical condition.

While there would be some risks involved in forcing information upon an unwilling hearer, irrespective of his state or his wishes, this is of course not what we are considering. What we are proposing is that the ill person should be the one who draws up the agenda and who brings up the topic when he is ready to deal with it. We mustn't then cheat by ignoring the opening he creates. Yes, the person may become upset, or weep, but that is not at all harmful. In fact, it is just converting the hidden upset into visible upset, not creating it anew. It's like finding out what your children or your students think of you. They do size you up; you can't avoid that. Your only choice is whether or not you let yourself find out about it. By handling the subject gently, you are highly unlikely to create any disturbance or emotion that isn't already there. Inappropriate silence is more likely to bring about problems. By bringing existing feelings into the open, you make them available for help and comfort.

Of course, some other people, not understanding this, may blame you for being the *cause* of the distress you elicit, but that is more of an expression of their personal problems than of yours. It is like the ancient Greek custom of killing the messenger who brings news of a defeat in battle, or like blaming the lightning rod if you don't like lightning.

The patient who asks you about his illness is usually also asking, "Can I talk with you? Can I trust you?" A proper response to that may be far more important to him than the scientific delineation of what name his disease has.

Weeping is something of which we're usually far too scared, and which can be highly therapeutic. It has never received the respect it deserves. You may allow the person the freedom to weep. Men, especially, may feel they need some sort of permission to cry, for they have been taught that terrible lie that says that it is unmanly to cry. Lauren Trombley (1976), a young psychiatrist dying of leukemia, wrote poignantly and with great insight of his responses to the situation: "People wrongly assume that a sick person should be 'protected' from strong, and particularly negative, feelings. The truth is that there is probably no more crucial time in a person's life when he needs to know what is going on with those who are important to him." Other people clearly describe a sense of satisfaction, of triumph, even of elation, on learning that they will die. As one young man put it: "Suddenly life is far simpler. Now I'm free from all the rules. What can they do to me now, if they don't like what I do? I can scrap all the stupid social games and pretenses, and do whatever I want to; there are no responsibilities except those I decide to accept. That's free."

It is often assumed that confirming the patient's suspicions of the nature of his diagnosis and prognosis deprives him of hope, but this is not so. He usually wants to know that it is serious, but not hopeless—and that's usually all that we can honestly say. The ancient Greeks used to consult the entrails of animals and make prognostications; nowadays the surgeons consult patients' entrails and make prognoses. They're not usually a great deal more accurate. The main useful function of the making of prognoses is to teach doctors humility.

Only in pediatrics and terminal care is it customary to insist on telling the family but not the patient, asking other people to make major decisions on his behalf. The motives may be authentic, but lying widens the gap between all of us.

Lying to a patient is rarely justifiable, but it is common practice. Such a lie is almost always found out; and it is rarely possible to undo the lie—to try to say, "Look, yesterday I may have lied to you about something of life-and-death importance—but today you can believe me!" Such a person invalidates himself as a source of further information and loses his capacity to reassure or comfort. Too often we find a maze of lies and evasions tying the whole family up in grim games of "I-know-but-don't-tell-anybody." The husband will say, "I know she has cancer, but don't tell her. She couldn't bear to know." The wife will say, "I know I've got cancer, but don't tell my husband. He'd worry too much." I've even had patients say to me, "I know it's cancer—but don't tell my doctor. It would upset him."

Truth is a vital drug; the only problem is getting the dose right. As Weisman has said: "Truth is not so bitter that it must always be downed in a single gulp, nor is it so poisonous that we must avoid it completely" (1972). A 19-year-old newlywed with cancer described responded in this way to the conspiracy of silence:

> I wanted to scream: "Dummy! How can TRUTH be a burden?!!" How can I face the truth, how can I deal with reality, if I don't know what the reality is? And if I'm not facing reality, then I'm not facing life, and I'm already dead anyway.
>
> My loved ones put on such a good show—sticking to their regular schedules, appearing unworried and calm—that I just thought that all my pain and suffering were not very important, and that no one cared very much. Having this kind of barrier in my family relationships was the *real* "burden."

We often put patients in a communicational double bind. Verbally we tell them they're fine, while nonverbally we tell them they're dying. We give double messages, saying "You are—and you're not. Death is so awful I can't talk to you about it: so don't worry about it at all." This is as contradictory as our usual double message when we are teaching children about sex: "Sex is a filthy, dirty, horrible thing—which you must save for the one you love."

Shneidman has pointed out that there are substantial and significant differences between ordinary conversation and professional discussion between doctor and patient (1976). In *conversation*, there is more concentration on matters of the world (events, things, and other people). Most of the talk is manifest, unambiguous, direct. What is said is largely what is meant, what is meant is largely said, meaning is overt. Conversation is usually between equals (exceptions or variations are with regard to age, status, etc.) and both participants have equal rights to require that they speak of and attend to their personal needs.

Talking with the dying person is certainly different. The content is more emotional, not only in mood and style but also in subject matter. It deals with latent and unconscious meanings. Communication can be more oblique, speaking "between the lines," implied, hinted at, metaphorical, poetic. It deals with generalities as well as specifics, with the eternal as well as the present. The exchange is not entirely between equals, for one is offering help and support to the other. While there may indeed be an exchange of benefits, and the therapist may learn and gain from his client, the consistent pattern is that one accepts the role of counselor, therapist, donor, and the other accepts the reciprocal role. The therapist has a catalytic function, offering a good reason for talking about what the patient is, literally, dying to talk about.

Knowing that you are dying is different from knowing anything else. Knowing, realizing, and acknowledging that one knows are, like denial, interpersonal events. *Realization* has two very apt meanings. It can mean the act of noticing and perceiving something that is already quite definitely there; and it can mean the process of making something real, of converting it from potential to actual existence. Some people seek to use these meanings strategically and interchangeably, as if by refraining from "realizing" in the sense of recognizing that it is there, we can avoid making it real; as if what we don't acknowledge won't "really" exist; as if external reality (whatever that is) can be managed by controlling our own cognition, our internal reality. In a sense, they're right.

REFERENCES

AITKEN-SWAN, J., and E. C. EASSON, "Reactions of Cancer Patients On Being Told Their Diagnosis," *British Medical Journal*, 1 (1959), 779–83.

GILBERTSEN V. A., and O. H. WANGENSTEEN, "Should the Doctor Tell the Patient That the Disease Is Cancer?" *Cancer*, 12 (1962), 80–85.

HINTON, J., "Facing Death," *Journal of Psychosomatic Research*, 10 (1966), 22–28.

KALISH, R., "Dying and Preparing for Death: A View of Families," in *New Meanings of Death*, ed. H. Feifel. New York: McGraw-Hill, 1977.

KELLEY, W. H., and S. R. FRIESEN, "Do Cancer Patients Want to Be Told?" *Surgery*, 27 (1950), 822–26.

KLINE, N. S., and J. SOBIN, "The Psychological Management of Cancer Cases," *Journal of the American Medical Association*, 46 (1951), 1547–51.

KOLLER, R., J. W. KENNEDY, J. BUTLER, and N. WAGNER, "Counseling the Coronary Patient on Sexual Activity," *Postgraduate Medicine*, 51 (1972), 133.

LIEF, H. I., ed., *Medical Aspects of Human Sexuality*. Baltimore: Williams & Williams, 1975.

MOUNT, B. M. et al., "Death and Dying—Attitudes in a Teaching Hospital," *Urology*, 4 (1974), 741–48.

OKEN, D., "What to Tell Cancer Patients," *Journal of the American Medical Association*, 175 (1961), 1120–28.

SHNEIDMAN, E. S., ed., *Death: Current Perspectives*. Palo Alto, Calif.: Mayfield Publishing Co., 1976.

TRIMBLE, G. Y., "The Coital Coronary," *Medical Aspects of Human Sexuality*, 5 (1970), 64.

TROMBLEY, L., *Ars Moriendi Newsletter* (Philadelphia), 1976.

WEISMAN, A., *On Dying and Denying*. New York: Behavioral Publications, 1972.

Living with the Dying

So, someone in your family has recently been diagnosed as suffering from a serious, potentially fatal illness. You may want very much to help that person, but feel very helpless about how to do so. You tend to feel very inadequate faced with a dying person, very aware of your own limitations. What can you do for someone who is confronting something as overwhelming as death? In fact, what the dying person usually wants and needs from us is not unreasonable. You can listen, with genuine interest and compassion; you can talk about whatever he or she may want to talk about; you can share a companionship that goes beyond words and may not need words. When I have asked many dying people what they feared most, "being left alone, deserted" was near the top of the list. The loneliness, the isolation they so often meet may be one of the most painful parts of the experience. And you can quite easily do something about that.

AWARENESS

The sociologists Barney Glaser and Anselm Strauss made important studies of the interactions between dying patients and hospital
staff and described various kinds of awareness of dying (1965,
1968). There is *closed awareness*—the patient does not know he is
going to die. The staff members do know, but strive to maintain the
patient's unsuspecting ignorance. This isn't easy, and usually involves much misdirection and avoidance, evasion and lying, and
the creation of a fictional future for the patient, because he will
certainly want to know something. He is unable to plan realistically
for his own and his family's future.

In the situation of *suspected awareness*, the patient is between
full ignorance and full awareness, in Weisman's state of "middle
knowledge" (1972). He suspects that he is going to die, but does
not know for sure. There is a sort of contest for information, as the
patient seeks direct and indirect confirmation of his suspicions and
everybody else tries to avoid providing clues. He must scan for the
signs, peep and sneak and eavesdrop. He must watch for moments
when the staff is off-guard, because he is unlikely to learn what he
wants to by direct questions. The staff may tell him, directly and
indirectly, that he is going too far and should be less inquiring
when he gets uncomfortably close to the truth. This is a highly
unstable state, with oscillating hopes.

Then there is what Glaser and Strauss have called the ritual
drama of *mutual pretense*, when both the patient and the staff
know that he is dying, and both tacitly agree in some way to act *as
if* this were not so. It is a subtle process, not always visible in detail
even to its participants. Part of the game is to pretend that they are
not even playing a game, to pretend that they are not pretending.
The staff are prime participants in this Mystery Play, an informal
and ad-lib masquerade, using such props and costumes as come to
hand. "Business as usual in spite of alterations" is signaled. Any
direct threats to the pretense, and all must act as if nothing had
happened. They avoid each other, cry separately, ignore it if the
mask slips momentarily. If they must bleed, they must learn to
bleed internally.

The observant spectator may see the patient offering cues suggesting that he may know, sly invitations to talk about it—which are briskly rejected by the staff, who scold him for talking of such morbid matters, and solemnly conclude that one should avoid talking to him too openly. The patient is extraordinarily tactful, and immensely careful not to embarrass others. One may talk about risky subjects as long as neither party seems at any real risk of "breaking down," or rather breaking through the pretense. Preferably, though, they should stick to safe topics—the food, the patient's sleep, minor complaints and their management. Bowels can be a most fruitful topic of conversation. The game can allow the patient some privacy for feelings and fears, but it limits the possibility for closer relations with family and staff. It can be a hard game to maintain when physical disablement or undeniable symptoms override it, and when it breaks down, there may be no other means of support available for patient or staff.

Finally, there is *open awareness*—both patient and staff know and acknowledge that he is dying. There may still be concern over the mode of death ("so long as I'm not in pain—and not a vegetable"). Other people's expectations may weigh heavily. Staff and family may expect—that the patient must remain calm, composed, and cheerful, and face death with his dignity (and theirs!) intact; remain in contact, cooperative and trusting. This is fine if all agree on the same standards and if it is practical to live up to them. Even if the facts are conceded, there may be strong differences of opinion about what is acceptable behavior.

LISTENING

Listening is very simple and yet can be very difficult to do. When the patient says something about death, suffering, anger, despair, or hopelessness, it makes us feel uncomfortable and even threatened. Often we pay no attention to what he has said, hoping that if we ignore it or pretend it wasn't said, he may turn to a more cheerful topic. Often he will do so, but it is our loss as well as his if this happens. The dying soon learn to be very considerate of our feelings, for they fear that we might not come back to see them at all if they upset us. So they discover that they are not allowed to talk about some of the things that worry them very much indeed, lest they lose us even earlier than they have to. In a sense, dying patients probably spend more energy and time taking care of us and our feelings—treating us—than we spend taking care of their needs.

At other times, family members or friends may even directly challenge the dying person who mentions his doubts or fears. "Don't talk like that!" he may be told, "Look how you're upsetting mother!" It's like our custom of routinely greeting people with "How are you?" We're irritated if they stop and tell us how they are—they're not supposed to do that. We're all supposed to pretend to be interested in other people's welfare, but only as long as they don't ask us to do any more than pretend. Next time someone says, "How are you?" try giving him a perfectly random response, like "Tuesday" or "cream cake," and see if he even notices.

The patient doesn't always make it easy for us, even when we are trying to listen to him honestly. Unsure of how you will respond, he will often approach a serious topic very obliquely. He may make remarks like "I really don't feel I'm getting any better" or "They're going to do more investigations tomorrow; I don't know why they bother." If we ignore such openings, he may go no further with the topic. But you could reply, "That must be very disappointing," or "Do you get worried about what's happening?" These responses address not only the words that were spoken, but the feelings that are expressed, and can make it much easier for the person to carry on discussing his worries, now or later.

TALKING ABOUT DEATH

Let the patient set the pace in the discussion of death and its related problems. Don't force someone to talk about it unwillingly—but don't pull back and hide when he wants to talk. So listen. In life, few of us have enough people prepared to listen to us, as we tell of our woes and joys and worries. While dying, it can be even harder to find a good audience. Though the art of creative listening is a skill, it doesn't demand excessive cleverness. You can begin the conversation by just sitting and waiting comfortably in silence, or by making a simple statement such as: "I suppose you're pretty worried by this illness." When you don't know what to say, maybe you shouldn't say anything just then. This is not to suggest that you should simulate interest. If you have to fake it, then maybe you need some help before you'll be able to give help to others. But the dying often have a lot to teach us, not just about dying, but about life and living, and their special perspective can be very helpful to us. So let us not be so hung up about our own grief and guilt and by our need to give in order to assuage these that we deny the patient the opportunity to give what he can give. You can't always give unlimited transfusions of hope. But you can always give honest interest, affection, and respect. You can learn something about how dying can be done, and how to appreciate your living. I remember one patient who expressed great concern over the long hours I was working—then, after a pause, added, "But you can go home at night."

We should allow seriously ill people to talk freely about their illness, their suspicions, and their knowledge. We can ask how they feel, making it clear that we anticipate a genuine answer rather than a simple, short, stereotyped response. The person may want an occasional confirmation that you understand. Active listening isn't hard to distinguish from passive politeness. You can certainly tell the difference, when you have some exciting news to share with friends, between someone who says insincerely, "How nice!" or "Great!" and someone who genuinely wants to hear all about it. We are often so aware of trying to judge whether the patient can "take the bad news" that we fail to notice that the patient is similarly judging our capacity to "take" it—and we often fail to pass the test. Patients are well able to recognize people who can't be frank about the illness. One woman said of her doctor: "I can't talk with him about dying—he feels we've all got to get better."

You may be put in the position of being told about the diagnosis and prognosis while the patient is not. This can be a terrible burden for you, but if you follow the approach suggested, the patient should soon be able to reveal to you what he or she knows, suspects, and fears. It is hard to understand why there is so much agreement that the relatives of a patient should be told (rather than the patient), why this should be so widely held to be a good idea. It breaks the usual rule that a doctor keep confidential all aspects of an adult's illness, unless and until the patient agrees that others should be told.

The most helpful everyday analogy to constructive early discussions of death with a dying person is probably seduction or courtship. You don't begin by speaking explicitly about the intimacy you may later share. You begin by making a remark that can be interpreted by a like-minded companion as an expression of interest in more explicit discussion. If both participants read each other's messages accurately, they become more explicit and direct by serial approximations. In talking with a dying person, remember to aim at communicational seduction, not rape.

Some people are scared to approach a seriously ill friend, lest he ask them directly about the nature of the illness. Yet this is very unlikely. If you should be asked such a question, it would be important to find out what the patient already knows about his illness, who else he has spoken to, and why he is asking you. It is never a simple question needing only a simple answer. You need to find out what is wrong with the whole communication system that surrounds the patient, and seek to improve it. You might ask: "Would you like me to ask your doctor to speak to you about this?" and see that the doctor is informed.

You can anticipate what some of the worries will be. A husband is likely to have numerous concerns: "How long have I got? How many months or years? Will the family be OK? How can I best provide for them? Will I be any good as a sex partner any more? What'll happen to my job? What will they think at the office? It may be all right now, but what'll happen later? How much extra work will it be for the family to look after me?" Let him know that you love him and will stay with him, for better and for worse. These seemingly obvious things may well need to be said aloud, even if you think they can be taken for granted. It may be hard to know when or how to help. When you want to step in with "Let me help you with that," you may get a gruff "I can do it myself."

A wife has very similar worries; for example: "I won't be any good as a wife or a mother any more. I'm not really a woman any more. What can I say to the children? I can't bear having people look after me."

Be prepared to touch. It's a primitive form of communication ("primitive" in the sense of being basic to us all, rather than in any pejorative sense). Touching can convey feelings that go far beyond words, and can comfort people whose state of consciousness or confusion has perhaps placed them beyond the reach of words. It can also help us to overcome some of the repugnance or even revulsion we may feel toward the disease that is now inhabiting the body we love. So be ready to hold hands, to hug, to stroke, without embarrassment.

Remember that the patient is alive, and treat him or her as a live person, capable of opinions and decisions. Whenever possible, in large and small ways, let the patient keep his or her natural authority and assert it. Of course, in time, someone may need to take the dying person's place within the household or family; perhaps you yourself will have to take over such functions. But do not do so too hastily. The dying person is powerless, beyond a certain point, to decide or influence the course of the disease, so it is especially galling not to be allowed to decide or influence anything else—to be prematurely deposed.

Be prepared to pay the patient the compliment of acting naturally toward him. Except when his condition is very fragile indeed, you can argue with him, disagree with him, laugh with him, tease him, cry with him, be quiet with him. One expects to be treated with consideration while one is ill, but it can be very unpleasant to be treated with unnatural solemnity and passivity for very long. It is hard to live if you don't matter to anyone, and harder still to die without mattering. Any mattering involves all the dimensions of living. As one patient of mine used to say: "I wish they'd stop treating me like I was made out of porcelain."

LIVING WITH DEATH

Apart from dealing with the special problems of communication with the dying, remember that most of one's time is likely to be spent in normal conversation. Remember at all times that although he may have additional special needs, the dying person is a perfectly normal human being, with the same special combination of interests, peculiarities, and opinions as before. Get to know him better, and talk about what interests him. Don't be too afraid of making mistakes or of admitting them. The patient doesn't expect you to be perfect, and may even be able to help you. The relationship can be more nearly equal than you might expect.

Let's consider the example of two patients. The first, Ivy, was a staunchly independent spinster who lived alone with her sister. One Christmas, her sister began to complain of indigestion and on investigation was found to have a stomach cancer, too far advanced for surgery. She died within a matter of months. About the time of the funeral, Ivy began to experience similar indigestion. She was in due course admitted to the same hospital, and an operation proved her to have an even larger stomach cancer, also too advanced for surgery. After the operation, the surgeons told her that all she had was an ulcer, and that she'd be well before long. But she remained in the hospital, and got weaker and weaker. I had treated Ivy some years before for a very different problem, and when I found out she was in the hospital, I went to see her. She was pleased to chat about what had been happening, but although the surgeons had assured me that she knew nothing about her condition, her conversation was barbed with broad hints about it. "They tell me it's just an ulcer," she said, and paused. "Strange, isn't it? Yesterday morning when I woke at six and I was so weak, my relatives had come all the way from Wales to see me—haven't seen them for years. And the chaplain was there." Another pause. "But they tell me it's just an ulcer!" Later, she asked, quite sharply, "Do I seem to be breathless?" "You don't look breathless to me," I replied, "Why do you ask?" "Well," said Ivy, "that's the way I'm going to go, isn't it?" Because I had responded favorably to this sort of test, Ivy took me into her confidence, and told me that she was sure she had exactly the same illness as her sister. She felt able to face up to her diagnosis, but she didn't know how to handle the doctors who insisted on playing these tedious charades about her "little ulcer."

Terry was another patient on the same ward. He had been a window-cleaner. He couldn't read or write, and he was very embarrassed about that. He too had been found to have a large stomach cancer upon operation, and although the surgeons believed they had been able to remove the tumor, they considered that the disease had probably spread beyond the stomach. He too was told that he had "just an ulcer." He surprised his surgeon, however, by insisting on seeing a psychiatrist immediately after the operation. "You say you've cut out the ulcer," he said, "but you haven't cut out the worry—and worries cause ulcers." When I saw him, he made it clear that he wanted to be able to talk to me so that he could review what had happened to him in his life, and he expressed his concern for his wife and children. Two themes emerged clearly in our first session, when he still officially knew nothing about his diagnosis. One was his search for a sense of meaning and accomplishment in his life thus far—had it been worthwhile? Had he made a good job of it? The other was his great concern that he should make arrangements so that his family would be well provided for "in case something happens to me." During the second session, "in case something happens" became "when something happens to me." He talked about how puzzling his illness was, because he'd had an ulcer before, "and it felt very different from this." He recalled a previous episode when he'd been having some hearing difficulties, and although the doctors had done all sorts of investigations, he'd never been able to get them to tell him what was wrong. He became very angry remembering this, and made it quite clear that he hated not knowing what was really going on. I accepted his feelings, and assured him that I never lie to patients, and that I was prepared to talk about his illness and any problems he had quite openly and frankly. He calmed down, and talked about how important it was to him to be able to trust a doctor like that. But he didn't make use of the opportunity that time; he was satisfied to have established his right to do so. On his next visit, he told me what he believed the diagnosis was, and I agreed, and we were able to talk about it in detail.

We can, by all means, communicate hope. It is seldom justifiable to give up all hope; though in time one's hopes may become more circumscribed, more limited, though still realistic. A person can hope he can go home for a time, that he can enjoy another good meal, or watch a film; that he will be able to see some friends or relatives who are coming from a distance.

Pay primary attention to what the patient wants. It is so easy, when preoccupied with one's own wishes, to insist on yet more specialists, or on flying the patient off to some famous clinic. Treatment of any medical condition, as we have seen, is rarely curative. Except for many minor conditions which tend to get better whatever is done about them, medicine rarely cures. Medicine is the science of prolonging disease and the art of making it bearable to live with. Much can now be done to help a person live a good while with illnesses, and to enable one to be more comfortable during this time. Changing doctors, especially if this is done more than once, prevents the patient from having a coherent course of any treatment and is likely to decrease both quantity and quality of life.

The dying person should be allowed to live his life the way he wants to, and as normally as possible. Too often we assume that once the diagnosis has been made, the person with a a serious illness must give up work, hobbies, even sexual activities, automatically. Is there not life before death? Let the patient decide these things himself, depending on how he feels. Let him continue to feel useful; for an enforced redundancy, especially when a person is feeling quite capable, can be one of the cruelest and least necessary aspects of a serious illness. Business and professional colleagues should be prepared to allow the patient to function in whatever way he can and wants to for as long as possible.

Don't keep children away from the dying—they can have a healthy, cheering effect on the patient, and they can help to keep the atmosphere normal and natural, for they don't automatically accept some of the unnecessary restrictions we so often place upon ourselves. Also, children have a right to be able to relate to their relatives and friends through all stages of life, including the last. Except in rare instances, hospitals should not prevent children from visiting in the wards. There is no risk that children will come to any harm by visiting seriously ill patients, and it can be an opportunity for them to learn about some of the realities of life. One reason death can become frightening for children is that they have so often been deprived of their rightful participation in the care for ill and dying relatives. Too often, their only experience of death is as something unmentionably awful that happens to a loved person after she or he has been taken away to a hospital. Before you rush to protest that children couldn't bear exposure to these realities, be quite sure it really is the children you are talking about, and not the frightened child within yourself who is speaking.

The elderly often seem to be able to face death more calmly than younger people, and may even welcome it. Especially when they have been suffering from chronic and debilitating illness, and when they are alone in life, death may not seem so awful. To far too great an extent in modern society, the elderly have been made redundant. They are treated as if they were already dead; they are often socially buried long before they are physically buried. And then we may spend more on the funeral than we did on the last year or years of their life.

At times, depression may become troublesome. Especially when a change in the sick person's mood develops slowly, it may take some time for you to become aware of it. Some people are particularly reluctant to admit to feeling sad; they may consider that it is "weak," or shows a "lack of self-control" to have such feelings. People who weep upset us, and the temptation may be to avoid it, to pretend that it isn't happening at all, or to escape if possible, with a gruff "There, there—I'll come back when you're feeling better." Don't be scared. There are times when it is very appropriate, very reasonable, very normal to cry. Let the dying cry, and be ready to sit with them while they do so, unless they want privacy. A man who weeps may be even more embarrassed and embarrassing—but let him know that it's all right for him to cry, and comfort him in his embarrassment. Don't overdo reassurance in any artificial sense—stick to the amount of hope you can believe in and share.

Don't become trapped by the illness. Some relatives feel obliged to live constantly with the illness, seldom leaving the bedside, and feeling guilty if they occasionally think of laughing or amusing themselves, or continuing with their normal life. But everyone needs and deserves a break from the constant pressure of attending a sick person; you will be a far more effective companion for allowing yourself some emotional, physical, and spiritual rest and refreshment.

Monitor your own feelings, for you will not be immune to the denial, despair, and other emotions the patient experiences. Don't be ashamed to admit that caring for a dying person can be a major strain for you, and don't hesitate to enlist the assistance and support of others. It is no comfort to the patient to see you neglecting yourself.

During the illness, you may often feel angry and put upon and exploited. Don't be ashamed of this, and don't let it lead to rejection of the patient or withdrawal from him. Be ready to admit, express, and discuss your feelings with the patient, your family, and the doctors and nurses. Sometimes, in the course of a prolonged illness, you may find yourself thinking: "I wish he would die and get it over with," and then feel appalled at your impatience and selfishness. A long period of waiting for the end, especially if the illness is stormy or given to recurrent crises or relapses, can be difficult to cope with; and it is natural, at times, to wish it were all over, for your sake and the patient's. However good the feast may have been, Damocles probably longed for it to be finished. At such times, as at other times in life, you'll have to forgive yourself for being human.

The patient may need special support with regard to his employment, if he plans to continue at work during treatment. There is evidence that cancer patients, for example, are discriminated against at work, even when they have survived the disease. Studies in California have shown that on returning to work, the patient may have lost seniority, health insurance benefits, possible promotions, even the job itself (see, e.g., Feldman, 1976). If this can happen to the person who has recovered from cancer, how much worse might it be for those who have *not* recovered, though they may have months or even years of working life ahead? Even among highly employable people, aged 25 to 50, working well when cancer is diagnosed, with high school education or more, and in occupations like registered nursing, management, and book-keeping, discrimination clearly exists.

Legislation may begin to improve the situation. In 1975, a bill was passed in California which aimed at eliminating job discrimination because of a medical condition. The definition of a "medical condition" included "any health impairment related to or associated with a diagnosis of cancer, from which a person has been rehabilitated or cured." More such laws are needed, and cure should not be required before protection is extended to the worker.

Nearly a quarter of a group studied by an American Cancer Society team (Feldman, 1976) had been rejected for jobs because of their cancer treatment; nearly a quarter said they had met discrimination at work; about a fifth felt that their working conditions or salary had been adversely affected. Relations with fellow workers were strained. Some people thought that cancer was contagious and avoided the patients. Others were intrusive and gossïpy or overprotective. The study also clearly showed that cancer need have no ill effects at work; a good proportion of the patients had had promotions and were able to return to physically strenuous jobs, and, even after disfiguring visible surgery, to return to jobs with a high degree of public contact.

Religious beliefs, as ordinarily expressed, have little to do with the way people handle death. Belonging to any religious group does not guarantee that death or suffering will be faced with more equanimity. One major study (Hinton, 1972), found that the recorded denomination of belief had no correlation with the amount of anxiety a seriously ill patient showed. More important was the way in which the person held his beliefs. For some people church-going is a habit, a reflex, a social occasion. Some use religious beliefs as an escape route, as a means of avoiding the realities of life, as if by behaving devoutly, they can gain personal exemption from such realities. None of these people gets much help in coping with death. Yet someone with devout beliefs (whether devoutly Catholic or devoutly agnostic), someone who has worked out a personal, coherent philosophy of life which enables him to make sense of life, can make sense of death, and can face it with less anxiety.

The dying person should certainly be offered every opportunity to keep to his usual religious practices, or to explore his beliefs and how the illness affects them, with whomever he finds an agreeable spiritual companion. There is no time for any of us to start heavy preaching of our own religious beliefs, or to seek a late conversion. If our own beliefs are indeed helpful in coping with death, then let us demonstrate this by a humility and sincerity in the care we offer. If the patient should want to talk to you about religious matters, of course he should be allowed to do so. It will be most useful if you can help him explore and define his own beliefs. Of what religion was his family, and how was he brought up? What effects have his life and his illness had on his beliefs? What is his concept of God, and of death? Even if the patient asks you about your own views, this is likely, in the first place, to be a test of whether you will allow the patient to talk about his own ideas. Once you know his point of view, you are in a better position to discuss your opinion in a way that could be helpful to him. By all means share your views then; but do not be judgmental or critical. No God gives you that right. We must be prepared to accept other people's differing opinions. Your beliefs may be a very real and absolute truth for you, and that is fine; but they need not be true for another. In some ways, religious problems seem to cause both medical staff and family members even more embarrassment than do sexual problems. However awkwardly people may handle either problem, they'll probably be calmer dealing with intimate sexual difficulties than with spiritual puzzlement.

Can there be any goals in thanatology, the care of the dying? Yes, but they must not become a set of externally applied rules of the right and proper way to die, as used to be laid down in the Middle Ages. Each of us has the right to die our own death, true to our self, and our style of life, helped by others to die comfortably and honestly, and without having to spend our last days playing sterile and self-defeating games according to someone else's rules.

It is not phony to claim that a terminal illness can provide a genuine opportunity for growth, or that there are important things the dying can teach us. Death and the prospect of death can bring things into focus, can separate the trivia from the genuinely valid aspects of life. "The prospect of execution concentrates a man's mind wonderfully." And indeed, when given the chance and the encouragement, the dying can make their last months or years substantially more meaningful than what has gone before. That is why those of us who work with the dying do not find it such an unrelieved burden of gloom and morbidity as many people suppose, for it is all to do with living—and living a vivid, valid life that wouldn't have been possible with the sterile games and pretenses with which most of us make do for most of the time. When the very existence of a tomorrow has become a present rather than a theoretical question, one must realize how unwise it is to keep postponing the simple pleasures, the reconciliations, the admissions that we care. It is then quite clear that people are always more important than possessions or rules, and that life can be lived honestly, and sincerely, and with real pleasure. Perhaps it ought not to take so much to bring us to realize this, but the dying can often teach us valuable lessons about these things. Working with such people has many unavoidably deeply sad moments. The more involved we are as helpers, especially with people with whom we don't have to have a relationship, the more often we will meet loss and grief. But we will inevitably, in the words of Dr. Ned Cassem (1974), learn more than we will teach, receive more than we give, and gain more opportunities for real personal growth than if we had avoided such encounters.

REFERENCES

CASSEM, N. H., "Care of the Dying Person," in *Concerning Death: A Practical Guide for the Living*, ed. E. A. Grollman. Boston: Beacon Press, 1974, pp. 13–48.

FELDMAN, F., "A. C. S. Volunteer," *American Cancer Society, California Division*, vol. 22, no. 2, 1976.

GLASER, BARNEY, and ANSELM STRAUSS, *Awareness of Dying*. Chicago: Aldine Press, 1965.

HINTON, J. M., *Dying*. Baltimore: Penguin, 1972.

WEISMAN, A., *On Dying and Denying*. New York: Behavioral Publications, 1972.

7

Planning for Death

There is probably no time when the average family is so vulnerable to confusion and exploitation, to compound their loss, as when a death has occurred. To a large extent, you can protect yourself and all your family from such exploitation by careful planning of your affairs. Every year, millions of families have to make major decisions and expensive purchases under conditions of emotional distress, pressure of time, and lack of information or experience. A Federal Trade Commission examiner once remarked that there are few, if any, industries in which the consumer is so disadvantaged or where his normal bargaining power is so diluted in a situation of such immediate need. *Caveat emptor*—Let the buyer beware.

BODY AND ORGAN DONATION

In the first place, you may wish to donate your body, or parts of it, for scientific and medical uses. The Uniform Anatomical Gift Act of 1968 sets the basic guidelines underlying the donor laws of each state. It declares:

1. Any person 18 years of age or older can donate all or part of his body after death for transplantation, research, or placement in a tissue bank.

2. A donor's valid statement of gift supersedes the rights of anyone else, unless a state autopsy law prevails and has conflicting requirements.

3. If a donor has not acted in his lifetime to specify a wish to donate, his survivors may do so, in a specified order of priority (spouse, adult son or daughter, either parent, adult brother or sister, guardian, or any other person authorized or under obligation to dispose of the body).

4. Physicians who accept anatomical gifts relying in good faith on documents provided to them in such cases are protected from legal action.

5. Where a transplant is planned, the fact and time of death must be determined by a physician *not* involved in the transplant.

6. The donor has the right to revoke the gift, and it may be rejected by those for whom it is intended.

Donation to a Medical School

You may donate your whole body to a medical school for dissection. This can be a valuable contribution to the training of doctors. Because there is often a shortage of bodies for dissection, your local medical school is likely to be very grateful for such a donation. A phone call to the university's department of anatomy will enable you to make the appropriate arrangements.

Usually a funeral director will take the body to the medical school, but the school may provide transportation, or an ambulance service may be used. A death certificate may need to be taken to the county board of health for a transportation permit. The rules vary from state to state. In some instances, the family might even be able to take the body to the school. In some states, only a funeral director may move a body. Most schools will pay transportation expenses within the state or within a certain area. The body should arrive within about twenty-four hours unless it has been refrigerated. You may give your body away, but you are not allowed to sell it. If you wish, you can carry an identification card on your person to record the fact of the donation (see Figure 7-1).

FIGURE 7-1 Donor Card

```
I, _____,

have donated my body for teaching purposes and scientific research to (name and

address of medical school): _____

_____

_____

For verification, call (phone number of school) _____

_____

Date _____ Signature _____

Address _____

_____
```

You should be able to expect that your body will be treated with respect. Some medical schools will, if requested, ultimately return the remains to the family in a sealed box, though others will not. Some will return the ashes. All will otherwise see that the remains are ultimately buried properly.

Other body parts can be donated. Eyes may be given to an eye bank for corneal transplants, the most successful type of transplant, which can restore sight to some blind people. Arrangements for donation of corneas should be made beforehand if possible, because the eyes must be removed within two to four hours after death and carefully preserved. This is more easily done in the hospital, though other arrangements can be made. It is not possible to bequeath your eyes to specific individuals; corneas will be used by the bank on the basis of simple rotation—for the next person who needs a transplant, irrespective of his or her ability to pay for it. In Canada, the Canadian National Institute for the Blind (CNIB) has established an eye bank; Canadians can obtain information at

CNIB regional offices. There are more than sixty eye banks in the United States, and Americans can check the local phone book for the address of the nearest one.

Ear bones can be donated, in the United States, to a *temporal bone bank*, for use in research into ear disease and deafness. Advance arrangements need to be made, because removal of the bones is a difficult and specialized procedure. For information, write to the National Temporal Bone Banks Center (Baltimore, Maryland 21205) or the Deafness Research Foundation (366 Madison Avenue, New York, New York 10017). In Canada, contact the Ontario Temporal Bone Bank (Banting Institute, Rooms 524-525, 100 College Street, Toronto 181, Ontario).

Kidney transplants are becoming more common, though there is often a serious shortage of suitable kidneys. In America, more information can be obtained from the National Kidney Foundation (116 East 27th Street, New York, New York 10010). In Canada, contact the Kidney Foundation of Canada (3785 Chemin de la Côté de Liesse, Montreal 379, Quebec), or its regional offices in each province.

Pituitary glands are used to produce growth hormone. An estimated five to ten thousand children in the United States suffer from a major lack of this hormone, causing them to be abnormally short and limited in growth. It takes some 300 pituitary glands to provide enough growth hormone to allow one child to grow normally for a year; thus the treatment is available, so far, to only a small proportion of the children who can benefit from it. This work is coordinated in the United States by the National Pituitary Agency (Suite 503-7, 210 West Fayette Street, Baltimore, Maryland 21202).

For information about tissue donation, you can contact the Tissue Bank of the Naval Medical Research Institute (NNMC, Bethesda, Maryland 20014; phone 202-295-1121) if you live in or near Washington, D.C.

The Living Bank has on file the names of over thirty thousand persons who have directed their next of kin to donate all or parts of their bodies for medical use. Some 60 percent want all their body to be used. The Bank (P.O. Box 6725 *or* 6631 Main Street, Houston, Texas 77025) has a twenty-four-hour telephone service (713-528-2971). It will send you a Uniform Donor Card (Figure 7-2) to keep in your wallet and a Donor Registration Form to return to the Bank. The card will direct those who attend you when you are gravely ill to notify the Bank immediately on your death.

FIGURE 7-2

UNIFORM DONOR CARD

of _____

(print or type name of donor)

In the hope that I may help others, I hereby make this anatomical gift, if medically acceptable, to take effect upon my death. The words and marks below indicate my desires.

I give: (a) ☐ any needed organs or parts

          (b) ☐ only the following organs or parts

_____

Specify which organ(s) or part(s) for the purposes of transplantation, therapy, medical research or education;

          (c) ☐ my body for anatomical study if needed.

_____

LIMITATIONS OR SPECIAL WISHES, IF ANY

Signed by the Donor and the following two witnesses in the presence of each other.

_____

Signature of Donor   Donor's Birthdate

_____

City & State where signed   Date signed

_____

Witness   Witness

THIS IS A LEGAL DOCUMENT UNDER THE UNIFORM ANATOMICAL GIFT ACT OR SIMILAR LAWS

Other items can also serve useful purposes. Spectacles can be sent to New Eyes for the Needy, Inc. (Short Hills, New Jersey 07076). Medicines left over from the last illness cannot be legally used again in North America. If they are clean and still in their original, labeled containers, they can be sent to the Pharmacy Department, Loma Linda Medical School (Loma Linda, California 92354), where arrangements are made for them to be used by missionary doctors abroad. Opinions differ as to whether such drugs are usable or valuable in the countries they are sent to, however.

Some people use the MedicAlert program to carry medical information about themselves and make it readily available in the event of an emergency. They can also have the Medic Alert medallion carry the information that they wish to donate organs at the time of their death. The address is MedicAlert (Turlock, California 95380; (phone 209-632-2371, or in an emergency 209-634-4917).

FUNERALS AND BURIAL

A funeral is an organized social response to death, involving some rites and ceremonies and the disposal of the body. The precise type of ceremony may be influenced by religious beliefs and social fashions; by the wishes of the deceased, the survivors' needs and opinions, and by community expectations.

The functionary whose business it is to provide services related to the funeral has undergone a number of changes of title and public image. In the nineteenth century, funerals were a responsibility shared by family and friends and the church. The local carpenter or cabinetmaker might "undertake" to help by constructing a box, and a carriage might be borrowed from the nearest livery stable. Then there emerged the *undertaker*, who provided such assistance on a more regular basis—and, in Philippe Aries' phrase, "the manipulation of the dead became a profession" (1974). About the time of the Civil War the *mortician* emerged. One early mortician, Dr. Holmes, was reputed to have "passionately" embalmed some 4,000 corpses in four years unaided. The function of the mortician, like that of a beautician, was to modify the uncomfortable realities of the body when we preferred not to see them directly. To allow the transport home of soldiers who had died in some distant battle without wasting a whole barrel of good brandy, the practice of embalming was reinvented and more widely used. A practice almost unknown in Europe, where it had been long abandoned, embalming helped to make the handling of death more resolutely a matter of commerce, of business, of profit. To complete this process it had to become more neatly packageable; it had to include an expertise, a technique people had to be persuaded that they needed—but would want the embalmer to do for them. Later in the nineteenth century the *funeral director* arrived. Like a TV or movie director, he moved beyond the manipulation of individual appearances and took charge of the production of an increasingly elaborate secular ceremony. One historian of the American funeral industry and establishment has spoken of "the dramaturgic role, in which the undertaker becomes a stage manager to create an appropriate atmosphere and to move the funeral party through a drama in which social relationships are stressed and an emotional catharsis or release is provided through ceremony" (Mitford, 1963).

No single new term has reliably succeeded these, but a further evolutionary stage is underway at present. It's not enough to be the seller of handy services and simple products or the *compere* of the commercial burial rites. Now the aim is higher still, a calling, a profession. Now we hear of "grief therapists," who claim a special therapeutic function in caring for the grieving as well as the deceased. Preachers of normalcy, they'll heal your grief with a better box with prettier trimmings and a higher tensile strength. (The emphasis on great tensile strength in advertising is intriguing. It's as if we're absolutely determined that if there is indeed to be a Day of Judgment when all shall rise again, we'll stay put.) That's quite a long way to come in a little over a hundred years.

Most states in the United States license funeral directors, and all license embalmers. The requirements usually include a minimum educational level of high school graduation, and some surveys have suggested that most men in the business have not had much more than this. In some states they have begun to require one or two years of college education, perhaps at least one year of study in a college of mortuary science or of funeral service education, followed by a state board licensing examination and a period of apprenticeship lasting a year or more. Quite elaborate sets of educational objectives were being developed in the early 1970s, outlining potential courses that would begin to look like those of the recognized paramedical specialties.

The Coroner

Under certain circumstances, the services of a coroner are legally necessary. In some areas, especially in Britain, the coroner is appointed by the local government; in most parts of the United States, the coroner is an elected official. Although the coroner may have medical experience, in most areas he need not be thus qualified. The medical examiner, with similar functions, is appointed by city, county, or state officials, or in some instances by an independent commission. He must be a doctor and in addition he is almost always a fully trained pathologist with special experience in forensic pathology.

The medical examiner or coroner must examine the cause of death in certain specific conditions: when someone dies who has not recently and regularly been under the care of a doctor who would otherwise be able to certify the cause of death with sufficient certainty, death by accident, and death by other than natural causes—homicides, suicides, deaths occurring in jails and other institutions, deaths arising from or related to industrial causes, and deaths that might be due to negligence. In such cases he requires a post-mortem examination, an autopsy, and such tests and examinations as will help determine the cause of death. He is then responsible for issuing the appropriate documents to record the fact and the cause of death. Sometimes, the investigation takes the form of an inquest, a formal inquiry, with or without a jury—a quasi-judicial hearing which will be able to hear witnesses and assemble the evidence.

In other cases, even when the death is clearly due to natural causes, the doctor may request an autopsy in order that more can be learned about the illness and its effects. In some instances, such a study can add greatly to medical knowledge. In this event, though, there is no automatic or official right to hold an autopsy, but the doctor will ask for, and need, the family's consent.

The Funeral Industry

The funeral industry was criticized with magnificent style in works such as Jessica Mitford's famous book *The American Way of Death* (1963). It has also been stoutly defended by several apologists for what they are wont to call "funeralization." They use old historical precedents. We are told excitedly in one recent apologia that the Oxford Text of the New English Bible uses both the words "embalm" and "coffin"; and names like Herodotus and Hammurabi are dropped, to establish the antiquity and respectability of modern funeral practices. The argument of historical precedent is surprisingly inept. The ancients also used to stone adulterers, which would be an extremely inconvenient practice to reintroduce in the modern world.

The major trade association, the National Funeral Director's Association, maintains a well-funded lobby in Washington and state capitals that brings powerful influence to bear on legislation in this field. The consumer interest has been far less well represented. Some states have passed curious laws restricting the individual's rights to have his corpse disposed of as he wishes, while necessitating higher funeral expenses, and without noticeably improving the general public good; but it is only quite recently that any sort of consumer lobby has begun to emerge to represent public interests in such legislation.

The size of the funeral industry is impressive. There were 1,977,000 deaths in the United States in 1973, for example, and official estimates calculate that there were probably some 23,000 funeral service and crematory establishments and some 45,000 licensed funeral directors and embalmers at that time. (Federal Trade Commission, 1975, 1977). The average cost of funeral and burial expenses is estimated at some $2,000. Gross receipts for the funeral homes and crematories were estimated by the U.S. Department of Commerce at $1.91 billion for 1973, $2.00 billion for 1974, and $2.12 billion for 1975, reaching a projected $2.80 billion by 1980. Then there are such related outlays as flowers (some $800 million annually), cemetery expenses (approximately $735 million annually), monuments and tombstones (about $450 million), and burial vaults (around $305 million). The total annual expenditure on items related to funerals would then be of the order of $4.2 billion. The federal government spends nearly $500 million a year on such expenses via veterans and other benefits.

All sorts of strange practices, in all walks of life and death, are justified on the basis of the argument that the public is merely being given what it wants. This reasoning is based on a false, mischievous, and distorted syllogism which, if fully dissected, would probably read something like this: In an ideal state, given a free choice from among a wide range of possibilities, an intelligent person would be likely to choose what he most wants and needs :: In this present, far-from-ideal state, offered a narrow and often artificial choice from among a limited range of possibilities, predetermined by other people to best meet *their* selfish needs, most people happen to choose X :: Therefore, X is what most people want and need.

Funerals are often discussed in terms of euphemisms dealing with "departure" and "saying goodbye," as if the deceased were indeed leaving for a cruise. The ancient Greeks used to put a coin in the mouth of the deceased to pay the boatman Charon for ferrying the body across the Styx. The journey has become far more expensive. Funeral ceremonies have been used to express affection for, or dread of, the deceased. Some primitive rites were intended to confuse the spirit, to protect the living from an unwelcome or sudden return. One aborigine tribe was reputed to remove the fingernails from and tie the hands of their dead, or tie or amputate the feet, to prevent them from digging themselves out of the grave. We use hermetically sealed iron caskets as if we shared these fears.

If possible, you should discuss the sort of funeral you want with the rest of the family, so that they can know what you want—usually the wishes of the deceased are unknown or ignored. Similarly, it is advisable for the family to discuss and, as far as possible, decide on what they want before funeral arrangements are made. In this way you can often plan the funeral you and your family want without having to buy services or materials neither wanted nor needed. By all means, question what you are offered, and ask for explanations until you are satisifed. The honest funeral director will have nothing to hide, and should be sincerely interested in assisting you with consideration for your feelings and your finances.

When a death has occurred and you must make the funeral arrangements, call your priest, minister, or rabbi. He will be able to counsel you on spiritual matters, and will also be able to help you with the practical details of arranging the funeral. Seriously consider holding the funeral service in the church. Your local funeral or memorial society will also be able to give you advice and help in arranging a secular funeral and burial. If you do feel the need to spend money to express your grief and affection, you do not have to purchase very expensive caskets or floral exhibitions. Most lasting and more useful memorials include gifts to hospitals, medical research, charities, and educational organizations. Think about it—how would *you* like to be remembered? Would you like to know that you were buried in elaborately crafted wood and metal and temporarily surrounded by flowers? Or would you prefer to have funds in your memory serve to educate and help others? Let the funeral concentrate on the spirit, the personality, and the affection rather than on the flesh and the body—the coffin can be kept closed, and need not even be present.

In some areas, owing to commercial pressures, newspapers refuse to accept funeral announcements containing statements like "Please omit flowers." This is an intolerable infringement of freedom of communication, and may make it difficult for your wishes to be respected.

Contrary to what may be suggested to you, present highly elaborate funeral practices are a comparatively recent and commercially sponsored development. They have no major respectable precedent in the Jewish or Christian tradition, both of which have stressed simplicity, modesty, and a de-emphasis of the body itself. Both major traditions emphasize a practical funeral dealing with uncamouflaged death; neither developed display of the corpse nor the excessive use of flowers.

In no major existing religion apart from the secular paganism of the funeral industry is there any belief or practice to resemble those described in standard works of the funeral literature suggesting that: "funeral service is a social function at which the deceased is the guest of honor and the center of attraction. . . . A poorly prepared body in a beautiful casket is just as incongruous as a young lady appearing at a party in a costly gown and with her hair in curlers."

Check on the state or local laws. You may well be encouraged to believe that cremation without a coffin or burial without a vault is illegal. But fortunately, most states have not chosen to interfere with human rights in this way. Cemetery officials often like vaults because they limit subsidence and make it easier to mow the lawns—but the practice is otherwise entirely unnecessary, and no significant problems arise in the many parts of the world where it is unheard of. All sorts of macabre accessories and artifacts are available—burial footwear, and whole ranges of special garments, inner-spring mattresses, and so on. These, too, are wholly unnecessary. No corpse needs a mattress, and people can be buried in a simple shroud or in their own clothes.

Before we consider the planning of the funeral, we should carefully consider the often questionable basis of the services you will be encouraged to buy and the relevant consumer protection advice with regard to the sales practices you may encounter. After due research, the Federal Trade Commission (1975, 1977) has proposed a Trade Regulation Rule to control funeral trade practices. In its related Staff Memorandum, the FTC Bureau of Consumer Protection states that the general marketing strategy of much of the industry seemed to eliminate low-cost alternatives to the standard funeral bylaws, regulations, and codes of ethics; to stunt the development of memorial societies; to make it difficult for the consumer to find out about prices before coming to the funeral home; and to confuse him, once he has arrived, about such prices and options as are available. It has been suggested that lack of competition in the industry has led to too many funeral homes, often far too lavishly equipped and heavily overinvested. To remain in business, such homes need to sell more expensive products.

It is important that you not be misled about legal, public health, or other requirements, and your funeral director should provide you with an explanation in print of local requirements.

Embalming

The decomposition or decay of a dead human body cannot be prevented by the use of current techniques of embalming, nor by any possible casket, burial vault, or other container, whether sealed, unsealed, airtight, or watertight. Embalming is *not* required by law except in very unusual circumstances, and except in such cases no one has the right to embalm anyone without specific authorization from the appropriate legally responsible person.

Occasionally, embalming may be required by law if a body needs to be transported over a long distance by common carrier, or if burial or cremation has for any reason to be substantially delayed. Some states require embalming if the death was due to certain contagious diseases. There is little or no real evidence that the corpse is ever, under normal circumstances, a health hazard, and none showing that current standard embalming practices are either effective or necessary safeguards. No major public health authority regards it as a useful health measure. Note that in some areas, for example, in Pennsylvania, the State Board of Funeral Directors requires that the body be buried or cremated within twenty-four hours of death (or removal from the hospital) if embalming is omitted. If embalming is to be omitted, the same board requires a statement signed by the next of kin stating that embalming is against the religious convictions of the deceased. Such requirements are unnecessary for the protection of the public, even if they may be unavoidable in some areas at present.

Embalming should never be legally required.

Many American funeral directors assume that embalming is desired unless they are specifically instructed to the contrary. Remember, in most cases, that embalming may help to preserve the body until shortly after the funeral. It does not protect the body indefinitely from the normal processes of dissolution, and indeed the later condition of a body, especially if it is buried in one of the "airtight" caskets you may be offered, will certainly be a great deal more unnatural and unwholesome than would be the case in the normal course of events.

Embalming involves draining the body of its blood and replacing it with embalming fluid pumped in through the arteries. The fluid, often colored and perfumed, contains such substances as formaldehyde, glycerine, borax, phenol, and alcohol, as well as water. A long hollow needle, a trochar, is pushed into the abdomen and the chest cavity, and their contents are pumped out and replaced with "cavity fluid." "Restorative work" may follow, using a wide variety of techniques (even minor surgery) and plaster of paris, wax, cottonwool, massage cream, latex, and other substances to remove the signs of death so far as possible and to restore the corpse to an appearance that often exceeds the glow of health ever achieved in life.

Much of the literature proposing the advantages of embalming implies that it usually leads to the long-term preservation of the body. Although a body can be preserved for years by techniques such as those used in laboratories of anatomy and research, it tends not to look very nice (rather discolored and leathery), so these methods aren't socially acceptable or commercially used. Embalmers in North America usually use a fluid diluted enough to leave the body as soft and normal-looking as possible, with enough preservative to help it last through the funeral. Preservation beyond a few days is not usually sought. Embalming is not a public health measure of any sort. The dead body is very much safer, more sanitary, and less of a public menace than the average living body. No competent medical authority considers embalming necessary for health reasons.

Yet embalming, in the words of a basic textbook on the subject (Strubb & Frederick, 1961), "forms the foundation for the entire funeral service structure. It is the basis for the sale of profitable merchandise." It is necessary as the basis for such other sales as open-casket viewing, cosmetics, burial clothes and shoes, and ornately lined and cushioned caskets. It is also most effective in keeping the consumer dealing with the same funeral home—you can hardly take the body elsewhere once they've started work on it. In some places, embalming is routinely begun on all bodies without benefit of permission from the family. Some people find the practice personally and esthetically offensive; for some, such as Orthodox Jews, it is prohibited by religious law. It will usually, by itself, add $50 to $200 or more to the cost of the funeral.

Viewing

There is no medically or psychologically valid case to be made in favor of corpse-viewing. What sort of reasons are put forward for such a practice? Well, let's consider an authoritative point of view. In a recent book, the executive director of the National Funeral Director's Association and a university director of mortuary science waxed enthusiastic about viewing (Raether & Slater, 1974). The body should be viewed "if it can be made viewable," for this serves several helpful purposes. Viewing the dead body, they assured us, makes those who survive more aware of the reality of death: "Seeing is believing." Secondly, they claim, proper restoration and preparation helps "to modify and remove the marks of violence or the ravages of disease," so as to "provide an acceptable image for recalling the deceased.... Viewing is therapeutic for people, regardless of age," and they see it as especially good for children. Instead of fantasizing, the child is enabled by the body's presence to comprehend the real meaning of death. No evidence is offered to support these assertions. I know of none that exists.

Embalmers may work hard to improve the appearance of the corpse, to help the family "preserve a beautiful memory picture." Shor (in Margolis et al., 1975, p. 249) writes, "First, the embalmer endeavours to restore the facial features to a lifelike appearance"; yet Pinette (ibid., p. 119) stresses the value of viewing because "visual confrontation confirms the fact that the one loved is really dead." Great care is taken to achieve an appropriately lively tone, to confirm the fact of death (surely a somewhat contradictory approach). Mayer (ibid, pp. 179–82), writing of the optimum funeral home environment, suggests that the best colors are "muted tones of red, yellow, yellow-orange ... tan, beige and taupe," although cool colors like blue and green may be used as "tiny, vivid accents." It is clear that this thoughtfully planned spectacle is believed to be of great value. Indeed, Nichols (ibid., p. 47) writes, "The funeral is an investment in the survivors' physical health, mental stability, and social behavior."

There is no genuine evidence that the "beautiful memory picture" conjured up with greasepaint, wax, and cottonwool is of any benefit whatever to the survivors. While the practice may allow each American citizen to emulate the dubious advantages of the Lenin mausoleum, let us not pretend that this is in any way a therapeutic process. It appropriately symbolizes the hollow preoccupation with appearances rather than true value, displaying the empty flesh, primped and painted like a prostitute, rather than remembering the qualities of the person's life. Finally reduced to an object rather than a person, people comment about "How good he looks" rather than "How good he was." Certainly our memory of the dead one will be important and valuable to us—but it is the living memory of all he was during his life that will remain significant, not just the false and prettified fetish of painted meat. This is no confrontation with the reality and finality of death, but rather an elaborate evasion. The major religious faiths discourage or do not allow such open-coffin funerals, and in this regard they are surely right.

Caskets

It is usually convenient to use some sort of container to hold the body for the duration of the funeral, such as a coffin (the familiar lozenge-shaped box) or a rectangular casket. These may range from a simple wooden coffin to a highly elaborate and ornate casket with satin lining, inner-spring mattress, and metal ornaments. Coffins range in price from a few dollars to hundreds and even thousands of dollars. "The casket is . . . the last material gift the survivors can give the body which once was a person," says a standard funeral text. Better by far to give your gifts to the living.

You may be misled into thinking that the state or local law

requires a casket, but this is usually not so. It is more commonly required by the regulations or policy of the cemetery or funeral home, and alternative homes or cemeteries may not insist on this. Similarly, the elaborately "sealed" caskets may be required, in a few states, when death is due to an infectious disease, but this is rare. Such "sealer" caskets with fancy rubber gaskets may cost $200 to $400 more than regular caskets, and serve no useful function at all. They are often not effective at sealing out air and water, and even if they do, the effect on the body is far more horrible than if no sealing is attempted. If you succeed in getting an airtight casket, you will seal in the anaerobic putrefactive bacteria which produce particularly unpleasant decomposition. You may be misled into thinking that special caskets can delay or prevent decomposition when combined with embalming, but phrases like "enduring protection" and "withstands the forces of time" in casket promotion are deceptive.

A casket is not required for prompt cremation, and suitable containers for this purpose are available at much lower prices.

Be very cautious when you buy a coffin or casket. Take your time and don't let yourself be hurried or confused. A reputable funeral director should be able to give you information about the prices of all his products and services over the telephone before you visit, helping you to choose the firm with which you wish to do business. Before he shows you caskets at the funeral home, he should offer you a list of all the caskets available for purchase, in ascending order of price. The least expensive caskets should be on display in the same manner as the others. One way of discouraging you from choosing the cheaper caskets, even when they are on display, is to show them in repulsive colors such as "silver taupe" (a nauseous silvery lavender-pink). Where this happens, be sure that other colors will be available if you ask. Ignore sales talk intended to disparage lower-priced goods, such as calling the cheaper caskets "tin cans" or "welfare boxes," or comments like "Do you really want to put her in *that?*" or guilt-stirring remarks about cheap funerals and how this is the last gift you can give or the last thing you can do for your loved one. You have already given your last gift—the casket is not a gift your relative will ever receive.

Vaults

A burial vault is a concrete, steel, or fiberglass enclosure built into the ground to surround the casket. It is supposed to "provide protection against the elements" and to "bear the earth load." It is unnecessary, and serves no useful purpose. Nowhere is it required by law, though some cemeteries insist on the use of such enclosures "to reduce the possibility of a grave cave-in." This, however, is never the serious possibility it may sound like. After some time, when the coffin has disintegrated, the earth may subside a few inches. This need cause no problems whatever, though if an elaborate tombstone is erected too soon it might crack or tilt slightly, or the operation of mechanical grass-mowing equipment could be slightly complicated thereby. In many other very civilized countries there is little difficulty in coping without vaults or lawn mowers.

When such a structure is required, it can be provided by the less expensive grave liner rather than the burial vault. The liner, which typically has no bottom, is usually made of wood or concrete; the more expensive burial vault is superfluous. It, too, may be purported to be airtight and watertight, and is never needed. Both may be sold by cemeteries as well as funeral homes—perhaps more cheaply. Liners cost around $20 to $125, while vaults usually cost $250 to $350, but *can* cost as much as $700 to $1,500. The wholesale-to-retail markup is seldom less than 100 percent and is sometimes as much as 600 percent. Some major cemeteries such as Arlington National Cemetery do not even require a liner.

Cemeteries

In choosing a cemetery, there are a number of factors you will want to consider. What sort of reputation does the cemetery have in the local community? Is it well maintained? Is it protected by adequate perpetual-care funds or endorsement trust funds to pay for upkeep in years to come, or backed by municipal or other funds? Prices vary considerably depending not only on the cemetery but on the location of the plot, and may vary between $150 and

$850 per individual grave. Do you prefer the sort of cemetery that caters to larger monuments, or the memorial park? Does the location of the plot matter greatly to you? There is a current trend toward what has been called "pre-need buying," meaning that one is now encouraged to choose cemetery plots as a general family decision, before one is needed. This can lessen the problem of unwise buying under the emotional stress of bereavement. A comparatively recent development has been the memorial park, which limits individual monuments to small, flat plaques, allowing the cemetery to appear as a large, landscaped lawn. This also allows for lower maintenance expenses, because large mowing machines can be used.

Some urban cemeteries are running out of space, and even the use of such methods as double-depth burial (two coffins in one plot, euphemistically called companion spaces) only postpones the problem. Graveyards occupy some 2 million acres of land, often in areas with major housing needs. Plans to relocate cemeteries generally meet great resistance, and burial grounds are generally immune from land-use legislation. Elsewhere, we have seen the development of such enterprises as the high-rise mausoleum, a twenty-story structure which could hold 129,000 bodies and allow funerals and visits at any hour of the day or night. A thirty-nine-story mausoleum has been planned.

Cremation

Though most American funeral services involve ground burial, a small but growing percentage of people, especially in large metropolitan areas, choose cremation. There were around 119,000 cremations in 1974—around 5 percent of funerals; an increase of some 74 percent over the previous ten years (Federal Trade Commission, 1975; 1977). In Britain the proportion of cremations is over 50 percent, and in Japan over 75 percent. In the United States most crematoriums are owned by private companies or corporations, whereas in Britain they are usually run by municipal authorities.

Some people prefer cremation, feeling that it is a quick, clean process that symbolizes both the finality of physical death and the return to natural elements. Others choose it because it can be much less expensive than other funerals (potentially less than $200 rather than $2,000 or more). Still others regard it as simpler and less ostentatious. In cremation, intense heat is used to reduce the body to its basic elements as ash in the course of a couple of hours. The ashes can be disposed of in a number of ways. Often, they are placed in a small metal, ceramic, or stone urn which can then be buried or placed in a niche in a formal memorial structure like a columbarium. Otherwise, the ashes can be scattered either in a memorial garden or in some place of special sentimental significance—in a garden, in the countryside, or at sea. Some states have laws prohibiting the scattering of ashes. Except as a means of protecting some business interests which do not need or deserve protection, such laws are wholly without justification.

In general, crematory charges range between $35 and $100. The purchase of a casket for cremation is not generally required by law. In fact, at least seven states now have laws prohibiting the requirement of one (California, Florida, Maryland, Maine, Minnesota, New Mexico, and Wisconsin). Enforcement of such laws is less than perfect, however. In some areas, a "suitable container" may be required by the state funeral board or an individual crematorium. This still does not necessarily mean a casket; simple containers of pressed wood, fiberboard, or even cardboard will suffice. Only in Massachusetts is there an absurd legal requirement insisting on a casket in all cremations.

Different religious groups vary in their views of cremation. Though there is no prohibition against cremation in the Bible, ancient Judaism practiced earth burial in all but exceptional circumstances. Today, Orthodox Jewish tradition is opposed to cremation, and Conservative congregations share similar views. Reform Judaism does not oppose cremation. The early Christian Church followed the Jewish tradition of earth burial, and cremation came into rather unfair disrepute—having been in common use in Greek and Roman culture, it was regarded as a pagan practice. Later, some other objections to cremation arose from those who interpreted the idea of the resurrection of the body very literally, believing that it had to be buried completely intact to allow resurrection. Later still, the modern cremation movement at the end of the nineteenth century was often supported by rebels against Church authority. Accordingly, the Catholic Church enacted some canon laws forbidding cremation or even cooperation with the practice. It was made clear, however, that the objection was not theological, but a matter of Church discipline. The Second Vatican Council permitted cremation and authorized priests to take part in such services. Protestant denominations are more permissive of it, freely allowing cremation.

Because cremation obviously does not allow later reexamination of the body as in exhumation after earth burial, it cannot be performed after any question about the cause of death has been raised until the cause of death is settled and any inquest is complete.

Simple Burial

In the coming years, further changes in funeral practices are likely. In 1971, the Catholic Church introduced a new liturgy for funerals, increasing participation in the service by those in attendance. Humanist and other nonreligious groups have developed forms of funeral service. The use of contemporary music and poetry and the expression of more modern lifestyles are becoming more common, and various churches are considering modifying their traditional forms of service to allow more flexibility and self-expression.

The trend is toward simpler, more personal funerals. A Methodist Church commission has recommended that the casket remain closed throughout the service and not be a status symbol. Unitarians have recommended prompt burial without embalming (cremation is preferred) with a memorial service a week or so later. Quakers, too, favor great funeral simplicity.

An important challenge to accepted funeral performances has been made by the nonprofit funeral and memorial societies that have arisen in over 120 cities across the United States and Canada, representing consumer interests in this area. Details of your nearest society can be obtained from the Continental Association of Funeral and Memorial Societies (1828 L Street, N.W., Washington, D.C. 20036; phone 202-293-4821). These societies have arrangements with local funeral homes to provide simple, dignified, and economical funerals for $125 to $350 in total. In Canada, contact the Memorial Society Association of Canada (5326 Ada Boulevard, Edmonton, Alberta T5W 4N7). Lifetime family membership in such a society usually costs $10–20, and membership can be transferred if you move. You are strongly recommended to join such a society.

FUNERAL PREPLANNING

Regrettably, although you may announce or record your wishes concerning how you would like to be treated after death, there is no way you can determine what will happen. Under common law, your body belongs to your next of kin or, in some circumstances, to other authorities—but not to you. They are free to decide how to dispose of your remains, whatever your wishes. Some states now have or are in the process of introducing laws to allow you to determine this, and to supersede the family's rights in this matter. It is to be hoped that this will become law in all states.

It makes a great deal of sense to plan and even to finance your funeral well in advance, both to ensure that your wishes are most likely to be carried out and to allow you to make a considerable saving. Remember, any financial saving on your funeral expenses constitutes better financial provision for your family and heirs. Memorial societies can be most helpful in making such arrangements. For a $15 fee, the American International Funeral Registry in Washington allows you to register instructions on how you want your body disposed of and what kind of funeral you wish. This commercial registry is not necessary, however, if you lodge a description of your wishes with your family and a cooperative funeral director. A format for doing so is provided in the Family Information Register and Planning Guide at the end of this chapter.

While some funeral directors cooperate in such planning,

others resist it, complaining that it will "lower the quality of the average funeral." The executive director of the National Funeral Director's Association is quoted as warning his colleagues, "If funeral directors insist on soliciting pre-need funerals, they are in fact pre-arranging the funeral of their profession" (Raether, 1964, cited in Federal Trade Commission, 1975). In fact, preplanning might indeed lower the cost of the average funeral, much to the public benefit, because the calm and unhurried purchaser and planner may spend more carefully and wisely than the grieving and shocked survivor. No honest funeral practices would be greatly threatened by wiser customer planning.

Kalish and Reynolds' study (1976) provides further evidence of consumer wishes: 79 to 89 percent of American blacks, Mexican-Americans and Anglo-Americans and 92 percent of Japanese-Americans rejected a big, elaborate funeral. Indeed, 58 to 63 percent overall (and 81 percent of Japanese-Americans) wanted a funeral with only relatives and close friends attending. Two-thirds of the blacks and 75 percent of the Japanese-Americans wanted the funeral in a church; half the Mexican-Americans and Anglos wanted services in a funeral home. About half of each wanted children under 10 to be allowed to attend. About 20 percent strongly objected to embalming (rather more Japanese-Americans, rather fewer blacks). While Mexican-Americans and blacks preferred burial to cremation by nearly 20 to 1, Anglos preferred it by only 3.5 to 1, and over half the Japanese-Americans preferred cremation.

Funeral Costs

Ask for and get a complete itemized list of the goods and services comprising the proposed funeral from your funeral director. Do not hesitate to question those items that seem excessive or to refuse unwanted items. Select, and pay for, only what you want. By all means shop around and compare estimates, and choose the cheapest prices available. This is thrifty and a compliment rather than an insult to the dead person. If you are told of any legal, public health, or religious requirements for any of the services, ask to see documentary proof of such requirements. If you don't understand any aspect of the arrangements or any part of the explanations you receive, ask again.

Typical average costs as of this writing could be:

Coffin or casket: $800 ($200 to more than $10,000; simple and entirely adequate containers can be $25 or less)

Funeral-home services: $200–$500 or more (depending on what is required—use of chapel or rooms, arrangements, notices, honorariums, flowers, etc.)

Embalming: $100 plus, and unnecessary

Transfer of body: $20

Burial permit: $15

Preparation room: $25

Hearse: $50 plus

Limousines: $45 each plus

Death notice (2 newspapers): $40

Certifications: $6–$50

Vault: $160 ($70–$1,500, and unnecessary)

Cemetery plot: $215 ($120–$5,000 plus)

Cemetery charge for opening and closing grave: $140–$160 plus

Monument or marker: $250 plus

You will probably need extra certified copies of the death certificate to collect insurances, burial allowances, and other benefits, so get about five copies. The funeral director will get these for you if you wish; otherwise you may obtain them for a nominal fee from the registrar of the state Public Health Department (in some states, the county clerk or one of his offices such as the Bureau of Records and Statistics or the Department of Vital Statistics). Call these offices first to be sure which is the appropriate one to visit. The principal death certificate is exchanged for a burial permit at that office.

Checklist of Funeral Arrangements

☐ Obtain death certificate from doctor.

☐ Register death; obtain burial permit.

☐ Decide on time and place of funeral or memorial service.

☐ Make a list of family, friends, and colleagues or employers to be informed, and inform each of them by phone.

☐ Notify memorial society or funeral home, and give clear instructions in terms of plan.

☐ If flowers are to be omitted, choose charity (or hospital, church, school, and so on) to which gifts may be sent instead.

☐ Write death/funeral notice/obituary and deliver it, in person or by phone, to appropriate newspaper(s).

☐ Notify insurance companies, union.

☐ Notify lawyer and executor(s).

☐ Arrange special household needs—answering callers, taking phone messages, caring for the children, food and housework. Where friends can help, let them know.

☐ Select pallbearers, where appropriate, and notify them.

☐ Where more distant family or friends should be notified by letter, list them and write appropriately.

☐ Check life and other relevant insurance and benefits, Social Security, credit union, trade union, military authorities, and so on.

☐ Arrange wake or reception, if planned, to follow funeral.

☐ Arrange transportation.

FINANCIAL PREPLANNING

We should take care to set our business, social, and emotional affairs in order. This prepares for death, though not in any gruesome sense, and allows for a more satisfying way of life. Such preplanning will help to lessen the morbid effects on the family when we eventually die, rather than leaving them with perpetually unfinished business. And such preplanning can help us to seek more honest and fulfilling relationships while we live, rather than searching for ways to buy off our "guilt-edged" insecurities after bereavement. Similarly, fewer of our plans and projects will come to an end with our own end if we have planned adequately for their continuance.

In 1969 the Institute of Life Insurance conducted a national survey and found that at least one adult had some insurance in over 80 percent of all the households studied (over 90 percent of adults aged 45 to 54). Most men and a majority of women were insured. The total amount of life insurance in force in 1971 was $1.5 trillion, but that's less than $26,000 per insured family (Life Insurance Fact Book, 1972). The 1976 study by Reynolds and Kalish showed cultural patterns in preparation for death. (In the figures quoted here, the first is for black, the second for Japanese-Americans, the third for Mexican-Americans, and the fourth for Anglo-Americans.) Many had taken out life insurance (84, 70, 52, and 65 percent), but not so many had arranged for someone to handle their affairs (24, 17, 25, and 42 percent), had bought a cemetery plot (22, 26, 12, and 25 percent), or had made out a will (22, 21, 12, and 36 percent). Far fewer had made funeral arrangements (13, 11, 8, and 14 percent), and very few had taken steps to donate their body or organs to medicine (2, 3, 1, and 8 percent).

Writing a Will

It is important to draw up a will. People often seem to feel upset by the very idea of making a will, as if they would somehow be signing a declaration of intent to die. In fact, a will is merely a legal means of expressing and effecting your wishes—your *will*—as to what should happen to your property after you die. If you die without a will (intestate), there are usually state, provincial, or national laws that will decide what should happen to your possessions and that will divide them among your survivors. But such regulations may not do so in the way you would prefer, or to the best advantage of your survivors, and will fail to make the provisions you wish.

If you die intestate, a court will appoint an administrator to serve as your executor. In New York, for instance, if there is no will, the surviving spouse is provided one-third of the estate by law (if there are two or more children), the children receiving two-thirds. The guardian administrator appointed by the court, who holds the children's funds until they come of age, must file an annual report—involving further fees each time. If a widow should need further funds to care for the children and if her share of the estate runs out before they come of age, she will have to petition the court and prove the need for the extra money—a process that will probably involve significant legal expense.

You could also forfeit major tax advantages by failing to make a will. Federal law, for example, exempts your survivors from paying federal death taxes if your estate is valued at $60,000 or less. In any event, you are allowed to pass up to 50 percent of the adjusted gross value of your estate to your surviving spouse tax-free. Thus, if a person with a $120,000 estate wills half of it to the spouse, he can avoid all federal death tax. Without a will, the tax on such an estate would amount to some $9,500.

The proportions into which your funds are divided are rigid. We've mentioned the common formula of one-third to the spouse and two-thirds to the children. In some states, if you died leaving no children, the estate would automatically be divided equally between your spouse and your parents—even if your parents were very wealthy and your spouse penniless; no allowances could even be made for special circumstances, such as a handicapped child.

You don't have to be rich to need a will. With relatively few restrictions, a will allows you to dispose of your affairs in precisely the way you wish. In the case of a very simple estate, if your financial affairs are not complex and, say, you merely wish to leave everything to your spouse, there is no reason why you should not draw up the will yourself. It needs to be clearly stated, without ambiguities; it should revoke and cancel all previous wills, and it should be signed by you in the presence of two witnesses who should sign it to validate your signature. However, in many cases it will be wise for you to get legal advice on how to take best advantage of the tax and other laws and to be sure that the will will really achieve what you expect, for it needs to be a technically accomplished document.

Further, your estate must be administered by someone to actually carry out your wishes. You can name an individual such as a member of your family, or your lawyer, or an authorized institution such as your bank to carry out this function—to act as *executor*. Again, if you fail to do so, an administrator will be appointed by the court to fulfill this role. The executor or administrator will be responsible for assembling your assets and winding up your affairs; for paying your debts, tax liabilities, and funeral expenses; and ultimately for distributing your estate to the people you named in your will.

Especially with a large estate, death duties and inheritance and estate taxes may create a complex affair, and competent legal assistance should be sought in planning and preparing the will. Little general advice can be given here, because the situation varies widely among states. The average legal fee for drawing up a will is $35 to $150, and you should discuss the likely fees with the lawyer in advance. Your local Bar Association may have a fee schedule you can check.

You don't need to itemize or list your assets or property unless you want specific items to go to specific people. You can change your will as often as you wish, so long as you go through the appropriate formalities. For certain of your assets, you will already have named beneficiaries—such as your life insurance, pension benefits, and U.S. Savings Bonds—so these cannot and do not need to be disposed of in your will. Also, you cannot dispose of property you expect to inherit but don't receive before your death, nor assets over which you will lose control after your death, such as income from trusts which you receive only during your lifetime.

There are certain things you should know in preparing a proper will. Though you're not legally required to write a will in any special way, some standard components of wills will help to make it more readily and easily processed:

1. Write it clearly and specifically enough to make your intentions absolutely clear and unambiguous.

2. Let the opening paragraph identify clearly who you (the "testator" or will-maker) are, with your address and the statement that you are knowingly making your will. Generally, you should include a clear statement that you are revoking any and all previous wills you may have made. Otherwise, there could be contradictory versions of your will that lead to costly confusion and delay.

3. It is common to state that burial expenses and legal debts, taxes, and costs of administering the estate are to be promptly payed as first claims against your estate.

4. Specify the way you want your assets distributed. You may decide on a series of specific bequests of money or property to individual people or charities, and leave the rest, what is called your "residuary estate," to your main heir. Remember that such specific legacies you make will usually take precedence, so if you give large amounts to others, and especially if the value of your estate falls, there may be little left for your main heirs. You may help to avoid this by specifying general legacies as a percentage of the total value of your estate.

5. As has been mentioned, you should appoint an executor to manage and settle your affairs.

6. You may wish to set up a trust, especially if you feel your heirs are too financially inexperienced to manage your estate; this may achieve some tax savings. Trusts are governed by so many laws and regulations that you will certainly need legal help to establish one.

7. Remember to make allowance for the possibility that the person(s) to whom you wish to leave your estate may die before you or, as in the death by accident of a married couple, your spouse may die at the same time as you. So include alternative instructions to deal with these possibilities. Remember, too, that subsequent events such as marriages, divorces, and changes in the financial status of those to whom you intend to leave your estate may require you to revise your will at a later date.

8. Type the will. Your handwriting may not be clearly deciphered, and such wills are often not accepted. Don't mix typing and handwriting. Fasten the pages of a lengthy will firmly together and initial and number every page and any corrections. The will

may be voided if a page is lost, misplaced, or replaced. Any changes, additions, or deletions that are not initialed to show they were made before you signed your will may make the provision or even the whole will void.

9. At the end of the will you must add your signature (don't add any provisions *after* this point), the date, and a clause that contains the signatures and addresses of your witnesses and a statement certifying that they saw you sign the will. Your witnesses must sign in the presence of each other and you. Generally, you will need two witnesses, though some states require three; three is thus the safest number if you have property in several states. *Never* use as a witness a person who will benefit in any way from your will.

10. Every married woman should have her own will. Even if she believes she has no property of her own, she will probably inherit at least some of her husband's estate and will need to decide how she wishes to dispose of that. Wives usually outlive their husbands, but they can't rely on this. Also a wife may need a will to name the guardian or trustee to care for her minor children in order to avoid later custody battles.

Probate

When your executor presents your will to the court to have it declared valid, he or she is *probating* the will. Estates may be handled by a variety of courts—the Superior Court in California, the Surrogate's Court in New York, the Orphan's Court in Pennsylvania, and in other states the Probate, County, or Circuit Court.

Revoking Your Will

Every state has different provisions for revoking your will. Generally it is done either by executing another will which clearly states that the previous will "is hereby revoked" or by signing a separate document declaring the will to be revoked. In either case, the document must be signed with the same formalities, including witnesses, as is the first will. When you write a new will, destroy all copies of the old one.

Revising Your Will

Check your will from time to time. You can revise it by writing a new will or by adding a *codicil*, which is a separate formal document altering or adding to the provisions of your existing will. It, too, needs to be signed with the same formalities and witnesses. Following are some questions you should consider:

Have you changed residence since making your last will? (If you spend your time in two states, both may claim you as a resident for purposes of death taxes, leading to double taxation or expensive litigation. Your will should make your principle residence absolutely clear and conform with that state's laws.)

Has a child been born or other changés occurred in the family since the last will was made? Have you married or divorced? Has any major beneficiary died?

Have you acquired any new business interests you wish to dispose of in line with any specific plan?

Do you wish to disinherit anyone? (Major changes in people's relative fortunes may fully justify this. State laws may interfere with your rights and freedom here. You generally *can't* disinherit your wife or husband unless he or she has abandoned you some time before and there was no reconciliation until death, or unless similar circumstances exist. Generally, widows are entitled to one-third or more of their husband's estate, and if a man leaves his wife less than this, the courts may grant it to her anyway. Numerous states recognize the wife's *right of dower*, meaning that she is legally entitled to use a third of her husband's estate while she lives. Equal rights for men are not fully established, but some states give the husband a similar claim on his wife's estate, called the *right of curtesy*. In some states where such rights no longer exist, the wife can accept the provisions of the will or renounce them and claim the share of his property she would have received if he'd died intestate—one-third or one-half, depending on the state.)

Storing Your Will

You should keep your will where it can be easily found by your executor when it is needed, and where it won't be stolen or lost.

Don't put it in a bank safe-deposit box, because this will be sealed on your death and the executor would need a court's permission to open it. In some circumstances the will itself may be removed, when no other contents can be, in the presence of a bank official.

Generally the will may best be lodged with your lawyer or trust company, in a fireproof vault. Keep a complete copy or duplicate of the will in your home for ready reference.

Your Executor

The more complex your estate, the more important it is that you should choose an executor able to handle the investments and properties involved. You may decide to name coexecutors, perhaps one a member of your family and the other a lawyer, bank, or trust company. The executor's functions include: submitting your will to the court for probate; taking title to all your property; seeing to the inventory and appraisal of all your assets; collecting all debts and money due to you, and paying your debts; filing estate tax returns with state and federal authorities; managing your estate and assets; paying out all your bequests and distributing your assets as you requested; and submitting a final account of your affairs to the court. The executor's commission and attorney fees are paid out of the estate.

Estate Tax

Federal law requires your executor to file an estate tax return for every estate with gross assets over $60,000. States may also impose death taxes and inheritance, transfer, or legacy taxes. Such taxes vary so widely in details and exemptions that one cannot generalize about them.

You may be able to reduce estate taxes and probate costs by various means. During your lifetime you may distribute a total of $30,000 among any number of beneficiaries, free of federal gift tax, all at once or over several years. You may give an additional amount of up to $3,000 a year each to as many different people as you wish. If you give more than this, you must file a gift tax return.

This is still useful, because gift tax rates are usually some 25 percent lower than estate tax rates. A married couple can make joint gifts of up to $6,000 annually and $60,000. The gifts must be made while you are alive; if you leave the same amounts to your family in your will, they will be subject to the full tax burden. The gifts must be completed at least three years before your death to qualify for exemption from tax.

Trusts

A *trust* is an agreement you can set up giving your property to a trustee or trustees to invest and manage to the advantage of the beneficiaries you name. Typically, the income from the sum invested goes to the beneficiaries, usually the surviving wife and children. There may be emergency clauses allowing the trustee to use the principal sum for major unforeseen expenses. You may want the income to go to your spouse during her lifetime, then the principal to go to the children; or the income to go to the children until they reach a given age, when they may receive the principal amount. It is usually best to name a specialist as trustee, such as a trust company or the trust department of a bank. There are many types of trust, such as a revocable living trust, in which the income is paid to the grantor (yourself) during your lifetime and which may be amended or revoked by you at any time. This can greatly reduce legal fees and taxes. It may be possible to make insurance policies payable to the revocable trust, escaping inheritance tax in some cases.

Life Insurance

Life and health insurance comprise another important way of providing coverage for your family for the costs of your illness and providing them with additional funds to protect their standard of living. You will need the advice of a competent and reliable insurance agent. Most states require that life insurance policies include a two-year incontestability clause (some companies offer a one-year clause). Such a clause states that if you live for one year (in some cases, two years) after securing the policy, the company must pay you benefits even if it turns out that you lied about your health when obtaining the policy.

Note that the proceeds of life insurance must be included when the gross value of your estate is calculated for taxation, but only if the policy was owned and paid for by the person whose life is insured or if he had control of the policy. However, a man's life can be insured by his wife, for instance. If she takes out the policy on her husband's life and is registered as the owner, then it will not be listed in her husband's estate and can escape tax.

The family may need the proceeds of life or accident insurance policies speedily to deal with immediate expenses. You will need a death certificate as proof of death, and shouldn't delay notifying the insurance company. When contacting the company, you should have available the policy number; the dead person's full name and address; date and place of birth; date, place, and cause of death; and your own name, age, address, and Social Security number. (Federal laws now require all taxpayers to provide their Social Security numbers to the insurance companies making payments to them.)

You can often choose how you wish the insurance benefit to be paid—as a lump sum, as a partial payment while the rest continues to earn interest until you take it, in serial payments, the interest only for the time being, or as a life income or annuity. Don't rush into deciding on this; seek good advice and consider the different possibilities carefully.

Joint Bank Accounts

Banks usually stop payment on all checks, as soon as they learn that one of the joint holders of a checking account has died. The surviving owner of a joint account will need to formally request the release of funds, and the bank will need to get the account officially cleared by government authorities; this can usually be arranged within a couple of days. Small bank accounts in the name of the deceased may also be released to the surviving spouse.

Safe-Deposit Boxes

You can rent a safe-deposit box from a bank or trust company to store papers or valuables. Such boxes are usually secure, though the bank or company does not usually insure their contents. Husband and wife may hold a box jointly, or either may hold a box individually with the other named as a deputy with a right to enter it, or withholding that right. In most states, banks are required to seal safe-deposit boxes (whether singly or jointly owned) immediately after the owner's death so no one can interfere with its contents. To open it, one usually needs a court authorization or must arrange for certain county and state officials to be present when it is opened and inventoried. Your bank can inform you of local regulations.

Friends may advise you to rush to the bank and clear out the box before the bank discovers that one of the joint holders has died. Remember that evasion of estate and inheritance taxes leads to fines and possibly imprisonment, and banks must keep a record of everyone who is given access to the box, with the date and time of their visit. It may be more practical to empty a jointly held box during a terminal illness.

Generally, states consider the contents of a jointly held safe-deposit box as owned equally by both tenants. It would be up to a survivor to prove that specific valuable items are solely his or hers. Proof may be aided if items belonging to each of you are kept in separate envelopes, duly marked, with contents listed. Usually when the will is probated, the executor will receive letters testamentary from the court, allowing access to the box with waivers for specific items, obtained from the estate tax section of the state tax department once they have inventoried the contents of the box.

Social Security Benefits

Most workers are covered by the Social Security system at some stage. Its benefits are not paid automatically but must be applied for. In the United States, lump-sum and income benefits are payable to eligible survivors who are covered by the Social

Security and the Civil Service, Veterans, or Servicemen acts. The commonest lump-sum benefits are between $211 and $255 from the Social Security Administration, and $250, as well as an allowance of $150 for a plot (where burial is not in a national or government cemetery), for most survivors of veterans or current members of the armed forces. Where there is no surviving spouse, the sum can be made available to the individual meeting burial expenses. Monthly income benefits may also be payable to survivors, depending on such factors as the insured person's income and the number of dependent children. Such benefits can be reasonably substantial. Further information is obtainable from your local Social Security and Veterans Administration office, and details of federal civil service benefits from the Civil Service Commission, Washington, D.C. In each case, when you are inquiring be sure you have the details the agency is likely to require, such as the deceased's full name and date of birth, the Social Security number of the deceased, the surviving spouse, and dependent children and proof of their ages; certified copies of the death certificate and marriage certificate; and approximate earnings of the deceased and the W-2 forms for the previous year. Don't delay too long in making claims, because back claims for monthly payments can't be made for more than twelve months, and the lump sum must be claimed within two years.

The monthly cash payments to the family may be made if the deceased held credit for a certain amount of work under Social Security at any time after 1936. No one needs more than 10 years of work, or 40 quarters, to be fully insured. While this status means that benefits can be paid, the amount will depend on average earnings. You will be fully insured if you had Social Security credit for at least one and a half years' work within the three years before you die.

Veterans' Benefits

If the deceased was an honorably discharged veteran, the U.S. government, through the Veterans Administration (VA), provides various benefits. The basic provisions include the following:

A reimbursement of up to $250 for burial expenses (over and above the Social Security grant)

An American flag to drape the casket

Free burial in any national cemetery (including the plot, opening, closing, and marking costs) except for Arlington

A headstone or memorial marker

Transport of the body to the burial place, if death occurs in a VA hospital

There are Dependency and Indemnity Compensations (DIC) related to any service-related deaths (even if the death occurs fifteen or more years after service) available to the widow (or widower), unmarried children under 18, children 18 to 23 if attending a VA–approved school, some handicapped children, and dependent parents. Payments depend on the pay grade of the deceased, and do not limit the receipt of Social Security payments.

If the deceased died during active duty, during active or inactive duty for training, or within 120 days of discharge from a service-related cause, a six-months' gratuity is awarded, a lump-sum payment of six times the veteran's monthly pay, between $800 and $3,000. Under the War Orphans' and Widows' Educational Assistance Act, the survivors may be eligible for financial support for up to 36 months of schooling or the equivalent in part-time studies.

There may be qualification for VA home loans; and even a death that is not service-related may entitle the surviving spouse and dependent children to pension payments, determined by current income and the number of children. Until remarriage, widows are also entitled to 10-point preference when applying for a federal civil service position. The VA will need a copy of the death certificate (if the veteran died out of service or outside a VA hospital), a copy of the marriage certificate, and copies of the birth certificates of dependent children.

In Canada, any member or former member of the Canadian armed forces is entitled to burial with military honors; a Canadian flag will be provided to cover the casket, or a naval or air force ensign, if appropriate. Various veterans' organizations such as the

Canadian Legion are often able to provide pallbearers or a guard of honor, if desired. A grave is provided for a veteran, or an allowance can be made for the cost of opening and closing a grave in the family plot.

If the deceased was registered in the Canada Pension Plan and contributed regularly since January 1, 1968, a death benefit is available, as well as survivor benefits. The nearest Canada Pension Plan office can provide further information.

Civil Service and Other Benefits

Various benefits are offered to city and state government employees, similar to federal benefits. For information about such benefits, contact the local office of the appropriate government agency. The family of former federal civil service employees may be eligible for benefits, and should check by writing the Civil Service Bureau of Retirement, Insurance, and Occupational Health (1900 East Street N.W., Washington, D.C. 20415).

Railroad workers' families are also eligible for special pension benefits, and should check with the union office. Other benefits may also be available to the family if the deceased was a member of a trade union, service or fraternal organization, or business or professional organization. Some offer life insurance policies or special funds for such families. Families often fail to claim such benefits, not knowing of their existence.

Your Car

Check with your auto club or the office of the state department of motor vehicles for advice on local regulations with regard to clearing the title to the automobile. If it is registered solely in the name of the deceased, it is part of the estate, though the survivor may, if there is to be no administrator handling the estate, secure release of the vehicle by presenting the state department of motor vehicles with an affidavit as to the owner's death and a statement that the survivor believes him- or herself to be entitled to ownership. In the case of joint ownership of the vehicle, check a copy of the title deed to see how your names are listed. If it states "X *or* Y," this should be a joint tenancy that will make it easier for you to take over the car; if it reads "X *and* Y," this is a common tenancy: you both own equal shares in the car and the share of the deceased is included in his or her estate.

Swindlers and Crooks

A range of rackets are operated by the meanest swindlers around—those who specialize in preying on the bereaved. Some call on you, pretending to be insurance agents prepared to pay off a $10,000 policy. They then reveal that it lapsed just before your spouse's death, but they can arrange payment in full if you'll just pay the final premium owed—perhaps $40 or $50. You'll never see your money again. Never pay anything to anyone who calls on you without first checking them out carefully. Phone the home office of the insurance company the person claims to represent. Pre-need buying of funeral services can be valuable—but check out the person who supervises and administers the funds of any agency offering "packages" of funeral services. A host of C.O.D. merchandise, supposedly ordered by the deceased, may arrive, along with claims of nonexistent debts and even expensive lonely-hearts services. Investigate every single claim before paying anything. Don't rush to acknowledge receipt of such items, let alone pay for them. Return every product or service you wouldn't have ordered yourself, and return them at the sender's expense. Don't sign up for anything until you're in a far more stable condition.

FAMILY INFORMATION REGISTER AND PLANNING GUIDE

To provide the best chance that your wishes will be known and respected, and to enable your survivors to use your help to deal with the multiple problems and decisions that will arise, it is wise to leave certain information. Much personal and family data may be urgently needed in the event of a death, and yet it may be difficult or even impossible for your survivors to gather it at such a time. The Family Information Register and Planning Guide that follows on pages 157–169 will, when completed, provide a record of significant family information for the use of the family and executors.

REFERENCES

ARIES, P., *Western Attitudes Toward Death*. Baltimore: Johns Hopkins University Press, 1974.

Federal Trade Commission, *Funeral Industry Practices*, Proposed Trade Regulation Rule and Staff Memorandum. Washington, D.C.: Federal Trade Commission, Bureau of Consumer Protection, Division of Special Projects, August 1975. Also *Report of the Presiding Officer on Proposed Trade Regulation Rule Concerning Funeral Industry Practices* [16 C.F.R. Part 143] [Public Record 215–16]. Washington, D.C.: Federal Trade Commission, 1977.

KALISH, R., and D. REYNOLDS, *Death and Ethnicity: A Psycho-Cultural Study*. Los Angeles: University of Southern California Press, 1976.

Life Insurance Fact Book. New York: New York Institute of Life Insurance, 1972.

MARGOLIS, O. S. et al., eds., *Grief and the Meaning of the Funeral*. New York: MSS Information Corp., 1975.

MITFORD, J., *The American Way of Death*. New York: Simon & Schuster, 1963, p. 15.

RAETHER, H. C., and R. C. SLATER, "The Funeral and the Funeral Director," in *Concerning Death: A Practical Guide for the Living*, ed E. A. Grollman. Boston: Beacon Press, 1974, pp. 187–209.

STRUBB, C. G., and L. G. FREDERICK, *The Principles and Practice of Embalming*. Dallas: Laurence G. Frederick, 1961.

FAMILY INFORMATION REGISTER AND PLANNING GUIDE

I. PERSONAL STATISTICS

HUSBAND

Name _____

Address _____

_____

Date of Birth _____ Social Security/
                                        Social Insurance Number _____
Place of Birth _____

    Father's Name _____

    Place of Birth _____

    Mother's Maiden Name _____

    Place of Birth _____

Occupation _____

Place of Work _____

Location of Birth Certificate _____

Any previous marriages? Yes/No _____

Separated _____ Divorced _____ Spouse deceased _____

Name of Previous Wife _____

Address (if divorced or separated) _____

_____

    Last Will and Testament _____ None _____

    Date Completed _____

    Location of Will _____

    Location of Second Copy _____

    Location of Citizenship Papers (if born abroad) _____

157

Military Service Record:

Date of Enlistment _____ Service Number _____

Branch of Service _____ Date of Separation _____

VA Number _____ Rank _____

Location of Military Service Papers _____

WIFE

Name _____

Address _____

_____

Date of Birth _____ Social Security/
Social Insurance Number _____

Place of Birth _____

    Father's Name _____

    Place of Birth _____

    Mother's Maiden Name _____

    Place of Birth _____

Occupation _____

Place of Work _____

Location of Birth Certificate _____

Any previous marriages? Yes/No _____

    Separated _____ Divorced _____ Spouse deceased _____

Name of Previous Husband _____

Address (if divorced or separated) _____

_____

    Last Will and Testament _____ None _____

    Date Completed _____

    Location of Will _____

    Location of Second Copy _____

Location of Citizenship Papers (if born abroad) _____

_____

Military Service Record:

Date of Enlistment _____ Service Number _____

Branch of Service _____ Date of Separation _____

VA Number _____ Rank _____

Location of Military Service Papers _____

FAMILY

Date of Marriage _____ Place _____

Location of Marriage License _____

Location of Divorce Papers _____ Date _____

Location of Adoption Papers _____

CHILDREN

Name	Present Address	Date of Birth	Place of Birth

RELATIVES AND CLOSE FRIENDS WHO SHOULD BE NOTIFIED:

Name	Address	Telephone Number

MEMBERSHIPS IN ORGANIZATIONS, CLUBS, SOCIETIES

Husband	Wife	Name of Organization	Status or Position	Person to Notify/ Tel. No.	Death Benefits Payable?

LOCATION OF OTHER IMPORTANT PAPERS

Life Insurance Policies ⎯⎯⎯⎯⎯⎯⎯⎯⎯⎯⎯⎯⎯⎯⎯⎯⎯⎯

Accident and Medical Insurance Policies ⎯⎯⎯⎯⎯⎯⎯⎯⎯⎯⎯⎯

⎯⎯⎯⎯⎯⎯⎯⎯⎯⎯⎯⎯⎯⎯⎯⎯⎯⎯⎯⎯⎯⎯⎯⎯⎯

Property-Insurance Policies ⎯⎯⎯⎯⎯⎯⎯⎯⎯⎯⎯⎯⎯⎯⎯⎯

Lease or Mortgage ⎯⎯⎯⎯⎯⎯⎯⎯⎯⎯⎯⎯⎯⎯⎯⎯⎯⎯⎯

Deed to Home ⎯⎯⎯⎯⎯⎯⎯⎯⎯⎯⎯⎯⎯⎯⎯⎯⎯⎯⎯⎯⎯

Tax Returns and Receipts (keep 3 years at a time) ⎯⎯⎯⎯⎯⎯⎯⎯

⎯⎯⎯⎯⎯⎯⎯⎯⎯⎯⎯⎯⎯⎯⎯⎯⎯⎯⎯⎯⎯⎯⎯⎯⎯

Others ⎯⎯⎯⎯⎯⎯⎯⎯⎯⎯⎯⎯⎯⎯⎯⎯⎯⎯⎯⎯⎯⎯⎯⎯

Current Income and Expense Records ⎯⎯⎯⎯⎯⎯⎯⎯⎯⎯⎯⎯

⎯⎯⎯⎯⎯⎯⎯⎯⎯⎯⎯⎯⎯⎯⎯⎯⎯⎯⎯⎯⎯⎯⎯⎯⎯

II. FINANCIAL DATA

PROPERTY

LIFE INSURANCE

Name of Company–Tel. No.	Policy No.	Beneficiary	Original Amount of Policy	Special Provisions

Insurance Agent _____ Address _____

Telephone No. _____

ACCIDENT, MEDICAL, AND PROPERTY INSURANCE

Name of Company–Tel. No.	Policy No.	Beneficiary	Original Amount of Policy	Special Provisions

BANK ACCOUNTS

(Include cash accounts with credit unions, savings banks, and savings and loan associations.)

Name and Address of Bank	Type of Account (checking, savings, etc.)	Location of Bankbooks, Checkbooks, Statements

SAFE-DEPOSIT BOXES

Name and Address of Bank	Box No.	Key No.	Persons Having Access to Box	Location of Keys

SECURITIES (stocks, bonds, etc.)

Company and Address	No. of Shares	Certificate Number	Date Bought	Cost when Bought	Location	Type, Details

PROPERTY/REAL ESTATE

(Separate property owned by married persons should be clearly indicated. Jointly owned property should be noted and explained fully with names, addresses, and interests of each joint owner listed separately.)

Type	Location	Location of Deed	Date Bought	Cost	Mortgage Held by	Other Details

MORTGAGES, PROMISSORY NOTES

Original Amount	Date Made	Name and Address of Maker	Collateral	Interest Rate	Location of Documents	Assignments or Cosigners

PEOPLE TO CONTACT *(names, addresses, and telephone numbers)*

Executors 1. _____

_____

2. _____

_____

Attorney _____

_____

Accountant _____

_____

Bank Official _____

_____

Cemetery Director _____

_____

VA Regional Officer _____

_____

Broker _____

_____

Mortgage Company _____

_____

RENTS, PENSIONS, ANNUITIES, ROYALTIES

Do you own any property on which you receive or are entitled to receive rent?   Yes _____

No _____ If yes, indicate your property rights, lease, and other details, and the basis or

amount of income resulting: _____

_____   _____

_____

_____

_____

Are you receiving any royalties, pensions, or annuities? Yes _____ No _____ If yes, indicate the source, address, and the income resulting: _____

_____

_____

_____

_____

_____

OUT-OF-STATE PROPERTY

Do you own property in another state or country? Yes _____ No _____ If yes, list details on a separate sheet.

TRUSTS

Have you created any trusts, or do you have any rights, powers, benefits, or trusteeship in other trusts? Yes _____ No _____ If yes, list details on a separate sheet.

OTHER PROPERTY OWNED

Check those which apply, and list full details on separate sheets. Interest in copartnership _____ Interest in an unincorporated business _____ Interest in life insurance on life of another _____ Debts owed to you by others _____ Amounts still due from outstanding claims _____ Leaseholds _____ Remainder interests _____ Farm products, crops, livestock, or machinery _____ Other _____

LIABILITIES

Check those liabilities which are outstanding on the date this document is signed, and list full details and location of relevant documents on separate sheet. Real estate mortgages or contracts _____ Notes payable _____ Bank loans _____ Credit union loans _____ Finance company loans _____ Personal loans _____

III. FUNERAL PLANS

Clergyman, Rabbi. Contact _____

at _____ (church or synagogue) to see my family and to

conduct the funeral. Telephone No. _____

Memorial, Burial, or Funeral Society Membership. Yes _____ No _____

Society's Name _____ Address _____

_____

Phone No. _____

Funeral Director. I would prefer that _____

_____ be asked to deal with the arrangements I specify below.

Cemetery Property Owned? Yes ___ No ___

If yes, Name and Address of Cemetery _____

_____

No. of Spaces Purchased ___ Plot No. _____ Deed No. _____

Location of Certificates _____

CARE OF MY BODY

My wish is that my body be: Buried ___ Cremated ___

Cemetery Preferred _____

Disposed of as Follows _____

Donated to _____ Medical School for Medical or

Anatomical Studies. Location of Agreement: _____

I give my permission for an autopsy (post-mortem examination) if the doctor considers it

necessary: _____

I do not wish an autopsy to be carried out: _____

I want to donate the following of my organs, if suitable local arrangements can be made:

Eyes _____ Kidneys _____ Other Organs _____

Location of Donor Card _____

Embalming is against my religious and personal beliefs, and I do not wish my body to be

embalmed: (sign) _____

SERVICE

I want there to be:

Immediate cremation, without embalming, viewing, or processions _____

Immediate burial, without embalming, viewing, or processions _____

A memorial service (without my body present) at _____

A funeral service (with my body present) at _____

A committal service (at graveside) _____

A private service, limited to family and close friends _____

An open service _____

No service of any kind _____

A closed casket _____ An open casket _____

Display and visiting of the body _____ No display or visiting _____

Embalming _____

Cremation: Ashes disposed of by crematorium ___

            Ashes buried in cemetary listed _____

            Treated as follows _____

_____

Other Arrangements as Listed Here (including a note of any scripture, literature, music, or other contributions to the service):

_____

_____

_____

_____

_____

Approximate Cost I Regard as Appropriate _____

Other Comments on the Costs or Qualities of Caskets, Vaults, Services, Memorials _____

_____

_____

_____

_____

_____

MEMORIALS

I would prefer that there be:

No flowers _____

Flowers at the discretion of my family _____

No limitations regarding flowers _____

Donations, instead of flowers, to the following: _____

_____

_____

_____

_____

_____

Religious Memorial Funds _____ Charities _____

Medical Research or Hospital Funds _____)

Even where the law does not as yet allow me the right to make these wishes of mine legally binding, I hope that my next of kin will consider these opinions to be morally binding.

Signed _____

Date _____

Children
and Death

Generally, we don't recall when we lost our immortality (unlike the loss of our virginity, although that's a less significant change). It is a more profound loss of innocence, though it more commonly occurs gradually. Often, it's related to the death of another, when one perceives oneself as in line for the same mortal inheritance.

We begin amid death, but we don't usually think of it that way. We are conceived and begin existence amid the death of dozens of ova and millions of spermatozoa, a horde of potential lives, which don't achieve life because we do. At birth, we leave a situation of predictability, security, and regularity to be suddenly thrust out into a strange, unpredictable, highly stimulating and puzzling world. Otto Rank (1931; 1941) believed that this first great shock was the source of all life's anxiety. Perhaps it can provide a model that echoes back to us on later occasions of disruptive change and loss. The earliest consistent source of severe anxiety is separation—being separated from the mother, deserted, alone, desolate, vulnerable, and unprotected.

Children's games like "hide and seek," and even throwing toys out of the crib, display an early concern with the disappearance and reappearance of objects. Realizing that things exist and then can "go away" or be lost, children assiduously practice the reassuring possibility that things can come back again. Loss-and-recovery games like "peek-a-boo" are played with others or with one's own reflection. Other children's games toy with death. "Ashes, ashes, all fall down!" echoes the deaths of the Great Plague. In other games we run desperately to avoid the touch of the person who is "It," lest we become "It," too. As adults, we're still running away from "It."

Life is sufficiently full of loss, separations, and nonreturns for the child to have many opportunities to begin to form these concepts. The young child experiments with plants and insects, and finds—not what makes them go, but what makes them stop. "All gone!" is a very early phrase learned by many children. Various studies now agree that the infant as young as 6 months of age is already beginning to distinguish being and nonbeing, just as she or he learns to distinguish "me" and "not-me." The concept of death and nonbeing is an essential part of defining life and being. Piaget (1929) has written of the child's development toward "object constancy," the realization that real objects last with some constancy and are not purely transitory phenomena. This is impossible without appreciating nonconstancy and the impermanence of other phenomena. Kastenbaum (in Feifel, 1977) refers to the 16-month-old boy watching a caterpillar that was inadvertently trampled by adult feet. After intently studying the remains, he announced gravely: "No more!"

You can't shelter the child from these facts of life; your only area of choice is how you will deal with them. The only approach that is guaranteed to fail is to try to ignore death. Neglecting to deal with the subject yourself just makes it more likely that the wrong person will tell the child in the wrong way. The child will be quite frequently confronted with examples of death—pets, relatives, and the full-color deaths on television and in films, in magazines and books.

Don't feel that you have to give the child final or wholly definitive answers. You can explore the issues together, and may learn from one another. The way you talk about it will be far more important than precisely what you say. Elegant words spoken fearfully or anxiously will not comfort; your warmth and caring will override the uncertainties of the situation. While you can choose what you say to the child, you can't choose what he will think. The less practical information the child is given, the more he will try to make sense of what is going on, using his own vivid imagination—and what he imagines is likely to be far more bizarre than the truth, and often more frightening.

Children have the right to know what is going on (they will always know that *something* is going on, and their fantasies, perhaps worse than the reality, will be made inaccessible to comfort when everyone is pretending that nothing is wrong). The child will always be able to realize that something very important is going on, and will feel excluded and especially alone if he is not told about it. Certainly, he does not need to share all the experiences of coping with a death as his elders experience it, but he cannot be excluded. A simple factual explanation, with responses to the child's own queries, will be helpful.

Some parents feel tempted to concoct a fictitious story about journeys and foreign places, in the hope that the child's memory of the dead person will slowly fade and that he won't press too insistently for further explanations of the absence. But however sad it may seem initially, the truth will ultimately prove easier to deal with; and the child needs, above all, to be able to trust you.

The sort of stories and equivocations we have so often used in the past can complicate matters. "Dad fell asleep and now he won't wake up again" can lead the child, very understandably, to fear falling asleep lest he, too, might not be able to wake up. "But you mustn't be sad about it!" Why not? And why is Granny crying so much if we mustn't be sad? "Mom's gone away, and she won't be coming back." Why did she go away? Did I do something to make her so angry that she went away? Why didn't she take me with her? Doesn't she love me any more? Dad's supposed to be going on a trip next month—will *he* come back? I'll sit and wait for her to come back. "God loved your Mom so much that he came down and took her away to live in heaven with him." How awful of him! How mean! Doesn't He know how much I love her? Why did He have to take her away from me?

We often try to find evasive words to avoid "die." So people "go to sleep," "perish," "expire," "are lost," or "pass away." (As a child, I read that Stalin "liquidated" his enemies, and began looking at the food liquidizer in the kitchen with a new respect.) Yet the modern media have made "death" a familiar word and a familiar sight. The direct terminology can be less frightening than the circumlocutions. "Gone away" is quite as desolate as "dead," and raises even more questions as to why you were left behind.

CAN CHILDREN UNDERSTAND DEATH?

The facts of death are natural counterparts of the facts of life. It is quite as obvious for a child to wonder, "Where am I going?" as to puzzle about "Where did I come from?"

It is generally agreed that a child's age is important in assessing how he is able to understand death, because the concept develops steadily as he matures. Remember that the age groups described below may give general guidance, but must not be applied strictly—children of the same chronological age may vary widely in their maturity.

Maria Nagy's research (1948) on children's concepts of death has been very influential. She proposed that their ideas develop in three stages between the ages of about 2 and 9. In the first stage, under the age of 5 or 6, death is seen as being like life under different circumstances—the dead person may be in the coffin, but probably breathing, thinking, and feeling. It is like the child's experiences of separation, and is not seen as final or permanent. It may be thought of by the child as being like sleep—from which you can wake up again; or like a long journey—from which you can return. It's like when Mother goes off to the supermarket, only it takes longer. It's puzzling that grown-ups are so upset about it, when they're so calm about other separations and journeys. "Yes, I know Granddad died—but why can't he come to tea?" Before the development of a secure abstract sense of time, "forever" is hard to grasp.

Between 5 and 9, Nagy believes, death is more often seen as an irreversible but not necessarily a general or an inevitable process, certainly so far as the child himself is concerned. It may be seen as an ending, and as something that happens to old people. The child, concurrently, will be conceptualizing life. There may be a stage when movement may seem to be the key, for example. Living things move, dead things don't. This works quite well, up to a point. But cars move, and smoke moves—are they alive? Granny moves very little these days—what about her? Death may be a rather more emotionless construct at this stage. In play and games, the child often likes playing at being killed, and may experimentally kill insects, and even small animals, being not yet entirely accepting of the idea that killing is bad or should be avoided.

Death may be personified, as a bogeyman, ghost, or skeleton, or as a bad man who comes to "get" you, though perhaps you can hide from him. From around the age of 6, fear begins to enter the picture more noticeably, and religious teaching about the Devil and the penalties for bad behavior may exaggerate this. The idea that children can die, too, may be recognized, and also the fear that the mother could die. There may seem to be a morbid interest in things associated with death, a preoccupation with death-related superstitions, and a persistence of the memory of dead animals that have been seen. Rhymes and jokes may stress bizarre and violent deaths. The child may now start to ask questions about the causes and consequences of death, which may be understood chiefly in terms of violence and punishment. "Maybe people only die if someone kills them, or perhaps as a punishment. Maybe mother died because I was naughty, or because I got angry and wished her dead." It will be useful to talk with the child about his fantasies, so that the issues can be clarified. But don't tell the child fairytales about the facts.

Gradually, the child's teaching about death becomes more realistic and less openly emotional again. By the age of 9, just as the child may no longer believe in Santa Claus, so death may be seen as due to more natural causes, and in the context of dying and possibly pain. According to Nagy, he will now see death as irreversible and inevitable, as part of the life cycle of all that live—

including himself. The child may also begin to learn to use the rhetoric of suicide, as expressed in such threats as "I wish I were dead" or "If I can't have that—I'll kill myself!"

Nagy's work, based on a study of Hungarian children in the years immediately after World War II, has been increasingly in question recently. It seems likely that her findings don't apply completely or directly to children in other cultures at other times, and that further social, economic, and cultural factors are also important. American children seem to focus on more realistic and organic and less fanciful explanations much earlier—by 5 or even as early as 3—and with less use of personifications. Children from lower socioeconomic groups are more likely to see death as the result of violence, in terms of stabbing, shooting, burning, bombing, suicide, crashes, and struggles. Middle-class children more readily think of death as due to old age or disease. Clearly, their experiences at home may have a great deal to do with this. It is often forgotten that quite apart from the development of the child's concepts of death, what she tells us about it will also depend on the development of her skills at expressing abstract ideas (and we can form abstract concepts before we can efficiently communicate them to others), and on her opinion of your capacity to understand, and hence what she is able to and chooses to tell you. What she says is very far from representing all that she thinks. It is also a mistake to assume too great a difference between children's and adults' views of death. Many adults express the same sense of personal exemption from its inevitability, show the same preoccupation with separation anxiety, use the same kind of personification, and so on, that some researchers have described as typical of children. The differences may be less in the concepts than in the imagery used to describe them.

Myra Bluebond-Langner's highly significant work with terminally ill children has shown clearly that children as young as 18 months of age come to know that they are dying and that this is a final and irreversible process (1978). She suggests that all views of death are present at all stages of our development, the view that is currently expressed depending on the social, psychological, and intellectual experiences and concerns at the time. For example, up to around 5 years of age, when a child is learning how to deal with separations and the feelings they arouse, the view of death as a final separation would be the major concern. Later, while learning the scientific explanations of other phenomena, the child may offer a more scientific explanation of death—without relinquishing the other views of death he has held.

TALKING WITH CHILDREN ABOUT DEATH

When someone in the family is dying, the child should be told as soon as is practical (and, if possible, by a parent or someone else close to him) and in a place that is familiar to him, such as home. The explanation of the death should be realistic and based on the facts, couched in words appropriate to the child's age. In discussing death with a child, it is important to be true to your own beliefs. If you have religious beliefs in some form of life after death, then share this with the child. Be careful to deal with his questions and to clarify the distinction between what happens to the body and what you believe happens to the soul or spirit. If you do not believe in life after death, admit that you do not know what happens to the person after death, but suggest that how one lives one's life until then does matter. Check out what the child himself believes, and never ridicule his ideas.

Don't give unnecessary details that you want to rehearse as part of your own mourning—but don't evade the child's questions. If you don't know how to answer a question, admit frankly that you don't know, or that you don't know how to explain. He will respect your honesty more than a hastily made-up, evasive story. You can anticipate and deal with some of his fears. Children fear pain especially—and may wish to be reassured that the dead person suffers no pain. They may fear that they have caused the death, wittingly or unwittingly, by wishing it or by being bad. You need not hide your own grief, though you have the right to your own privacy. Let the child remain with the family at this time; don't send him away without a very good reason.

Some of the books listed under "Recommended Reading" in

the Appendix can be most helpful in planning your discussion with the child.

John Bowlby's studies (1974) describe three stages in children's natural grief response. At first, the child protests vigorously, cannot fully believe that the person is dead, and may try angrily to find ways of getting the person back. This is followed by a period of disorganization and grief, as he begins to accept the reality of the loss. Finally, there is a stage of greater calm as the child begins to reorganize his life, despite the loss. These responses are really the same as those seen in adults.

When you are dealing with anybody concerning death, especially a child, don't stifle grief. One of the idiocies of our culture is the prohibition of the frank display of emotions which makes it so unfashionable to be sincere in public, and pretends that it is unseemly or "hysterical" to have or express feelings of grief. Because we may be upset by others' feelings, we teach children to keep them hidden. "Big boys don't cry," we warn boys. "Pull yourself together." Crying is a perfectly normal and healthy expression of emotion and can provide a valuable release of tension. Hiding feelings of sadness, tenderness, or sympathy may be obtuse—but it has nothing to do with courage.

Grief is a perfectly normal response to loss, neither a disgrace (needing to be hidden) nor a disease (to be cured). If one is not allowed to grieve, then one has left the job undone—and later problems may arise from this thwarting of a natural and ultimately healing process.

While some people may be too shocked, initially, to show their grief, don't regard this as an admirable norm. "He took it so well," we say, mistakenly. "He never cried." Allow the child to express grief and to cry. He doesn't need to "be brave." Bravery in such circumstances is a peculiar and frequently overvalued quality, often in fact equivalent to insensitivity, cultivated foolishness, and a staggering lack of imagination.

Another fear commonly aroused in children when a death occurs is that of being abandoned. "Who will take care of me?" "Who'll be the next to go away and leave me like this?" You may be confronted by the question "Will you die, too?" On such an occasion, you need to explain that ultimately everyone will die, but that you have a normal life expectancy, and hope to be around until the child is grown up and well able to look after himself—and that, if anything were to happen to you, you have made suitable arrangements for others to look after him.

This, of course, raises the question of what arrangements you have made. Consider seriously who would be able to help, and who you would want to take care of *your* children should you and your spouse die, perhaps in an accident. Consider what values you would like to attend their upbringing, and what arrangements could be made to ensure their care with as little disruption of their lives as possible. It is far from morbid to take such precautions; it is a way of guaranteeing the quality of your children's lives. Especially if the child has already experienced the loss of one parent, he may need to be informed and reassured about such arrangements.

Children can also feel very guiltily responsible for a death. Probably all children have wished that their parents and other people were dead, in moments of anger, and they may even have stated it openly. "I hate you, I wish you were dead." Should any misfortune actually befall the person concerned, it is easy for the child to imagine that his aggressive feelings somehow caused the harm. Some parents even unthinkingly add to the confusion by such remarks as "You'll make Mommy sick if you carry on like that!" or "You'll be the death of me yet!"

Early in their lives, children should be allowed to know that it is normal and OK to feel angry and even violent, though we need to find nonviolent ways of handling such emotions. Children should be assured that anger in no way contradicts love, and that they can be angry with their parents, just as their parents can be angry with them, without lessening the basic love they have for one another. The child is less likely spontaneously to voice these fears of responsibility for causing the illness than other concerns, but may nonetheless need the reassurance. You might say, for example, "All children sometimes get very angry at their parents, and they may even wish that something bad would happen to mother or father. But that's a way of showing how cross they are, for they don't really want it to happen. And they won't make it happen."

"Sometimes, later, someone you love may actually get sick, but this is not because of those bad wishes or angry thoughts. Your wishes and thoughts, by themselves, can't hurt other people." You may also reassure the child that the deceased parent knew and understood how much the child loved him or her and that the parent loved the child very much.

Other reactions can be seen—flat denial that death has occurred, for example, perhaps with persistent claims that the dead relative will return. There may be angry and hostile responses— toward others ("The doctors didn't give him the right medicine!" or "Why did Mommy make Daddy go away?"); toward himself ("It's my fault; I was bad"); or toward the dead person ("Didn't he love me? Why did he leave me when I need him so much?"). The child may seek to replace the dead relative by trying to reassure himself of the affection of other relatives who could act as substitutes, or by identifying himself with the person he has lost, imitating her mannerisms and traits, or complaining of her symptoms.

What do you say to the child whose parent has committed suicide? It's tempting to try to hide the cause of death, but the child is likely to find out sooner or later, and may find the secrecy all the more disturbing. Except, perhaps, for very young children who might not appreciate the distinction, you could tell the child that his parent killed him/herself. Again, you need to reassure him that this was not his fault. The child may wonder: "Didn't Mom love me enough to want to live with me?" You might say that you do not really know why she did this, but that you think she had a problem she felt she couldn't deal with. You would explain that killing oneself is not a good way of solving problems.

When the parent has died of an illness, reassure the child that the parent loved him very much—so that he doesn't fear that she deserted him or that he might have driven her away—and that she knew how much he loved her. Let him know that Mom was very sick, and although the doctors did all they could to help, she eventually became too sick to live. He may ask, "Am I old enough to die?" and may need to know that this is possible, but that people usually die when they are older than he is. Assure him that the other members of the family will continue to love and care for him.

Be prepared to answer his questions and to share your emotions. Yes, you both miss her very much, and you both feel sad. Remember how important it is for the child to keep to the regular events of his life. When so large a part of his life has changed, inevitably, due to the death, it is comforting for him to be able to otherwise keep to his regular schedule. Amid all the unusual activities in the bereaved household, it may be hard for the child to find his way and to be able to be fed and to rest at his usual times.

Realizing that someone became sick and died, children may become concerned about illness in general and with physical symptoms. The child may not understand the nature of the illness, and may worry that she could catch the disease. You can stress that most people recover from most illnesses, and that she is not at risk. The distinction between major and minor illness needs to be made.

Animals and pets may play a part in helping a child discover and understand death. Flies, beetles, and birds can provide emotionally neutral demonstrations of death, and can be the subject of more or less detached curiosity. Children may for a time seem morbidly interested in dead things, and may collect and bury a variety of dead animals. The death of a beloved pet will cause real grief. It is important not to try to hide the facts. The pet didn't run away; it's dead. Children need to discuss the experience of loss and to mourn. They need to know that their pet is dead, and thus not in pain or lonely. Children may want to devise some sort of ceremony and bury the pet, and this should not be discouraged. Don't hurry to get a replacement pet until the mourning is finished. Then get a new pet—a different one, with a different name. We lose, and we establish new relationships, though none of us is readily replaceable.

The natural order of events demonstrates that death is as inseparable a part of life as birth; the birds and the bees teach both lessons. All things have a lifespan; after a time of being, they cease, but they are replaced.

One of the lessons the child learns from the death is that grown-up people are not all-powerful and all-knowing. You don't have to have glib answers for all their questions; you can search together for understanding, and share your own ideas. You can answer questions quite simply.

What is dead? Dead means not alive any more. When it is dead, the body is still and peaceful. It doesn't breathe, or move, or hear or see anything, or feel. It simply stops. It doesn't hurt or worry at all.

Will I die? Will you? Eventually, we all die, but not yet. We don't want to die, and it's hard to imagine it, because we've probably got a long life ahead of us. One day I will die, probably after you've grown up and are able to look after yourself.

Grandad's getting really old—will he die soon? Probably sooner than we will, because he's older than we are. But not for a while.

If she's sick, why doesn't the doctor make her better? That's what the doctor is trying to do. Doctors can usually make people better, but some sicknesses are too severe, and then the doctor can't make people better even when he tries hard. Even then, he can do a lot to help sick people be as comfortable as possible.

Where do people go when they die? What happens to them? When people have died, we usually bury them. We put their bodies in a special box and bury them in the ground in a place called a cemetery. We have a special service called a funeral, when the people who loved the person who died get together to remember him and to comfort the people who were closest to him. Some people are cremated instead. Then the body is put into a sort of furnace which turns it into ashes. The body can't feel anything at all.

What is the child's place with regard to the funeral? Obviously, this depends on individual circumstances. The very small child may be unwittingly disturbing at the ceremony, and unable to understand what is going on or to benefit from being there. Older children probably have a significant personal opinion about whether or not they want to go to the funeral, and their wishes should be respected. Especially when the child decides to attend, he should be told what will happen at the service and the burial, so he can know what to expect. There may be questions about cemeteries and graves, and these, too, should be answered as honestly as possible, with as much detail as the child requests.

The child's different sense of time may well mean that he

recovers from his grief more quickly than the rest of the family. Be grateful for his return to normal activities in which he can again get absorbed; don't feel you need to impose your grief upon him; don't be shocked that he seems at times to show less sadness than you. Continue to make natural references to the person who died, as part of normal conversation; avoiding such references may continue to imply that something unnaturally awful has happened. Children often love souvenirs and mementos by which to remember the people they loved, and should be helped to live with good memories of the dead. The child may also respond to loss by regression and begin to speak and behave in a more babyish fashion, seeking more attention and comforting.

Of course the death of a parent presents a special difficulty. It is with the parents, especially with the mother, that a child learns and practices the ability to love. With help, he can find another person to love. Otherwise, the child might remain attached to a fantasy of the parent who has died, or be frightened to love anyone else again. A boy may grow to manhood suspicious of women, expecting them to abandon him if he loves them. He may become promiscuous, loving and leaving women before they can leave him and hurt him; or he may hesitate to love at all. If he loses his father, and the opportunity to learn from a male person as a model, this may cause other difficulties. The mother, having lost her spouse, may devote her entire life to her son, from whom she expects to gain all gratification. Similarly, father and daughter may become excessively dependent on each other after the mother's death. Let the child continue to be your child, not a substitute for your dead spouse. Remain close and comforting, but don't become too exclusively intimate.

After the period of mourning, the surviving parent may remarry. Children who have not yet fully accepted the finality of the death may at first resent someone they consider an intruder in the family. In this case, it will help if you make it clear that this is a new relationship, deeply felt in its own right but not supplanting the earlier relationship.

EFFECTS OF CHILDHOOD BEREAVEMENT

Early experiences of bereavement can have lasting and possibly serious effects on the child. Some studies (Kastenbaum & Aisenberg, 1972; Furman, 1974; Seligman, 1975) have shown that people with psychiatric problems later in life are more frequently found to have lost a parent early in life than other people. Depressed adults, for example, are more likely to have been orphaned during childhood, especially before the age of 4. Children who have lost a sibling may also show disturbance. They may show a fear of doctors and hospitals, regression in behavior, and fear that they themselves could die at any time, perhaps at the same age or from the same cause as their sibling. The child may feel somehow responsible for the death, or feel that she should have died instead, and now doesn't deserve anything good in life. She may brood over the bad things she said or did to the dead sibling, and may need help to recall the good parts of their relationship. Emotional crises have been reported later in life when people reach the age at which a parent or sibling died, or when their children reach the age at which they themselves were bereaved.

THE DYING CHILD

The dying child takes a while to realize that he is dying, and his needs, worries, and questions vary at different stages in his illness. Our best insight into the process has been provided by the work of Myra Bluebond-Langner (1978) among children with leukemia. She finds that when first diagnosed, the child is worried about the seriousness of his illness and about feeling sicker than ever before. While achieving his first remission, he usually grows interested in his drugs and treatments and their side effects, and hopes for a lasting recovery. The first relapse or return of symptoms arouses doubts, and he begins to think about the possibility that he will always be sick. As the illness continues, he becomes more concerned about its chronic nature, wondering if the suffering will ever end. The death of a fellow patient often precipitates the realization that he, too, will die.

Children seem hesitant to express the extent of their awareness, lest it lose them the companionship of their parents. They're very aware of changes in the behavior of those around them. They also seem interested in sharing with other people what they know, but only when they're sure the other person will stay with them, whatever they say. We should let them avoid and conceal with those who feel most at ease with mutual pretense, and let them talk openly with those who accept that situation confidently. Listen carefully to the child and follow the cues he gives you. Answer what he asks, in his own terms, and help him to do what he wants to do.

The death of a child can place major strains on a marriage, especially on one that has weakened to the point where the child or children are all that the parents now have in common. When a child dies—especially the first-born, or the only child—the parents may blame each other for negligence or carelessness, or for not feeling the loss deeply enough, and may break up. No adequate studies have been carried out, but some authorities estimate that as many as 75 percent of couples may separate after the death of a child, especially if they do not seek competent help. We always feel guilt and responsibility; and where the death is due to hereditary illness, for instance, these feelings are difficult to avoid, even if they are inappropriate.

In the death of one's child, one has lost one's own future, one's own foothold in immortality.

REFERENCES

Bluebond-Langner, Myra, *The Private Worlds of Dying Children.* Princeton, N.J.: Princeton University Press, 1978.

Bowlby, J., *Separation.* New York: Basic Books, 1974.

Furman, E., *A Child's Parent Dies: Studies in Childhood Bereavement.* New Haven: Yale University Press, 1974.

Kastenbaum, R., and R. Aisenberg, *The Psychology of Death*. New York: Springer Publishing Co., 1972.

Kastenbaum, R., "Death and Development through the Lifespan," in *New Meanings of Death*, ed. H. Feifel. New York: McGraw-Hill, 1977.

Nagy, M. H., "The Child's Theories Concerning Death," *Journal of Genetic Psychology*, 73 (1948), 3–27.

Piaget, J., *The Child's Conception of the World*. London: Kegan Paul, 1929.

Rank, O., *Psychology and the Soul*. New York: Perpetua Book Edition, 1961.

———, *Beyond Psychology*. New York: Dover Books, 1958.

Seligman, M., *Helplessness: On Depression, Development and Death*. San Francisco: W. H. Freeman, 1975.

Euthanasia and the "Living Will"

They shoot horses, don't they?

THERAPEUTIC FRENZY

The doctor was 68 when he was found to have a large stomach cancer. Five years earlier he'd had to retire from practice after a severe coronary thrombosis which had greatly reduced his freedom to move about. His disease was already very far advanced when it was first discovered. An exploratory operation revealed it to be widely spread through his abdomen and liver. It was impossible to remove. There were secondary growths of the tumor in many vertebrae, throughout his backbone. Because he was a doctor, he was told what had been found, and he fully understood what this meant. Despite increasingly large doses of powerful pain-killers, he was in constant pain from the disease.

Ten days after the operation, he collapsed owing to a massive blood clot in the lungs (pulmonary embolism) and was very near death. A resident doctor performed an emergency operation for the removal of the clot, on the ward, and revived him. When he'd recovered, he commended his young colleague's skill and presumed good intentions. But because the pain from his cancer was now more than he wished needlessly to endure, he asked that no further steps be taken to prolong his life should he collapse from any other cause. He made sure everyone knew his feelings and, being a doctor, even got hold of his case records and wrote a note to this effect.

Nonetheless, two weeks later, when he suffered another coronary, and his heart stopped, he was resuscitated by the emergency team. That night, his heart stopped four more times, but was artificially restarted each time.

His body recovered, though his brain did not, and the body was carefully kept going for a further three weeks, decerebrate, with bouts of violent projectile vomiting and convulsions. Blood transfusions and complex intravenous feeding were kept up, maintaining his normal body chemistry. He was given antibacterial and antifungal medication to prevent infections, especially to prevent pneumonia, which might complicate the tracheotomy that had been done to keep his airway clear. Finally, his respiratory center began to fail, but as preparations were being made for an artificial mechanical respirator to take over this brain function, his heart stopped. He did not respond to further resuscitation attempts.

Who, one wonders, was treating whom for what? Physicians in a modern hospital appear to have no capacity to stop their therapeutic enthusiasm, or to temper their drive to do whatever they are capable of doing with any consideration of the patient's feelings and wishes. This has led people to seek ways of controlling what might happen to *them* under similar circumstances. This increased public interest has made itself evident in support for legislation to allow voluntary euthanasia (opinion polls have reported as much as 70 percent agreement in the general public) and in the popularity of signed statements of one's wishes such as the "Living Will." *Euthanasia* itself is an almost unusable term, being applied to everything from its original meaning of "good death" to Nazi atrocities. Most alternative terms proposed so far are even more ugly, however, including *self-deliverance* and *benemortasia*.

EUTHANASIA AND THE LAW

The law concerning euthanasia in most countries is in disarray, though it is usually interpreted and twisted as far as possible in bona fide cases of euthanasia to avoid severe punishment of those responsible for "mercy murder." Special categories of mental illness have been invented to allow juries to find sane people "not guilty by reason of insanity"—a purely temporary insanity.

Not all responsible judicial bodies are humane in their interpretation of the laws and rules, however. In 1976 and 1977 in South Africa, Dr. Alby Hartman, a popular surgeon and general practitioner, was punished by the local medical council for having speeded the demise of his moribund and severely suffering father. A nurse complained to the police, and Dr. Hartman was tried and convicted of murder. The judge sentenced him to be detained until the court rose—then adjourned, so he served a sentence of some 30 seconds in custody. But then the council tried him again. Although its disciplinary committee recommended only a suspended sentence, the council threw out this decision and struck him off the medical register. They ruined his medical practice, despite petitions from his patients and from colleagues throughout the country. He eventually found a way to support himself—ironically, by selling life insurance.

So-called mercy killings do not fit into any of the existing categories of American law. They are not murder in the first degree, which is killing "with malice aforethought"—deliberate, premeditated, and with malicious intent and cruelty. This does not really apply to killing with love aforethought, and with the deliberate intent of ending the person's suffering. Nor are "mercy killings" murder in the second degree, which generally applies to death caused by reckless and dangerous action, with implied malice and "regardless of human life." They are not manslaughter, which may imply unlawful killing without malice, but either in a sudden quarrel or unintentionally while committing another unlawful act.

One problem is the extent to which the law is uninterested in motives—it cares far more about *whether* you killed than *why*—

188

and it does not generally allow the illegality of an act to be mitigated by the quality of the motivation for it. In 1933, a law promulgated in Uruguay stated that "the judges are authorized to forego punishment of a person whose previous life has been honourable, where he commits a homicide motivated by compassion, induced by repeated requests of the victim." To a lesser extent, German and Swiss law also allow honorable motives to be taken into account.

Some would make a distinction between *active euthanasia* (actively taking steps to produce the death) and *passive euthanasia* (allowing a death to occur by *not* intervening). In 1957, Pope Pius XII dealt with the question of whether a respirator can be turned off when a patient is in a final and hopeless coma, and decided that continued use of the respirator is not morally obligatory in such cases. While the law does not generally oblige us to be Good Samaritans, there are circumstances in which any of us, especially doctors, could be held criminally and civilly liable for not giving lifesaving aid. The law is especially murky in this area, but tends to more fiercely punish acts of commission than acts of omission. Though the distinction may in some cases be rather academic, most people seem to find it morally easier to condone omission than commission, even when the result is the same. Several polls have shown that a high proportion (80 percent or more) of American doctors favor "negative euthanasia," and a similar proportion admit to practicing it on occasion. Other moralists insist that the decision not to keep a patient alive is as morally deliberate as a decision actively to end a life.

It is sometimes objected that to have any part in ending a life or allowing a life to end is to play God—for determining the end of life is His prerogative. It has been called a violation of the property rights of God. This argument simply won't do. If it is wrong to interfere with the timing of death, surely we would not be allowed to delay its arrival by our treatments and cures.

A more realistic problem is that of deciding whether a person has made a free decision for voluntary euthanasia. We must be sure that such decisions are authentic, and not due to a temporary depression capable of being alleviated, or an alteration of body chemistry, or pressure from relatives. The Voluntary Euthanasia Bill proposed in Britain in 1969 suggested a thirty-day waiting period after a person declared his decision for death by euthanasia (defined as "the painless inducement of death"), a declaration that could be revoked at any time during that period. This would allow time for the remedy of temporary pressures influencing such a decision, even though it might not remove the basic medical problem.

THE "COMMITTEE OF THE PERSON"

And what of situations in which people are unable to make such a decision for themselves, such as the infant or child, or the unconscious or mentally incompetent adult? One possible way of dealing with this in regard to adults is suggested by an innovative law introduced in New York State in 1966 as Section 100-A of the Mental Hygiene Law. This allows one to designate a person (or people) to act as a "Committee of the Person" on his behalf in the event of his becoming incompetent to act for himself. The committee, designated by the person himself and appointed by a court, is then entitled to carry out his instructions and directions as he or she understands them. The documents for establishing such a committee are drawn up and witnessed in the same manner as a will. By this means, it is possible for you to make your opinion clearly known and have it carried out by someone you have selected, informed, and instructed. Your family might not be so well able to act on your behalf owing to conflicts of interest, greed, spite, very different opinions, or simply their own emotional distress at the time. A group appointed by the court might be more impartial, but uninformed about you, your opinions, and your wishes. More widespread adoption of the "Committee of the Person" approach by other states could be useful.

Otherwise, legal guardianship of confused and legally incompetent patients ordinarily falls to the next of kin. The guardian's duty is to judge what he sincerely believes the patient would prefer under the existing circumstances, based on his knowledge of the patient—*not* to decide what he himself would prefer to do under such circumstances, unless there is absolutely no specific knowledge of the patient's preferences.

If the doctor or hospital involved has good reason to believe that the family or guardian is not acting in the patient's best interests, they may petition a court to appoint a temporary guardian. In such cases as the refusal for religious reasons to permit blood transfusions, the position is becoming clearer. Freedom of religion exists, but it includes no right to cause death. You may *believe* in human sacrifice, but you may not *practice* it.

Either the "Committee of the Person" or the legal guardian approach could supplement the legalization of voluntary euthanasia to help deal with the case of the person unable to express his own preference.

Before the famous Quinlan case of 1976,* there was no legally sanctioned procedure for stopping treatment (though physicians have done so, when they were convinced it was in the patient's best interests, throughout medical history). If the Quinlan ruling becomes widely established by subsequent court decisions, then a relatively clear procedure could be outlined to get consent for stopping treatment without criminal liability. Under the terms of this ruling, the consent of four parties would be required to stop treatment:

1. The patient's implied consent, as well as the overriding rule that the other parties can only legally consent to the ending of life support if it is in the patient's best interests

2. The consent of the family, guardian, or immediate next of kin

3. The consent and agreement of the attending doctors that "there is no reasonable possibility of return to cognitive and sapient life" or that "there is irrefutable evidence that biological death is imminent"

4. The consent, where the preceding parties agree, of the hospital ethics committee "composed of physicians, social workers, attor-

In the Matter of Karen Quinlan (Washington, D.C.: University Publications of America, 1977) reprints the complete legal briefs, court proceedings, and decision in the Superior Court of New Jersey.

neys, and theologians," which acts as a "safeguard for patients and their caretakers" by exploring "all of the options for a particular patient," allowing discussion of the individual situation, and allowing the responsibility of these judgments to be shared"

There have been many attempts to draw up criteria to guide such decisions, such as that produced by an interdisciplinary group—the Ad Hoc Committee on Treatment Termination Criteria—at Drew University. This group proposed the "Drew Criterion," similar in structure to the Quinlan ruling. It proposes that if there is "permanent loss of all cognitive function" with "permanently impaired understanding so as to offer no reasonable hope of recovery," or where the doctors assess the "dying process" as "being in its last stages" (a much vaguer criterion), then where family members agree and the patient's preference is known "by written document or reasonably implied," the family "may justifiably consent to withholding active treatment on new complications or emergencies, while continuing life support already instituted, so as to allow the terminal illness to take its course" (see Oden, 1976). This criterion has the disadvantage of attempting a wishy-washy variation of passive euthanasia by withholding extra resuscitative measures, but withdrawing none—which may not be helpful if irrationally excessive resuscitative measures have already been instituted before the decision is reached.

DOCUMENTS LIMITING TREATMENT— THE RIGHT TO DIE

Another approach to the problem of not being able, at the relevant point, to communicate your wishes effectively is evident in the proliferation of documents like the "Living Will," by which a person communicates in advance, in writing, his or her preferences with regard to terminal treatment. Should you decide to record your wishes, there are several alternatives open to you. You can sign one of several standardized forms, or you can prepare a document that specifies your individual views.

Such documents have important differences. Some call for steps that are not generally legal, or not likely to be carried out. Some reject the use of *all* artificial means of life support; these would, if strictly interpreted, include all medications, pacemakers, oxygen—even hearing aids and bandages. Most focus on the point when there is "no reasonable expectation of recovery," though this is usually a more or less uncertain estimate of probabilities—and, as we have discussed before, actual recovery from illnesses is comparatively rare. Some request that life should be ended in the event of any "permanent physical disability"—yet this could include failing hearing or the loss of a toe.

There are other problems with such documents. Some ask for termination in the event of "any condition requiring the use—beyond two weeks—of mechanical equipment for breathing, heart action, feeding, dialysis, or brain function, without a prognosis of full recovery of my vital organs." (In hardly any illness can a doctor guarantee a prognosis of *full* recovery.) This would rule out effective treatment for many conditions in which substantial recovery is likely, but where two weeks is too short a period for making a reliable prognosis. Some ask that the signer's life be ended if the person is "deprived of independent mobility," yet not all of us would want to die if our only major problem was loss of the ability to walk. Other doubtful conditions for seeking death include experiencing "only partial consciousness" (don't faint or get drunk). In general, the treatment-refusal documents try to anticipate incredibly complicated contingencies which involve too many variables to be anticipated and qualified, leading to self-defeating oversimplification. It's like trying to draw up a document that would enable someone else to choose a wife or husband for you and being irrevocably tied to the results of that decision.

The other difficulty the courts have found in dealing with such "wills" is the problem of deciding whether the person's earlier preferences, however clearly expressed, are still firmly held once the hypothetical situation has become real and present. While it may seem to us, when we are healthy and active, that the loss of mobility, for example, would be intolerable, most people do not find it intolerable once it has occurred.

The "Living Will"

The Euthanasia Society of America, founded in 1938, had relatively little impact in the first three decades of its life, and its advocacy of euthanasia attracted only around 4,000 members. In 1968 it reorganized, becoming the Euthanasia Education Council and shifting its emphasis to the individual's right to die with dignity by refusing life-prolonging procedures. Since then, its membership has risen to approach 100,000. One key component in its increasing success was the development of the "Living Will." The council has received over 750,000 requests for copies of the will, which has gone beyond its twenty-second printing.

In the "Living Will" (see Figure 9-1), the signer anticipates a time when *he cannot make or communicate decisions about his condition and treatment* and *there is no reasonable expectation of recovery, and curative treatment is no longer indicated* (a condition in fact applicable to almost all states of illness); *he rejects "artificial means" and "heroic measures"* (with the difficulty of deciding which, of all possible measures, are extraordinary or heroic—some would include only those which are particularly painful, excessively expensive, or otherwise repugnant to the patient); and *he asks for the administration of drugs to alleviate suffering "even though this may hasten the moment of death."* The document thus does not request an act of euthanasia, but relies on the possibility that drugs used to relieve symptoms may also hasten death, indirectly but unavoidably. In fact, although this can occur, effective symptom control need not shorten life at all.

It is estimated that more than 200,000 Americans have signed a "Living Will" and placed the document on record. Copies can be obtained from the Euthanasia Educational Council (250 West 57th St., New York, New York 10019). It is advised that you have your signature witnessed by two other people, to establish that you are of sound mind and signing voluntarily. If you intend to have such documents used, make multiple copies of them once they have been signed and witnessed. Lodge the original with your lawyer and have other copies readily available, perhaps giving one to your physician and one to your next of kin. Its chances of being recog-

FIGURE 9-1 The "Living Will." (Reprinted by permission of Concern for Dying, 250 West 57th St., New York, N.Y. 10019.)

TO MY FAMILY, MY PHYSICIAN, MY LAWYER, MY CLERGYMAN
TO ANY MEDICAL FACILITY IN WHOSE CARE I HAPPEN TO BE
TO ANY INDIVIDUAL WHO MAY BECOME RESPONSIBLE FOR MY HEALTH, WELFARE OR AFFAIRS

Death is as much a reality as birth, growth, maturity and old age—it is the one certainty of life. If the time comes when I, _____ can no longer take part in decisions for my own future, let this statement stand as an expression of my wishes, while I am still of sound mind.

If the situation should arise in which there is no reasonable expectation of my recovery from physical or mental disability, I request that I be allowed to die and not be kept alive by artificial means or "heroic measures." I do not fear death itself as much as the indignities of deterioration, dependence and hopeless pain. I, therefore, ask that medication be mercifully administered to me to alleviate suffering even though this may hasten the moment of death.

This request is made after careful consideration. I hope you who care for me will feel morally bound to follow its mandate. I recognize that this appears to place a heavy responsibility upon you, but it is with the intention of relieving you of such responsibility and of placing it upon myself in accordance with my strong convictions, that this statement is made.

Signed _____

Date _____

Witness _____

Witness _____

Copies of this request have been given to _____

_____

_____

_____

---

nized as valid may be increased by periodically, perhaps annually, redating and initialing it to indicate that your decision has not changed.

The California Natural Death Act

Such documents as the "Living Will" are at present not legally binding, though they may be morally persuasive. Bills involving the "Living Will" or variations of it have been introduced in thirteen state legislatures in an attempt to obtain formal legal standing. In 1976, California passed the Natural Death Act, which aimed to resolve the "considerable uncertainty in the medical and legal professions as to the legality of terminating the use or application of life-sustaining procedures where the patient has voluntarily and in sound mind evidenced a desire that such procedure be withheld or withdrawn." Its preamble states: "The Legislature finds that adult persons have the fundamental right to control the decisions relating to the rendering of their own medical care, including the desire to have life-sustaining procedures withheld or withdrawn." During 1977, Arkansas, Idaho, Nevada, New Mexico, North Carolina, Oregon, and Texas, in addition to California, passed right-to-die laws. Similar bills continue to be considered in most other states.

The California act does not authorize euthanasia. No doctor is empowered to decide not to treat a patient, or to take steps to end a life, and relatives are given no rights or immunities under the act. It provides for a form (Figure 9-2) in which the patient states in advance his intention to withhold his consent to some types of treatment in certain circumstances. It also includes several safeguards. The witnesses must not be relatives of the patient, nor anyone likely to benefit under his will. The directive can be revoked at any time without any particular formality. However, in the event of the revocation not being acted upon, there will be no liability if the doctor did not have actual notice of the patient's change of mind. If the patient is conscious and mentally competent, the doctor must ensure that the steps he proposes to take are in accordance with the patient's wishes.

The California act specifically states that death resulting from the withdrawing of life-sustaining measures does not constitute suicide, and that the doctor will not be guilty of any criminal offense, liable to civil action, or guilty of unprofessional conduct. For the doctor to refuse to act under the directive will not attract civil or criminal liability; though if he fails to pass the matter over to another physician who *is* prepared to carry out the directive, he will be guilty of unprofessional conduct. Anyone who forgets a

FIGURE 9-2 Natural Death Act, Directive

I _____being of sound mind, willfully, and voluntarily make known my desire that my life shall not be artificially prolonged under the circumstances set forth below and do hereby declare:

1. If at any time I should have an incurable injury, disease or illness certified to be a terminal condition by two physicians, and where the application of life-sustaining procedures would serve only to artificially prolong the moment of my death and where my physician determines that my death is imminent whether or not life-sustaining procedures are utilized, I direct that such procedures be withheld or withdrawn, and that I be permitted to die naturally.

2. In the absence of my ability to give directions regarding the use of such life-sustaining procedures, it is my intention that this directive shall be honored by my family and physician(s) as the final expression of my legal right to refuse medical or surgical treatment and accept the consequences from such refusal.

3. If I have been diagnosed as pregnant and that diagnosis is known to my physician, this directive shall have no force or effect during the course of my pregnancy.

4. I have been diagnosed and notified at least 14 days ago as having a terminal condition by _____M.D., whose address is _____ and whose telephone number is _____. I understand that if I have not filled in the physician's name and address, it shall be presumed that I did not have a terminal condition when I made out this directive.

5. The directive shall have no effect five years from the date filled in above.

6. I understand the full import of this directive, and I am emotionally and mentally competent to make this directive.

---

directive in someone else's name or willfully conceals knowledge of someone's revocation that results in the hastening of that person's death will be subject to prosecution for murder.

A directive's validity lapses after five years, when it must be re-executed. Because there was concern that insurance companies might insist that their customers sign such a directive as a condition for being accepted for insurance (to save the company the cost of expensive life-sustaining equipment), such requirements are specifically prohibited by the act.

No other state legislature has enacted similar laws, nor has any formally recognized the "Living Will"; there have not yet been cases in which the courts have established legal precedent for the use of such documents, nor have they yet been shown to be practical, workable, and without serious disadvantages. Still, the public response to the "Living Will" has made it clear that there is a considerable general wish for some such legal provision.

"The Christian Affirmation of Life"

"The Christian Affirmation of Life," a document that has been widely distributed and discussed, originated with the directors of the Catholic Hospital Association in 1974 (see Figure 9-3). It was intended to represent a specifically Christian point of view and to avoid some of the shortcomings of the "Living Will." The "Affirmation" makes additional requests of the doctor. It asks that the signer be told the truth and be considered a vital member of the decision-making team—serious omissions from the "Living Will." It includes an affirmation of faith and asks specifically for appropriate spiritual care and prayers. It does not include witnesses, for it is not intended to be a legal document. It is not meant to be used in court to command adherence to the patient's wishes, but is for the purposes of "reflection and meditation" and relies on moral rather than legal authority. Copies may be obtained from the Catholic Hospital Association (1438 South Grand Boulevard, St. Louis, Missouri 63104).

Alternatives

Another version of such wills (Figure 9-4) is a more legally formal statement that specifically refuses consent for life-prolonging procedures and declares that this refusal is to remain in force until the signer revokes it in writing. The signer seeks to relieve all physicians and other personnel who withhold treatment from any legal liability for doing so.

INFORMED DISSENT

Probably all attempts to specify in advance under which precise conditions one would or would not wish to have the doctors aban-

FIGURE 9-3 "The Christian Affirmation of Life." (Reprinted by permission of the Catholic Hospital Association.)

To my family, friends, physician, lawyer and clergyman:

I believe that each individual person is created by God our Father in love and that God retains a loving relationship to each person throughout human life and eternity.

I believe that Jesus Christ lived, suffered, and died for me and that his suffering, death, and resurrection prefigure and make possible the death-resurrection process which I now anticipate.

I believe that each person's worth and dignity derives from the relationship of love in Christ that God has for each individual person, and not from one's usefulness or effectiveness in society.

I believe that God our Father has entrusted to me a shared dominion with him over my earthly existence so that I am bound to use ordinary means to preserve my life but I am free to refuse extraordinary means to prolong my life.

I believe that through death life is not taken away but merely changed, and though I may experience fear, suffering, and sorrow, by the grace of the Holy Spirit, I hope to accept death as a free human act which enables me to surrender this life and to be united with God for eternity.

Because of my belief:

I,

request that I be informed as death approaches so that I may continue to prepare for the full encounter with Christ through the help of the sacraments and the consolation and prayers of my family and friends.

I request that, if possible, I be consulted concerning the medical procedures which might be used to prolong my life as death approaches. If I can no longer take part in decisions concerning my own future and there is no reasonable expectation of my recovery from physical and mental disability, I request that no extraordinary means be used to prolong my life.

I request, though I wish to join my suffering to the suffering of Jesus so I may be united fully with him in the act of death-resurrection, that my pain, if unbearable, be alleviated. However, no means should be used with the intention of shortening my life.

I request, because I am a sinner and in need of reconciliation and because my faith, hope, and love may not overcome all fear and doubt, that my family, friends, and the whole Christian community join me in prayer and mortification as I prepare for the great personal act of dying.

Finally, I request that after my death, my family, my friends, and the whole Christian community pray for me, and rejoice with me because of the mercy and love of the Trinity, whith whom I hope to be united for all eternity.

Signed _____

FIGURE 9-4 Refusal of Consent for Life-Prolonging Procedures

To any and all doctors, hospitals, health personnel and others treating me during my final illness:

I _____hereby make this statement in the presence of witnesses, to declare and record my express wish and desire that: in the event, due to illness or accident, that my condition becomes terminal and without reasonable hope of recovery, then I do not wish to be kept alive by the use of drugs, treatments or machine. I wish to receive adequate medication for proper control of my symptoms, but nothing beyond what is necessary for that purpose. I hereby specifically withdraw my consent for any such primarily life-sustaining treatment, and this withdrawal of my consent shall continue unless and until I revoke it in writing. Should I, in the course of my illness, subsequently become legally incompetent or unable to communicate my wishes to those treating me, then this document should be considered as continuing to withdraw my consent to any further treatment not directed primarily at symptom relief. Any and all doctors, nurses, hospitals and institutions that honour my wishes and intentions as expressed in this document, are hereby formally held free from any and all liability on behalf of myself, my heirs, successors and assigns.

Signed _____

Dated _____

Witnesses: _____   _____

_____   _____

---

don attempts to prolong or sustain one's life are doomed to failure. They must always oversimplify; they must always neglect crucial aspects of the relevant circumstances that will be important but are unknowable now. With regard to the needs of the sentient individual, it is essential to improve legislation to guarantee every person the right to as much information as she wishes to have about her illness, about the treatments, both existing and proposed, about effects and side effects, and about her prognosis. The principle of the necessity for *informed consent* for medical treatment should be more assiduously enforced and assured, for it is far too frequently ignored or abused. Further, there should be a clearly recognized right to *informed dissent*. One should be enabled specifically to refuse certain treatment modalities once informed about their advantages and disadvantages; such dissent from particular treatments relative to one's own individual circumstances should be enforceable. The position with regard to the patient no longer capable of communicating her wishes can be met both by the prospective use of specific informed dissent (when there is time to foresee likely pathological events) and by the wider adoption and use of the "Committee of the Person" approach.

In the context of the proper doctor-patient relationship, the abuse of the best interests of the patient by uncontrolled therapeutic frenzy should be less common. The training of physicians, too, must stress not only *how* to treat, but *when* to treat—and when *not* to treat.

REFERENCES

"Funeral Industry Practices," Final Staff Report to the Federal Trade Commission & Proposed Trade Regulation Rule. FTC Bureau of Consumer Protection, Washington, D.C. (June 1978). 560. PB.

"Legislative Manual 1977," Society for the Right to Die, 250 W. 57th Street, N.Y. 10019. 1978.

ODEN, T. C., *Should Treatment Be Terminated?* New York: Harper & Row, 1976. (The Drew Committee Criteria are printed and discussed in this book.)

10

Suicide

Dear Mary,
You deserve something better. I tried, but I'm
all wrong. Thanks for your help. It'll stop
hurting soon. Love, Bill.
Suicide note

THE EPIDEMIC

Suicide has become a widespread epidemic in our time. The statistics vary in detail, but are uniformly alarming. One estimate suggests that someone, somewhere, tries deliberately to kill himself about every minute throughout the day. About sixty to seventy times a day, the attempt will be "successful" (for in the macabre terminology commonly used, the "successful" suicide is the one who dies). There may be more than 100,000 attempts per year in America. Some 25,000 deaths from suicide are reported every year in the United States, and the actual number is certainly much higher, probably around twice as high. Recent British studies show that nearly 10 out of every 1,000 attendances at hospital accident and emergency departments are due to self-poisoning, a prevalence rate of 430 per 100,000 of the population, figures far higher than earlier estimates. This means that over the course of just one year, 1 person out of every 230 of the adult population of London attempts suicide by means of poison. Attempted suicides may account for some 15 percent of all acute emergency medical admissions, forming the second most common category (Shneidman, 1976).

Suicide threatens us not just as an unpleasant reminder of mortality, but as a demonstration of the uncomfortable fact that we can bring about our own death. In a way, it is almost insulting, when the rest of us are scared of death and trying hard to live, to find someone who seems to regard life so lightly or so distastefully as to discard it. One way people try to deal with this is to regard suicide as a particularly odd type of behavior unique to insane and peculiar people. The truth is more important but more frightening: suicides are us. We make it more dreadful by the way we treat the victims—the suicide and his survivors. Albert Camus insisted that suicide is the only truly serious philosophical problem, for judging whether or not life is worth living is the fundamental question. All other questions come after that one.

Many of us contemplate suicide at some time in our life; once we recognize this as a potential choice, we can hardly fail to consider the possibility when things get really difficult. But most of us, most of the time, realize that however much suicide may look like an appropriate response to the troubles confronting us, it is very seldom the best option open to us.

Some people gamble with death by various means. Some play Russian Roulette with one bullet in the six chambers, or with only one chamber unloaded. They may play "chicken" in cars or on motorcycles. One teenager who'd taken a rare and deadly poison smiled as he waited to see whether he'd survive it, and said to me: "When I was a kid, we used to play 'chicken' on the railway line. I was always the last to jump off. I wonder whether I've jumped off in time this time."

What of those who mismanage their lives and neglect to take proper care of themselves—such as the diabetic muddling his diet or his insulin, or the woman with severe liver disease who continues to drink? What of the accident-prone, like the repeatedly "unlucky" pedestrian? It is now clear that a significant proportion of car accidents are partly or completely suicidal in origin. For some people self-damage is a way of life—smoking, overeating, drinking heavily, choosing jobs or playing sports that are unduly dangerous. It is recognized that even a substantial percentage of homicides are partially or largely precipitated by the apparent victims.

Suicide is rude. In England it was a felony, like murder, until 1961—a crime against the monarch. The suicide discards our rules and society's values. He asks us questions we don't want to hear. He seems to be passing judgment on us all. Some people, choosing to die publicly, use death as a weapon and rub our noses in the mess they leave. The suicide threatens our omnipotence, slaps us in the face and calls our advice, love, and help useless. By a supreme act of projection, he makes us feel as helpless and hopeless as he himself feels.

At times, suicide seems to be sought as a sort of magical means of achieving unrealistic but devoutly desired ends. There may be fantasies of revenge: "I'll die and then they'll all be sorry, and I'll enjoy seeing that." There is the death-rebirth fantasy—"I'll be a phoenix"—the attempt to make a new start by destroying the bad old self and rising from the ashes. "I am insoluble—I'll destroy me and start again."

Although anyone might kill himself if sufficiently desperate, research studies enable us to draw a partial picture of the most likely victim (see Shneidman, 1976; Lester & Lester, 1971; Farberow, 1979). The "typical" suicide is a male Caucasian; single, a widower, divorced, or separated; adolescent or over 65; probably living alone, unemployed, redundant, or retired; and depressed, possibly having made a previous suicide attempt. He may abuse alcohol or drugs and may have shown difficulties in coping with previous stresses. He may well be suffering from an existing and possibly chronic physical illness. It is likely that he will have mentioned, perhaps even threatened, suicide in recent months; he will probably have seen his doctor recently (one study showed that two-thirds of suicides had visited their family doctor in the month before their death; 40 percent in the previous week).

As in so many other areas of activity, men are more lethal than women. Approximately twice as many men as women are "successful" at suicide, although women *attempt* suicide far more commonly. Men tend to use more dangerous and surer methods, and to be more adept at using lethal weapons. More women take overdoses of tablets—also a dangerous technique, but far more variably so. Single, separated, divorced, and widowed people have a higher suicide rate than their married peers. Caucasians seem to have a higher rate of suicide than other racial groups. Unfortunately, this is one aspect of Western culture which migrants and immigrants quite readily adopt. Black Americans who move from the South to the northern big cities tend to show a marked rise in incidence of suicide; and middle- and upper-class blacks are beginning to approach the suicide rate of their white fellows. There is a particularly striking increase in the suicide rate of young American Indians.

Statistics, of course, may provide reasonable information about a large population but relatively little information about individual people. However, they show that urban communities have higher suicide rates than rural ones; that people with no children are more likely to kill themselves than those with offspring; and that people with significant and chronic physical illnesses are more prone to suicide, as are alcoholics and addicts. The rate of death by suicide is high among the elderly, but there has been a substantial increase in the death rate from suicide among the young over recent decades. During the late 1960s suicide was the tenth leading killer in the United States, the third most common cause of death in the 15–19-year-old group, and the second most common among college students (see Shneidman, 1976). Numerous pressures contribute to this, including difficulties in competing in the academic ratrace, problems in coping with personal relationships, and failures in both areas leading to feelings of incompetence, rejection, and abandonment. Many of these suicides take place at home, and the lack of communication and understanding between the parents and the child is often very striking. Even when the parents and the teenager are ostensibly discussing an issue, they are often talking *at* one another, but not listening *to* one another. Parents appeal to their own authority—though such authority hardly exists if one has to appeal to it. Teenagers, in turn, emphasize their group norms and the differences between their own and their parents' life-styles. The more disapproving and critical the parents become, the more teenagers emphasize their differences in order to find some areas of life where parents are patently not qualified to judge them. All members of the family seem to forget that we can communicate accurately and with love without necessarily agreeing on many issues. Love and respect thrive on understanding, not on agreement. But excess emphasis on agreement to petty policies and restrictions can make it difficult to talk about much more important matters.

Suicide in the elderly is also a major problem (ibid.). Men and women over 65, while forming less than 10 percent of the population, make up more than 25 percent of deaths by suicide. This frequently occurs in the context of depression and poor physical health. Some ominous features of the general behavior of the elderly are self-neglect; unaccustomed solitariness; gloomy ruminations and self-recrimination; and feelings of uselessness, redundancy, and rejection. Recent bereavement and economic and emotional insecurity may also contribute to the decision to give up.

Obviously, individual self-damaging acts may vary in the extent to which death is sought or likely. Edwin Shneidman (1976) has categorized the *lethality* of intent with regard to the probability of an individual killing himself in the immediate future as follows:

High lethality—expects his actions to result in death

Medium lethality—ambivalent; some expectation of death

Low lethality—no conscious wish to die, but some small element of risk

Absent lethality—no lethal intent

As far as one can see, genetic and inherited factors are not involved to any substantial extent, though cultural and early environmental effects may influence national and ethnic differences in suicide rates. Being the first-born child and coming from a family in which other suicides have occurred may have some predisposing influence. The person who kills himself may be a more rigid and inflexible personality, finding difficulty in coping with changing circumstances and having a negative view of himself. Suicide is considerably less likely among people who have stable, lasting, satisfying, and unambiguous relationships with other people than among those who are isolated or who are surrounded by stormy and resentful relationships. Loss and disruption of important close relationships increases the risk. Drinking precedes many acts of suicide.

Some myths about suicide should be cleared up, for they can lead to dangerous mistakes. People are often surprisingly unmoved by suicide threats, believing that "those who talk about it never do it." Quite the contrary: almost everybody who commits suicide has talked about it, in some way, to somebody else. So suicide threats should always be taken seriously. Sometimes the potential suicide talks about it directly, sometimes indirectly. "I just feel weary of life," he may say, "I can't face carrying on much longer." One may hear a more bitter, vengeful approach: "They'd be sorry if I weren't around any more," or "You may not have to put up with me much longer." Often, once a person has finally decided on committing suicide, his mood may lighten—he may look relieved and more cheerful, for the certainty he has chosen may be more comfortable, for a while, than the uncertainty that preceded it. If there have been other good reasons for expecting a risk of suicide, one must not relax one's guard too soon.

The suicide often agrees to put his life at risk to register an emphatic protest against his circumstances, or to seek to correct an intolerable element within his life. He may expect to live or, in a muddled way, expect both to die and to be around to reap the benefits of the effects his action may have on others. Menninger (1966) spoke of the three deadly wishes intertwined in an act of suicide—the wish to die, the wish to kill, and the wish to be killed.

Some people nowadays use suicide like they use drugs and alcohol—as reality solvents, to dissolve and alter reality as they experience it. What gets destroyed may be themselves, but what they actually wish to destroy may be external reality.

Suicide is not common among cancer patients, and is usually in response not to terminal illness itself so much as to its unnecessary effects—the disruption of personal relationships and badly treated symptoms. It may also depend on how the illness affects one's self-image. Suicide attempts seem to be more common among patients who have cancer involving the head and neck than among those whose cancer affects other parts of the body—the psychosocial deformity, in addition to the physical, may be too much to bear. Certainly, in some such circumstances, a "rational" decision may be made to commit suicide in the absence of any mental disorder. However, the decision may also represent a relievable depression, or a response to intolerably inadequate but improvable care. One cannot too readily or too glibly classify the nature of suicidal ideas in such circumstances. Just as it would not be justifiable to seek to prevent suicide under all circumstances, it is not justifiable to support or encourage such attempts too readily. The situation may not be as gloomy as it initially seems, and a patient may be able to find a far more fulfilling way of life than he or she had previously thought possible. As one such patient said to me after some weeks of therapy: "My God, how much I'd have missed if you'd just let me go ahead and kill myself when I wanted to!"

HELPING THE POTENTIALLY SUICIDAL PERSON

Sometimes you may be concerned that someone in your family, even in the absence of severe physical illness, is potentially suicidal. In such an instance, you would want to get professional advice and help, but may want first to decide whether your fears are realistic. Don't shrink from mentioning suicide, though obviously you should do so tactfully. I doubt that any person, even (or especially) an intelligent or sensitive one, hasn't at some time thought about suicide—so you're highly unlikely to suggest the idea to someone who has never considered it. It's probably far more dangerous if no one knows that he's thinking about it. He may actually want to discuss it with you—most people who eventually kill themselves, as we have said, at least try to talk to someone about it before they act. One may begin talking about the subject in many ways. "How does the future seem to you?" "Just how low do you feel at times?" "Does it sometimes seem that life isn't worth living?" "Have you ever thought of harming yourself when you felt like that? What did you think of doing? What would happen if you did harm yourself?" If the person says he did think of suicide but has changed his mind, ask him to explain why he gave up the idea—does it sound convincing? Explore the possibilities of his finding more constructive ways of dealing with his difficulties. Don't get too deeply locked into endless involvement in the suicidal ruminations themselves.

Sometimes the very depressed, confused, or seriously physically ill person may seem remote, inaccessible, withdrawn, and silent. Treat the person as sentient—as capable of understanding and remembering what you say, even if that person cannot say anything to you—up and beyond the point of death. People often receive better than they can transmit. The person may be able to respond to very simple requests or orders when she can no longer speak; she may be able to understand even when quite mute. So it can be perfectly appropriate to address yourself to the seriously ill person, however unresponsive that person may be. Introduce yourself and say why you're there. Let her know you will be receptive if she wants to say anything, but that otherwise you will try to anticipate her wants and needs as best you can. With the withdrawn or silent conscious person, one might say: "It seems hard for you to talk now. That's all right. But I want you to know I'm trying to help you. If there's anything you can say to me about what's happening to you, and how you feel, it would help me to help you." If the person tries to reply but hesitates, be patient. You might suggest some of the reasons for the hesitation and ask if they apply.

Never stand at the bedside of a mute, delirious, or apparently unconscious patient and discuss that person's affairs in terms you would not use in her presence if she were fully alert and responding.

Learn to tolerate silence. Listening can take much more skill than talking. Permit silence to continue when necessary to encourage the other person to speak, or to share an emotion that goes beyond words. Resist the temptation to leap into every pause.

Anger can be especially hard for you to deal with. Angry is one thing a seriously ill person can be when he or she is too helpless to be anything else.

Anger is a common reaction to frustration, and it may often be displaced from a target that isn't available (fate, God, the illness, the boss, the rude nurse who just went off duty), or from a situation that occurred earlier in the day when the person couldn't say anything, onto a target that *is* available—you. Accept and identify the anger. If you're puzzled about why the person is so cross with you, say so. Did you provoke the patient? Perhaps your brusqueness, sarcasm, or moralizing may have caused it. When people feel especially handicapped by their illness or problems, your own good health, energy, and cheerfulness may accentuate the bitterness the patients feel about the capacities they are losing. People often become especially angry when they feel helpless or passive and dependent. You may be able to ease this by letting such people play an intelligent part in deciding what happens to them. Obviously, in the course of an illness, many decisions may need to be made by the doctor—the specialist. But too often, all decisions are taken away from people who are perfectly capable of making them, or at least of sharing in making them.

DEPRESSION AND SUICIDE

Because depression is now one of the most common diseases as well as a potential killer, you should learn how to recognize it. It is not well known that depression as a disease incorporates far more than a change of mood. Usually, yes, there is an obvious depression of mood—the person feels miserable and sad to an extent that is out of proportion to the problems he faces; and eventually his mood will no longer be responsive to external events. Sometimes a depression may follow an obviously disturbing event—perhaps a major loss like a bereavement. Often, however, there may be no obvious "cause," and people may be very puzzled about this. Yet the precipitating factors of a depression may be far from obvious. In searching for a cause for his depression, the person may often worsen it, for he will sit and review every possible cause, examining every unhappy event in his life—and *that's* bound to be depressing. It may be very difficult to recall when the process began, for depression is one of the sneakiest illnesses around. One of the first structures it invades and destroys is hope. Whatever the objective realities of the situation, the future looks dark and hopeless, and there seems to be no way things could improve, no way to cope with one's problems. Even gloomier thoughts arise. The depressed person may feel sure he's going mad, or that he has cancer or some other dread disease. Thinking itself can become difficult and slowed; the simplest task becomes hard to handle; and making even quite obvious decisions may seem impossible. "It's as if my brains were steeped in treacle," one old lady told me.

Lacking energy, the depressed person feels tired however much she tries to rest. Sleep is often disturbed. Some depressed people sleep a good deal without feeling refreshed by it; commonly sleep is restless and unprofitable, with early-morning wakening—waking at maybe four in the morning, a very black and dismal hour, feeling profoundly miserable and unable to return to sleep. Sexual activity often declines, adding fears of impotence or frigidity to the problem. The person loses pleasure in all activities, till even the things that most reliably pleased him are no longer enjoyed. He often withdraws from other people, becoming more solitary, and often completely preoccupied with himself alone, in a completely negative and self-denigrating way. Performance at work and in family functions declines, and personal appearance may be neglected.

A depressed person will often postpone the idea of suicide, realizing that however empty life feels, he is needed by his children or friends, and that he has still an important part to play in the lives of others. This may be initially protective; but it can lead him to a more dangerous interpretation of the same situation once he begins to think: "They'll be better off without me—I'm no good for them." Yet a properly treated depression need not cause any lasting problems for other family members, while there is evidence to suggest that a parent's death by suicide may cause later difficulties for the children, and may even influence their later susceptibility to suicide.

What can you do about it? Watch out for the warning signs

described. If you have any reason to suspect that a member of your family, or someone else you know, is considering suicide, be prepared to talk with him about his feelings, and also let his family doctor know of your concern. Don't scoff at him, don't argue about the details. Listen with acceptance of his feelings, and with empathy—you may help a lot by giving him the opportunity to vent his feelings of pain, bitterness, and helplessness. Let him know that you understand, as far as you can, and that you care. But never fake it. If you can't genuinely understand and care, you shouldn't be talking to him at all. He needs no further demonstrations of uncaring misunderstanding. In that case, mention your concern to someone who can cope better—and still be sure to involve the family doctor. Listen carefully, and encourage the depressed person to discuss his problems and the way he has tried to cope with them. Make it absolutely clear that he can express his feelings frankly, however strong and negative they may be. Find out what matters for him in life, what holds real meaning for him. Stress what possibilities still exist for him to continue a meaningful life, or even to increase its meaning. Emphasize that proper professional help is available, and that other ways of dealing with his problems will be sought and probably found.

You can contribute a good deal to those who subsequently do help the suicidal person. You can be readily available and can use your close knowledge of the person—and he can't reject your help by accusing you of being "paid to care," which is often a way of rejecting a professional therapist. Arguing with the person isn't helpful, even if the objective facts of the situation contradict his statements. State your view of the facts clearly and gently, but remember that it is the subjective facts (the situation as he experiences it) he is suffering from. He may be confused about what he really wants in life and how to go about getting it. Talking to a sympathetic and reflective listener may help him to clarify his feelings, fears, and plans.

The person may hesitate to talk about suicidal ideas as such, as he may not want to arouse your disapproval or anxiety. Until he is able finally to decide that he doesn't want to die, he may not want you to be able to prevent him from harming himself, lest you take away one of the few options he may be able to see open to him. In other cases the person may be greatly relieved that you brought up the subject and pleased to talk about it. Don't try to tell him there's nothing to worry about, or urge him, "Pull yourself together" or "Snap out of it." Do you think he would choose to be that miserable if he could readily choose to be otherwise?

If you believe anyone is actively considering suicide, don't leave him alone until the crisis passes or until further help is available.

Your role may be very important, but don't try to handle the situation alone. Get professional help—increasing numbers of doctors and others are being trained to handle the problem of suicide, and most psychiatrists should be able to help. Similarly, some social workers and psychologists have been specially trained to deal with such problems. No matter who eventually takes charge of the case, you can remain a valuable member of the caring team. Keep the therapist fully informed of all you learn about the patient's condition and how it changes during treatment. Cooperate fully with the therapist's advice and plans; even if, at times, you feel sure you have a better idea, you lack the training that would help you to fully understand the situation. Make your suggestions to the therapist. Moreover, a patient is always better off with one coherent plan of treatment than with a smorgasbord of tidbits of different people's advice.

One important function you can fulfill is to reduce the risk of an impulsive suicide bid resulting from a sudden decision. If, as is likely, your relative or friend is being treated with medication, help him make sure that he takes it in the correct amounts and at the right times. If possible, take charge of the medicines yourself rather than allowing the patient to leave them lying around at home. Remove all weapons or potential weapons—not sneakily, but openly and with full explanation of your actions and motives. Remove also other medicines. Remember that people sometimes take an overdose of someone else's medication—so if you are taking medicines for any reason, keep them secure.

In any case, and at any time—in fact, right now—go through the family medicine cabinet. Remove all extra drugs and medicines and either flush them down the toilet or take them to your local pharmacist, who can dispose of them safely. No family needs a stockpile of drugs. Not only may the drugs change in chemical composition over time and lose any value they once had, but they provide a constant risk of overdose, accidental or deliberate, by adults or children. Except for medications you are presently taking under a doctor's supervision, don't save drugs—they won't save you.

Your local suicide prevention center or other crisis service may be able to help, as may such call-in services as the Suicide Prevention Line, Teenage Hot Line, Problems in Living Line, and the Samaritans.

When someone has attempted suicide and survived, continue to treat him with compassion. Too often, people treat the survivor as a double failure—he was so incompetent at life that he tried to kill himself, and so incapable that he couldn't even manage that. The family may feel great anger toward the survivor: "How could she do this to us? Didn't she love us enough to spare us this? Didn't she think of the disgrace she was bringing to the family?" It's a little like the mother whose child has been missing for some hours, till she becomes very anxious about his well-being. When he finally returns, safe, her initial relief and gladness may be replaced by anger, as she smacks him: "Don't you *ever* do that to me again!" Remember that even after the crisis has passed, the person who has been driven to the point of suicide will have emotional and other problems and will continue to need and deserve your caring and help.

BEFORE YOU KILL YOURSELF

What if this section you have been reading sounds like a description of your situation? What if you yourself are considering the possibility of suicide, if you don't want to carry on living?

Above all, call someone for help. Suicide is much too big a decision to make alone. However hopeless the situation may seem to you—there is hope. However much it may seem to you that your problems are insoluble and that there's no other way out—there is another way out. This is not mere Pollyanna optimism, no Micawber-like false cheer; this is not just soft-talking persuasion. I have met thousands of people in times of acute psychological stress. Many of them were convinced that there was no longer any point in living, and they wanted to die. These were true feelings, but not true or valid conclusions. So far, I have yet to meet one person for whom suicide was in fact the best way out; and those who gave themselves a fair chance to explore alternatives indeed found aggreeable alternatives.

One of the great advantages of sharing your situation with others, however great the temptation to nurture your misery in solitude, is that, from their position—caring but slightly separated from your situation—they are often able to see alternative courses of action that might not be apparent to you. One thing does seem clear, in our present state of knowledge—death is irreversible. Once you have killed yourself, there will be no opportunity to change your mind, for no one will be able to bring you back to life for another try. So don't take an irreversible step until you are sure beyond doubt that no alternatives are possible—and *you cannot reach that conclusion on your own*. Often you are just too close to be able to see the alternatives. (It's much easier to find your way out of a maze with the advice of someone who is in a position to see the whole maze and its entrances and exits and patterns.)

So don't be afraid to call openly for help or advice. Your request will be taken seriously by anyone capable of understanding distress. There may be a local suicide prevention center or call-in service that can help. If those alternatives aren't available to you, call a hospital, your family doctor, a clergyman, or your local police station. If you can't decide, call a relative, a friend, a neighbor. If you can't find the appropriate telephone number, call the operator and she can help.

Be prepared to be frank. Tell whomever you contact about how bad you feel and what plans for suicide you may have made. If you phone someone who doesn't already know you, give your full name and address and your telephone number, so they can call you back, if need be. As soon as possible, get to visit a professional counselor. Tell him about your situation, and take his advice. People sometimes fear that by calling for professional help they may get trapped and somehow forced to continue living whether they want to or not. Well, there are measures that can be taken to protect you, even without your agreement—but you can make those unnecessary by allowing for the possibility of hope. Ultimately, though, there is no way in which anyone, or any hospital, can totally prevent you from harming yourself if you remain determined to do so. As a human being, aware of the possibility of suicide, you have a permanent, built-in ejector seat. Like the ejector seats in planes, it can really only be used once—but there's no need to use it now.

You are in the position to make what could be the best investment of your life. Seek out properly trained professional help, and invest one month of your time and collaboration in trying to see whether you can't make something better of your life. At the end of that time, you could still kill yourself, if you insist. Or, if you have begun to realize the possibility of help, you could review your investment.

Should one part of your personality be allowed to decree death for every other part of you? One young man I treated provided another argument against suicide. "Just because my brain is feeling miserable," he said, "that's no reason for me to allow it to put an end to all my other organs, which can't speak for themselves. Even if my brain feels hopeless—my feet are enjoying themselves, and my liver is doing well!"

The more miserable you feel, the harder it may be to let yourself trust other people and talk with them. But if you're reaching the point of considering suicide, how much worse could things get?

It's a good idea for you to act so as to reduce the chances that a sudden impulse may lead you to harm yourself in a way that you would later regret. So get rid of all tablets, pills, and medicines in the house; if you have guns or other weapons, get a trustworthy friend or your local police station to look after them for you. Remember, too, the real risk that your suicide attempt may have a better chance of maiming you than of killing you, and may only add to your problems rather than relieving them. Commonly used drugs in overdoses can leave you with all your problems intact—plus ulcers, stomach hemorrhage, buzzing in the ears, deafness, or a severely damaged liver. You don't need that.

Perhaps you are considering a suicide attempt with other ideas in mind. Again, discuss these with a suitable counselor, for you may find it's not such a good idea as it seems. Some people attempt suicide as an act of vengeance: "They'll be sorry when . . ." or "I'll show *them* how strongly I feel!" Are you sure they'll feel sorry? Does it matter how they'll feel when you're no longer around to know how they feel? Are there not better ways of convincing them of the way you feel—which would allow you to be around to benefit from the situation? Some people try suicide, especially by an overdose of drugs, as a way of escaping, hopefully temporarily, from a situation they find intolerable. They say things like: "All I wanted to do was to sleep and sleep—and I hoped things might be better when I woke up." That's a very messy and chancy way of trying to achieve a respite of peace. You can gain better and more constructive relief by sharing your problems with someone else who can help to the extent that's useful. You can get away from the awfulness of things better by visiting friends once treatment has started.

It's no good trying to run away from your problems, physically or geographically, whether you run into a coma or to California. The problems will still be with you when you get there; and in strange territory, you are likely to be less well equipped to cope with them. Instead, act to increase your options, to increase your degree of freedom. Self-damage or self-destruction inevitably reduces your range of choice. Competent medical and psychological care should serve to increase your capacities to live the sort of life you value and find meaningful, not to cramp your style into someone else's conception of normal.

It is often argued that to deprive a person of his right to end his own life is to abridge or limit his freedom. Yet few suicides who are rescued from an attempt complain about that curtailment of their freedom, or regret, except briefly, having been saved.

It is easy to find "good" reasons for killing oneself, though they are not usually correct or true reasons, or reasons you would accept if someone close to you proposed them for himself. Marshal your arguments, and then consider them this way: if your close relative or lover gave you the same arguments as reasons why you should kill him or her, would you accept, and go ahead? Most of the arguments in favor of the rationality of most suicides rely on sophistry and clever debating tricks. Suicide is an emergency exit we all have, but like most such exits, we need not use it; the door locks behind us once we're out, so we can't change our mind. Suicide is inappropriate as a style of life; it rarely provides an appropriate or authentic death.

For some people, suicide is a variety of rebellion against God. One of my patients ruminated as follows: If only He is permitted to decide when we live and when we die, are you usurping His control over life and death? Or are you carrying it out as part of His plan? Must He work His will through external events, or through your own actions? Maybe you don't really want to destroy the life God gave you, but to destroy what that life has become, to seek to regain something more like the original life you started out with. But that's too hasty, too rushed, too irreversible; too false an attempt to *force* what must happen spontaneously. Rebirth can't be demanded at gunpoint, but must be gained through suitable work. It's too literal to concentrate on altering the body rather than altering the life.

What are you expecting from death? A pleasant sleep with a nice reawakening in benign and friendly circumstances? Are you really sure that's what lies ahead? Do you see it as "an easy way out"? The many hundreds of people I've known to attempt it would insist that it's not easy and it's not the way out. You'd better be absolutely right, and certain that you want to die. You won't be able to change your mind if you find it hasn't improved things. After you're dead, you won't be able to correct any mistakes. You don't know what death is like. You've never experienced it. You may have been asleep, drunk, anesthetized—but you've always been able to wake up again. Death's not like that.

Would you stop anyone from killing him- or herself? Why? Why not?

Remember the likely effect of your act of suicide on others, especially your family and friends. Perhaps by concentrating on your incapacities, you may try to convince yourself they'll be better off without you. But if you're the sort of person that cares at all about other people, they *won't* be better off without you. They will be diminished by your death, and may be very severely affected by it. Edwin Shneidman (1976) refers to them as the "survivor-victims." We don't know what lies in store for *you* after your death—we do know what lies in store for them, and it's not nice.

THE SURVIVOR-VICTIMS

Natural death leads to the complex pain of grief in survivors, as will be described in the next chapter. Death by suicide, self-willed death, leads to an even more bitter type of grief. Every year there are probably some 750,000 people in the United States alone who are seriously affected by someone else's suicide. This kind of death is an especially cruel reminder of the limitations of our power to save another.

Among the emotional responses particularly prominent are guilt and blame. One may blame oneself for failing to prevent a suicide or, worse, for causing it to happen. "Why didn't I stop him?" "Why didn't I believe her when she threatened to kill herself?" "How did I drive him to do it?"

You can do a good deal to help the suicidal person who is not entirely certain he wants to seek death; you can be vigilant and cautious, discourage him from harming himself and encourage him to find other ways of coping. But it is important to realize that no one can prevent someone else from killing himself if he has firmly decided to do so. You may have been able to prevent the preventable; don't berate yourself for failing to prevent the unpreventable.

In ambivalent mixture with sorrow is anger—"How could she do this to us?"—and shame at being tainted with the stigma of the act. One may also feel sheer relief. You may have lived through a good deal of anxiety with previous suicide attempts and threats, and through the infectious gloom of the person's depression. It is natural to feel a sense of relief that this is over. You can too easily feel guilty because you feel angry or relieved—then angry at feeling guilty.

Above all, there is the question: "Why?" The period of questioning may be protracted and painful. I recall seeing a distinguished lawyer whose 17-year-old son had killed himself a year earlier; he had sat in the cellar of the family home and shot his head off. It was totally unexpected. The parents, who were genuinely involved with their children, were astounded. The father was left with the unpleasant task of cleaning up the cellar. Cleaning up the family's lives took longer. Faced by the awful, unexplained reality of this act, he responded, after the initial shock, as a lawyer might. He collected the evidence. He retraced the last few months of his son's life as far as he could, and spoke to as many people who had known the boy as he could. He collected photographs, interviews, dates, and data. He went over his son's room again and again, seeking clues. All he found was a carefully preserved copy of a poem about suicide, cut out of a magazine two years before. The poem had been written at the age of 15 by another young man who eventually killed himself when he was 17.

When visiting friends bereaved by suicide, approach the family as you might approach anyone in sorrow. Offer your caring by all means, and allow them to express their feelings freely. Avoid prejudice and judgment. Whatever your personal views on the morality and ethics of suicide, this is no time for offering either condemnation or support of the act. Save your arguments, for or against, for some suitable formal debate.

Let the family members talk through the guilt, anger, and recriminations if they want to. Though the whole social situation may have played a part in leading up to the suicide, individual recriminations are not useful. None of us, in any of our relationships with anybody, could bear the sort of scrutiny that the survivor-victims turn on their relationships. We have all done and said things that are regrettable, especially with the pernicious wisdom of hindsight, once someone has died. But we have not killed anyone by so doing. We must forgive ourselves for having had a normal human relationship, and look also at the constructive and creative aspects of it.

REFERENCES

FARBEROW, N. L., ed., *Indirect Self-Destructive Behavior*. New York: McGraw Hill, 1979.

LESTER, G., and D. LESTER, *Suicide: The Gamble with Death*. Englewood Cliffs, N.J.: Prentice-Hall. Inc., 1971.

MENNINGER, K., *Man Against Himself*. New York: Harcourt, Brace & World, 1966.

SHNEIDMAN, E. S., ed., *Suicidology: Contemporary Developments*. New York: Grune & Stratton, 1970.

11

Grief, Loss, and Bereavement

A CORRESPONDENCE*

Dear Dr. S——,

I met you recently in Heidelberg at the Conference. My name is Celine and I was there with Kurt. I am writing partly to inform you and partly out of my own need to survive. Kurt died last Tuesday. The results of the autopsy are not yet finished, but there is little (no!) doubt in my mind that it was suicide. My burden is in being the only one who was close enough to him to be able to make any sense of it all. I spent the last 3 days with him constantly, 24 hours a day; the last 2½ months with him, living together. I am suffering from the pain of the personal loss of a loved one (and my most significant "other"), and I feel it would help me through the process of mourning if I could understand it all better. Of course it's too late to save him, although I was *not* trying to be his therapist—how could I have been: I loved him. But I feel an understanding would leave me more peaceful, relieve me of the burden of carrying all this information and not being able to use it. He has found his peace. He

*Correspondence published with permission.

wanted to die, much of the time. Now I am seeking my peace—in living on. Will you help me?

In retrospect, I am astounded at my innocence, as I am now astounded at my own health and determination to go on. Earlier, 2 months ago, Kurt admitted having plans for suicide (an overdose of something—alone!). Since then, he seemed to come out of his long-lasting depression and begin to actively reach for life. But he still had regular dips into depression again. The last week, he was simply withdrawn and did what he could (successfully) to hide it from me. Once he said, "I've known much joy with you, but it isn't happiness . . . I want to die." Later, he wrote that he had "lost control" when he admitted wanting to die. To him, self-control did not mean self-discipline as I think it does to most healthy people, but it meant isolating, hiding, suppressing his inner core, his essential self. He was such a private person, so controlled, that he didn't know *himself* where or what that inner core was. *That* was what frightened him, I think. He believed that I could see it in him—and that I could *sense* it. He hoped to learn about it, I think, through me. He strived, tried, struggled to feel it, to feel some significance to life. He opened himself to me and saw nothing there.

On his birthday, weeks ago, he wrote: "At 35, not much time. This should be a really good time. The only presents I want are self-forgiveness and the courage to live. . . . This has been a hellish day. God save me. Half of my life has been lived. What a disaster. Could get worse? Yes, by getting shorter and older."

Last Monday, he fell asleep quicker than usual, slept deeply, snored loudly, all night, and still when I left for work at 7 a.m. Tuesday. Later I found an empty "Dalmadorm" bottle which I'm convinced was full on Saturday. His secretary got help at noon. His stomach was empty. His heart was revived, but he died in hospital at 1 p.m. . . . I remember the water running a very long time that last night, and him coming out of the bathroom and making an excuse (?) that he was very thirsty. But he didn't drink his Scotch at bedtime like he always did.

I wonder if it isn't easier for me to separate, just because his withdrawn self which I couldn't completely reach, prevented the cementing (or reciprocation) of my own emotional investment. . . . My problem—the most painful part—is not understanding. And yet, even understanding *now* better than *then* also hurts, because I'm afraid I failed to save him. I'm sure I didn't cause his death, but I'm not clear whether he somehow hoped I would consciously read the subtle signs of his intent. Was I just too dumb, or insensitive? Okay, and if I missed the chance of saving him, can I forgive myself? And, how?

. . . Perhaps I want to classify what happened. Removal. Distance. Some closure to this tragic puzzle. He shared his suicide with me— touching me, dying in bed beside me all night, knowing I would soon know. It was the best he could give me, for he couldn't stand to share his life with me. He couldn't even stand to live it himself. Yet he gave me a deadly burden—a torture. Could it be that the fixed aim narrows the range of vision, and that he was too far gone to consider anyone else? Or could it have been the nearest thing to a loving act he could make?

Please, Dr. S——, can you help?

Celine

●

Dear Celine,

. . . I greatly respect the pain of your loss, the flood of questions that surround you, and the unavoidable regrets. I share your impulse to understand; and the wish that one could have been of more help. It is very easy to move from one's sorrow that it could have happened at all; to the wish that it could have been prevented; to the assumption that there must have been something that one could have done, to prevent it; to self-recrimination for not having prevented it— though, finally, there may not have been anything more that you could have done.

. . . Of course you were not his therapist (he allowed none), you were far more valuable as his lover. There was clearly more that you could give him, and more that he could receive, in that relationship, than he evidently would ever have allowed from a formally therapeutic relationship. Perhaps he could allow you near, at a time when no-one else was allowed near, because of your innocence; because you could give him nourishment without overwhelming, and without threatening to remove from him his right to do what he ultimately did. . . . Often, when a person becomes so depressed, he ceases to allow the outside world any fair chance of helping. He would hide the depth of his despair. Deception may become an act of love in its intentions even if not in its effects, as a reluctance to share the void with people one values, lest they be tainted by it, or drawn into it, and lost. You may have acted as a mirror, in whose reflection, in your obvious love for him, he could catch glimpses of a self you could see and believe in, which he could experience briefly through you. . . .

I understand the guilt. Of course you didn't cause his death (in a way, you may, recently, have caused his life) but it feels like it. . . . You were given a puzzle you were not really meant to solve, by a man playing Russian Roulette with a bullet in every chamber save one. You may have been the empty chamber. But had that empty chamber come round for the first shot, there would still have been other shots, and other bullets. . . .

. . . There is also the anger. How could he die on me, thrust this so much unwanted result on me? Oh yes, there can be anger. And that is as normal as the grief. How selfish, how inconsiderate the dead can be! How bitterly we can resent their having so finally excluded us!

. . . There is also, in your most moving letter, a strong sense of a reconciliation. He chose to share his death with you. Might it have been, even though a bitterly unwelcome gift, the most loving act he could offer at that time? He may very well have felt that the gift of his life was of no benefit to you at all; he may have feared that you might come to share his emptiness, to become contaminated by his grief. . . . Perhaps he wanted to set you free: can you accept the freedom?

Please feel free to write again, as and when you need to; and feel free not to write, when and if you do not wish to. I am content to do whatever will be helpful. . . .

M. A. S——

•

Dear Dr. S——,

It doesn't feel adequate to just say, "Thank you for your letter." Now, when I feel unraveled, or just before bed, I re-read your letter—instead of agonizing over Kurt's diary. You seem to have given me "permission" to accept the subjective reality which comforts me most. Yet, at the same time, let me see this as a slightly white-washed version of reality. It's as though I can be enchanted by the man, and see through my enchantment at the same time, without spoiling it. . . . .

. . . I can see the risk of Kurt's insistence on doing it all by himself. I have reached the more humble realization that although I (and only I) could do it, I nevertheless could not do it alone (I alone am not God, but perhaps all of us together are?).

. . . Now I keep getting a barrier effect. "This is far enough." Now I want to stop all this. I want to go on. In a rational way, I'm glad to be out of it. What a trap for me it would have been if he'd continued to live and hadn't got better! I've only just now learned that I'm *not* pregnant. (First reaction—relief; second—deep grief, as though I were letting go his seed, so now he's all gone.)

Yes, Dr. S——, I think I can accept the freedom his death has given me; I am making a fresh start. . . . In time, I believe there will be another man I'll allow near. I don't know if I'll feel enchanted enough to love, but I certainly hope so. It's what I want. Without love, life seems so grey. I'm trying to be patient while my insides heal. I still ache physically, as if most of my chest and stomach had been torn out. But I don't feel empty, like Kurt did. I have a strong sense of myself, my integrity. Something has to be there to be aching.

. . . I would feel more secure if I could write to you again, if you wouldn't mind . . . I carry all the memories with me when I pack up, as I'm moving apartments. The grieving is not over. Mostly, I am despondent, while trying mightily to hang on 'till normal interest in things returns. . . . Please stick by me, just a little longer. It feels like a life-line.

Celine

●

Dear Celine,

. . . I am pleased that you have found a more acceptable version of subjective reality (all reality is subjective: we only think people are being objective when their prejudices coincide with our own). Now you have accepted your freedom; soon you will celebrate it. Your insight into the truth of therapy is greater than was his: you are the essential and necessary—but not sufficient—agent in your own growth. It cannot occur without you, but that is no reason to believe that it has to be done by you alone. Therapy can be a most seemly variety of human communion. . . . Your new start will be a creative act. If you have learned to let people near, you can certainly now allow others near; others who may be able to give love with less pain. I don't think you'll avoid love for long. The healing of that raw internal ache will come. Your grief's work will be over before long. One comes to realize that it is an honor to the dead, not disrespect, to move through grief to acceptance and further growth. The despondency will dissolve; the pleasure in the little things in life will return, first to be enjoyed alone, then to be shared with others. . . .

M. S——

●

Dear Dr. S——

. . . My task seems to have been almost impossible, in that I had to bring to bear both grief and anger (practically extreme opposites, to me) on one subject. As long as I faced only the grief and not the anger, the anger seemed to turn on myself and convert to depression. But there didn't seem to be room for both at once. In any case, something major has changed in me—some value—and my suffering seems over. I am very tired, as if from jet lag.

First came the poignantly sharp pain of being told the news that first day, surely as traumatic as any physical assault. (I've since been unable to seriously worry or fear the unknown. It's as if everything bad has happened to me that could, and now I feel very little. Nothing will be worse.) Then the denial. Then the heavy realization, followed by despair. Then the feeling of nothingness—the hardest of all to handle, when I felt totally blank. My dreams of terror—morbidity, death, maiming—were gradually replaced by a period of seeming refusal to dream. Access to self cut off. What a relief it was to have my first dream of anger—pounding Kurt on the head with my fists, hammering him into the ground. Anything felt better than nothing. I wallowed in it, gave full vent to my resentment at having to go through any of this, and the cost. I didn't deserve it!

But then, reflecting on what I deserved and what I might want now, and on what would be a fresh start, I realized that to some extent, I put myself in that position. How easy it would be for the "fresh start" to be really a repeat of the same pattern. I was struck by the similarity between grief and a drug addict's withdrawal. I'd been infatuated by (addicted to) Kurt, and stopped dead in my tracks was like going "cold turkey."

. . . Hope returning, what I want is to successfully sustain and deepen a love. I remembered Jan, who I'd known before Kurt. I realized what I was longing for was all the good qualities I never really appreciated in Jan . . . to shorten the story, I found he hadn't given up on me. When we met again, seeing where we stood, we were both frightened to death of making a crucial error. I couldn't decide at first. My emotions were still too slippery. As soon as I stopped trying to force myself to be decisive, something inside went "click," and I simply knew. Like a soft and warm "breath" expanding from my center. A kind of readiness (not a resignation as it would have been earlier) to go on with a healthy relationship. This is more than just starting anew. I'm changing my old self-destructive patterns.

For now, it seems the grief work is taking a break—or, perhaps it's over. It all seems long ago, and my attention is on present and future concerns. The image of Kurt I carry in my head seems to have changed (no longer idealized). I am not even the same person as then. But isn't it amazing how life surges on; how new growth germinates from the ashes? For about a week it's been slowly "dawning" on me that the depression has lifted. I even feel a little excited about it—it feels so good to be happy and productive again.

Helpful, too, has been the opportunity to help other people in similar situations . . . and recently bereaved. I didn't try to reason them out of their feelings; my own recent experience has taught me to respect those feelings . . . as a result I feel stronger myself for having had something to give again. The power of grief is so overwhelmingly great, worse than any physical pain. I wish this could be made more widely known. Grief is simply not publicly acceptable after about two or three weeks. I think it might be a good idea to renew the wearing of black or an armband, and encourage the "victim" to wear it as long as the hurt is incapacitating.

I think I'll never stop missing Kurt and regretting that my fantasy about "how it could have been" never came true. But it may fade to the level of regretting that one found out as a child that there was no

Santa Claus. Even now, though, while the missing is still recent, it is not nearly so painful as the rejection and loss of self-esteem. That part, the personal damage, is healing now to the point that I'm feeling almost like a warm fluid is spreading in me, the return of sanity. . . .

With gratitude,
Celine

Eighteen months after her bereavement, Celine wrote again:

Yes, I am still well. In fact, even better. Daily, I live tangible evidence of my triumph. I have made use of the crisis and emerged as a more mature, more playful, very content person. (That must sound awfully self-satisfied.) Now I'm very involved in the process of my own aging, including, of course, death as a pinnacle. I can't conceive yet just how that will actually be so, but then I also had no prior notion of how I could come out of the bereavement, either. It's a great surprise to me to find that aging is a positive experience. I seem to get more and more glad to be living. Yet, if my time weren't finite, it probably wouldn't work. I just believe that because I am going to die, the quality of my life experience is increased. And conversely, to the extent that I live fully and richly, the chances of experiencing death positively are enhanced. . . . My bereavement was by far the most influential event in my life. It caused more change, positively, than any other single thing.

BEREAVEMENT

Bereavement is a universal experience, but only recently have we begun to study and to understand it better. There are many estimates of the extent of the problems. The average age of widows at the time of their husband's death is 56. About one out of every five children in the United States will lose one parent to death before the child is 16. Eighteen percent of Canadian women over the age of 14 are widowed, and one-fifth of all new widows created each year are under the age of 45. Three-quarters of the women who become widows at 45 can expect to live for at least 25 more years.

The ratio of widows to widowers is about 4:1, owing to the lower mortality among younger women and the tendency for women to be younger than their husbands. Remarriage rates among the widowed are considerably lower for women than for men (see Bequaert, 1976). Thus the emphasis in the literature is usually on the widow and her needs.

The loss of any object or person with whom one has a significant relationship leads to grief, a complex emotional response including sadness, anger, and guilt. It is an unavoidable accompaniment of attachment to anyone or anything. Bereavement is part of the price of love.

THE EXPERIENCE OF GRIEF

The experience of grief can best be conveyed by considering the descriptions of the bereaved themselves. C. S. Lewis (1961) described grief as a long valley, where any bend may reveal a wholly new landscape, or the same scene you thought you'd long since left behind. Despite the partial recurrences, the sequence doesn't quite repeat.

> *Joan:* When I woke up, I knew something was wrong. He felt so cold, and there was a funny noise when he breathed. I shook him, but he wouldn't say anything. I couldn't wake him at all. Then the noise stopped—and he stopped breathing. I didn't know what to do. I sat and stared. I don't know how long I sat there. Then I went next door and told Mrs. King that something had happened to Fred. I think she called the ambulance and the doctor.

> People were so kind, at least they tried to be. I felt angry at them, especially the doctor. I felt like he should have done something to prevent it. I don't know what, but there should have been something. And I felt awful about the way I reacted. I kept asking "Why Fred? Why did it have to happen to him?" It seemed so unfair. It just didn't seem possible that something so bad had happened to us. They told me I had to hold myself together, for the sake of the children. I knew how much I loved them, but it didn't seem enough, somehow. Why should I carry on?

I still can't realize fully that it's happened. I keep catching myself doing things as if he was still here. I'm talking to someone and I find myself thinking, "I must tell Fred about that." I keep waiting for him to arrive home from work, and start to get up each time I think I hear the car. Other times, I really do manage to forget about him for a while—and then I feel guilty when I realize I wasn't thinking of him. It's as if he's at least alive in some way while I'm thinking about him; and as if he'll finally be dead when I've forgotten.

I look around me when I'm on the bus or out shopping, and I sort of resent the other people who aren't suffering like I am. I burst into tears in odd places, like in the supermarket.

•

Doris: For some time I felt in a dream, as though everything was going on around me, but I wasn't really there, and it had nothing to do with me.

•

Betty: I was very bewildered and shocked, and I felt very childlike. I wanted to be cherished and made a fuss of and praised for being good. And I felt lost and wanted people to direct me and tell me what to do and show me how to do it.

After the first phase of numbness and spiritual concussion comes the second phase with the typical "pangs" of grief and intense feelings of yearning and pining for the person we've lost, with anxiety, fear, and bewilderment. We recognize intellectually that it's no use walking the streets calling and searching for them, but there's a gut-level urge to do so. One mourns the irretrievable loss of the familiar.

Peter: The grief is paralyzing, I'm so weary and lazy and yet so busy. Disbelief—how could it have happened? Greed, as I want to get every detail, as if something important must have been overlooked and discovering it will set everything right again. Find the missing piece and maybe we can reverse this awful thing. There must have been something I could have done, should have done, didn't do: why didn't I prevent it? Why did she do this to me? You left me, damn you! Do I have to go around as your bloody widower from now on? No, I don't mean that. But how could you leave me at a time like this? Not fair; what time would ever be suitable for such a loss? Senseless, totally senseless, pointless.

There must have been some sort of mistake: I'm just not the sort of man these things happen to. I've been cheated! I've been robbed! I'm so alone. She did this without me. She did something I couldn't join, and left me behind. After all that—nothing. My boundaries have been breached, and something seems to be flowing out, like a broken egg. Humpty-Dumpty, I never really appreciated you before!

One weeps a lot. One weeps the unsaid, the undone, the unlived things. If one could say more of it, do more of it, while we live, maybe that would reduce the bitterness. Maybe we could run our lives so there is less unfinished business, rather than building up an accruing and accumulating debt.

There's a time for mourning, weeping, for singing old songs, for retreat and isolation, prayer and contemplation; and then for crawling out to face others again, creeping back into place. For a time, I give in to the feelings, not censoring them all, not running a blue pencil through my unscripted thoughts and emotions.

I am, so literally, *at a loss*—that's where I am. What to do? What point in doing anything when the one thing I want to do above all others can't be done? The finely tuned structure of my world included her, like the keystone of an arch. Now the structure is tottering and needs rebuilding. All I can see now are the gaps, the holes, the damage. Yes, I suppose all the other stones are still there, in the rubble. I could rebuild. But as yet I have no plan, no energy.

•

Mary: I still keep his pajamas under his pillow. I went over to his side of the bed to sleep. . . .

The responses of other people can be awkward. C. S. Lewis described how he could see other people, as they approached him, debating whether or not to greet him, whether or not to mention it; and how he hated it, whatever they decided. "Perhaps the bereaved should be isolated in special settlements, like lepers," he suggested.

Ann: People did come around at the beginning, and then gradually they dropped off, and I was very hurt. People who'd been close friends for years began to avoid me. As a couple we had so many friends, and now there were hardly any.

•

Mary: Men I used to hug when greeting them now shy away, for their wives resent it now. We've become adversaries, rivals. I remind them both that one of them will be in my position one day. And the wife seems sure I want her husband now.

However impossible it may seem at first, one does gradually accomplish the grief work, as one works through the pain of the loss. Within some six to twelve weeks of such work, there is usually some noticeable lifting of mood, and an improvement in the physical complaints. More satisfactory and thorough resolution is usually achieved within six to twelve months, though there is wide individual variation in responses.

EFFECTS OF BEREAVEMENT

The first year or so of bereavement is often a time of greater risk of health problems. As many as 50 percent of bereaved people perceive their general health as impaired; they use health services more often. There is, for instance, a 240 percent increase in consultations for depression, insomnia, and similar symptoms, including headaches, dizziness, fainting, blurred vision, skin rashes, excessive sweating, indigestion, difficulty in swallowing, vomiting, heavy menstrual periods or loss of periods, palpitations, chest pains, shortness of breath, frequent infections, and general aches, nervousness, fears of nervous breakdown, feelings of panic, "peculiar thoughts," nightmares, trembling, loss of appetite or excessive appetite, loss of weight, reduced working capacity or fatigue. There is an unusually high proportion of widows and widowers, especially recently bereaved, among people coming into psychiatric care for the first time (Parkes, 1972).

Even mortality may be increased. One study (Rees & Luttans, 1967) reported that 4.8 percent of a bereaved group died in the first year after their loss, as compared with .68 percent of a control group of similar people who had not been bereaved. A group of American researchers (Young et al., 1963) found an increase in the death rate of widowers over the age of 54 of over 40 percent in the first six months. A high proportion of the increased death rate after bereavement seems to be due to heart disease, especially coronary thrombosis (so the "broken heart" is a very real phenomenon) and there is early evidence that vulnerability to other diseases may be increased.

MOURNING AND RITUAL

Death disrupts the established social system, and the damage is repaired in various ways. In some societies, the kinship system provides for a rapid replacement of the lost person by the closest available substitute—often by remarriage to the husband's brother or the wife's sister. Modern Western society is less accepting of very prompt substitution, placing more reliance on inheritance laws and life insurance instead. In Hindu society, it was regarded as a correct and appropriate act for the widow to burn herself to death on her husband's funeral pyre. This *sati* or *suttee* was supposed to be voluntary, though there was great pressure to comply. Nowadays, the widow in our society often suffers instead a forced redundancy and neglect, a sort of social *suttee*.

The modern small family unit, isolated from the extended family, is more at risk. There are fewer people and resources within the family itself, and less help available from the extended family. As late as the early years of this century, parents frequently died before they had finished raising their children. The extended family provided quite effective substitutes without disturbing the basic lines of kin affiliation or the children's property rights.

There's a need to account for and explain the loss, and to give it some special meaning. Lack of religious beliefs that can make "sense" of the loss leaves few alternatives for many people. Remembering and reminiscing is a common and useful process, and shouldn't be stopped by friends who think it is "being morbid"; it is also a process of exploring the meaning of the life.

Various acts of mourning have clear purposes. They openly acknowledge the reality of death and explain it once more in whatever way the current system of belief conceptualizes death. They allow for the open expression of grief, but in controlled and socially acceptable circumstances and forms; and they allow gestures of consolation and support from friends and relatives. For one final occasion, the dead person takes a central position in a social event, along with his bereaved relations. The rituals may honor the dead and define the shape they will take in our memories, or make preparations for the soul's journey or the life in another world.

Rituals serve to provide a temporary structure at a time when the removal of an important part of your personal and social structure has left you adrift. They give you *something* to do when there's nothing to be done and you feel you must do something—without your having to search to be creative in devising something to do. Rituals can give you a set of familiar practices to turn to when the shape of life has become unfamiliar. In my experience, families with no body to mourn over (when someone has been lost at sea, for example, or missing and believed killed in war) find it far harder to accept and adjust to the loss. There is no definitive event that marks such a death; it remains uncertain in time and place; there is no way of sharing it formally with family or friends, no real opportunity for leave-taking. In such cases a memorial service should be held, to serve at least some of these purposes.

Funerals and mourning customs help to strengthen and reaffirm the solidarity of the family and the social group, and to reconstitute them. They are therapeutic rites for the living, as well as commemorative and propitiatory rites for the dead.

Yet there has been a general decline of the rituals and customs surrounding death in recent years. Dress customs, like wearing black, are now relatively rare; the custom of pulling the blinds or covering the mirrors in the house is rarer still. When a funeral procession passes, few people stop; and those men who wear hats don't take them off. November 11—Armistice Day in World War

I—used to be a major expression of prolonged shared national mourning in Britain and many other countries; today it is barely noticeable.

There is relatively little guidance available at present concerning how society expects bereaved people to behave. Now we seem to hope that they will simply cease to trouble us as soon as possible. Even comparatively recently, there were clearly stated expectations. In the 1920s and '30s, such interpreters of the Establishment as Emily Post could describe the protocol in detail. It was understood that no woman should appear at the graveside. An elderly widow was expected to remain in mourning for the rest of her life, wearing deep mourning clothing with a crepe veil for a year, black clothes for the second year, and perhaps a lighter veil after that. A widower should not attend a dance for a year, a son not for six months, and a brother not for three months, according to Post's etiquette. Such formal rules were quite strictly adhered to, and deviation from the norm was held improper and regarded as showing a lack of the proper emotions.

Today, even though we don't have such rigid social rules surrounding the "proper" expression of grief, there are those who seek to impose their ideas of grief behavior on the bereaved. For instance, there is the grisly fiction of "Grief Therapy." It claims therapeutic benefits for open caskets and corpse viewing and seeks to charge for the exhibition of professional sympathy. If even sympathy can't be given away for nothing these days, then perhaps we have even more to mourn for. Where grief merits intervention, this should be under the direction of trained and experienced professionals. No seller of death-related merchandise is suitably trained or sufficiently unbiased to provide such therapy.

You may, naturally, find help from your religion. Men and women of faith can be of great benefit to the sorrowing, perhaps by sharing their faith and exploring together how it is possible to cope. Many people of previously unquestioning faith find it severely strained by death. "How can a God of Love allow such suffering?" is a frequent question, and one to which we must find our own answers. Some people have had very unhelpful encounters with their minister or priest, and many do not feel greatly helped by what they see as empty recitations of pious quotations at such a time. One family I knew were rebuked by their priest for their sorrow and mourning, for he insisted that this revealed their imperfect faith in the Life Hereafter. "Your husband is with God and the saints," he insisted. "You should not weep, but rejoice." I am sure God forgave him for his lack of compassion and understanding and even of simple tact, but the family found it harder to forgive. Faith can be a major comfort; the trappings of faith can be used pettily and meanly by people of limited comprehension.

It is becoming more common for clergymen of all denominations to receive training in dealing with these personal and spiritual crises, and thus it is becoming more likely that people can find appropriate help from them.

PATHOLOGICAL GRIEF

Occasionally we see what is called a pathological grief reaction, where bereavement begins to become an illness in its own right. It occurs when death is still emotionally denied long after the fact—even if it has been intellectually acknowledged. The mourner is obsessed with a chronic, desperate hope that the dead person will return, though perhaps in part dreading this possibility. The mourner may still talk of the dead person in the present tense, and may have repeated dreams about him, often involving thwarted attempts to save or rescue him, in a recurrent struggle. Such mourners may lose the thread of their own life, becoming increasingly preoccupied with the one they have lost. Visiting the grave may be difficult or impossible because of the finality it represents; or the grave may be frequently visited and looked after with elaborate care, as if to continue the relationship with at least the remains of the person.

There are three main ways in which the reaction to loss may go wrong and cause further problems. There may be delayed grief, in which the bereaved person seems to show little obvious sorrow at first. This person sets about the reorganization of her life with great energy and calmness, though often with poor judgment and an unnecessary sense of haste. Usually, at some later date she responds with devastating grief to some far less important loss or more distant bereavement. In the second kind of pathological grief, there may be a more permanent inhibition of the grief, which may then come to be expressed in physical and neurotic disorders. In chronic grief, there may be an acute stage of despair indefinitely prolonged, with the person in a long-lasting depressed state, anxious and miserable and obsessed by sad memories. A part of this type of pathological grief may be the process that has been called "mummification." This type of grief was demonstrated by Queen Victoria, who carefully kept everything in the palaces as Prince Albert had left it, and even maintained a daily ritual in which his clothes and shaving water were laid out. In "mummification," the possessions and surroundings of the dead person are socially embalmed and kept unchanged for years.

The nature and quality of the death may be related to a more turbulent outcome or less readily resolved grief. Such deaths include, for example: (a) death by suicide or death otherwise perceptibly "self-inflicted" (some types of accident and deaths due to self-neglect, such as failure to seek or follow medical advice); (b) death seen as especially untimely because of the deceased's youth, promise, recent marriage, or having nearly or just achieved important goals; (c) a death in which the bereaved had to be distressingly involved in the terminal care (dealing with such problems as intractable incontinence, personality deterioration, or delirium); (d) death in which the bereaved believes he or she has objective reasons for guilt, whether justified or not (having perhaps failed to take fairly obvious measures to protect the health of the deceased—the mother whose child died when she left it alone, or the husband who underestimated or mocked his wife's illness, or as in the case of the girl whose fiancé died trying to save her from drowning); (e) other factors, such as the possibility that the death resulted from someone else's negligence, or was the result of murder; (f) death that is unconfirmed and where there is no body to bury; (g) death that is especially sudden or unexpected; or (h) death that is unduly prolonged and drawn-out, occurring long after it was expected (involving guilt that one had wished the person would "just die and get it over with").

Another factor that may be related to pathological grief is the nature and depth of the relationship the mourner had with the deceased. The more mature the relationship, the more likely that the reaction will be a deep sadness, without guilt, and moving to an acceptance fairly quickly. When the relationship has been less mature, more dependent, more ambivalent and stormy, the reaction is likely to be complicated by guilt, anger, and continuing ambivalence. Those who have not yet completed their emotional business with the one they mourn may strive to keep that person "alive" until it is finished, refusing to accept the fact of death.

Other factors may be relevant in predicting pathological grief reactions. Sudden deaths appear to produce greater stress among young widows. In a lingering illness, they might have a chance to prepare themselves, but the unexpected loss of the spouse seriously limits their capacity to cope; many do not regain full functioning and equilibrium for an especially long time. They may be less likely to remarry than widows who had more time to prepare for their spouse's death, and may be so involved in their own grief that they are unable to deal with their children's needs, leading to later disturbances in the children. In much older widows, it appears that a long fatal illness of the spouse leads to poorer adjustment, especially medically.

Anniversary reactions are often seen, in which the loss is re-experienced on an important date associated with the deceased—the anniversary of the death or wedding, or the birthday of the deceased. Similarly, problems often arise when a person reaches the same age as that at which his parents died.

REACTIONS TO STILLBIRTH AND THE DEATH OF CHILDREN

Stillbirth can be a peculiarly stressful experience of loss. Not only is it often unexpected, but it arrives at a time when a particularly significant and happy occasion has been awaited. When months of anticipation, hope, and preparation are interrupted by a miscarriage, stillbirth, or death of a newborn, there is the loss, not of someone you knew, whose personality you had experienced, but of the beautiful, talented child you had anticipated, an idealized child you had expected and planned for. The loss of a potential person, of someone who was supposed to be but now will never be, is difficult to accept. There can be a strong sense of failure, of inadequacy at having failed to produce a normal, healthy child; of guilt, perhaps, at having failed to ensure its survival; of anger at whatever or whomever else is viewed as being responsible for the loss; and of waste at the uselessness of all the preparations made during the pregnancy, both physical and emotional—the wasted months. You worry that some sin of omission or commission during the pregnancy might have caused the death. The medical and nursing attendants are usually appalled, and the baby is usually hurriedly hidden away. There is a conspiracy of silence, and no one wants to mention what has happened.

The support of others in such deaths is most important. The sense of a void can be limited by using what is tangible and can be remembered. In many cases, the parents should be allowed to see and touch their dead baby, so as to have someone real to remember. They should be able to name the child, to take part in the certification, and to have a funeral with a marked grave.

Marriages can be greatly stressed by the loss of a child, and divorce seems to be frequent after a child has died, for example, from leukemia. Where the marriage survives, there is a tendency to replace the child with a new birth before long. The next child may inherit all the fears and overconcern aroused by the dead sibling, with results that may be unfortunate. The restitution phenomenon can be shown on a larger scale, too. At Aberfan in Britain in 1966, 116 children died in a disaster. In the second year after the tragedy, the birth rate in the village showed a sharp increase which lasted for three years, then returned to normal. Altogether, 152 children were born in excess of the expected birth rate, though not generally to the bereaved mothers (only 12 of the 100 bereaved mothers had more children). The community, without apparent planning, expressed its grief by acting to restore itself.

HELPING THE BEREAVED

Allow, help, and encourage the expression of the emotions the bereaved feel, which may include sadness, depression, guilt, hopelessness and helplessness, relief, anger, and protest. Expressing and talking through these feelings help to lessen the emotional pressure. Allow the person's mind to defend itself—denial and stunned disbelief are natural responses and can be protective in the early days—but also provide the opportunity for a gentle confrontation with reality. Support and help the person deal with his realistic problems in planning and decision making by giving him the opportunity to discuss his alternatives. Try not to end up making decisions for him, though. Sustain his appreciation of reality, mildly challenging his tendency to seek magical ways of meeting his wishes. As he gradually relinquishes the lost relationship, let him explore the positive and negative aspects of it in his conversation.

Medication is not usually needed or helpful. Family and acquaintances often ask doctors to provide drugs to "knock her out," to "calm her," to help her "not to break down," or to "stop her from being upset." The normal expression of feelings at this time is not an illness and does not need to be treated. It is not useful to try to postpone the emotional turmoil, either, and inducing a possible dependency on drugs or alcohol at this stage will only add to later problems. People who are given large amounts of tranquilizers usually feel more disturbed: "I felt worse because I couldn't weep. It was a sort of chemical straightjacket. I felt as if I wasn't able to mourn properly."

It can be very helpful for you to visit the bereaved person after you have heard of the death, to offer your sympathy and your help. Some books of etiquette imply that the condolence call (as they tend to label it) is an uncomfortable formality. Yet it is surely a simple and straightforward act of humanity. It demonstrates one's concern, and reassures the mourner that she isn't as alone in her sorrow as she may feel. It helps to show her that there are others who care about and try to understand her grief and are prepared to share it with her. Despite her major loss, she can be reminded of the many genuine contacts she has with other members of the community. Certainly, it may not be easy to make the call—you feel awkward at intruding upon someone at such a time. It is so much easier to stay at home and try to persuade yourself that "of course she'd rather be alone just now. She knows she can always call on us if she needs anything." But much as one may need and appreciate help, it can be very difficult to bring oneself to ask for it. And the bereaved shouldn't have to beg. Remember, too, that visits may be valuable during the weeks and months after the funeral, when solitude may be all the more oppressive.

The bereaved often feel that no one can appreciate the depth of their feelings, and truly we cannot share their private suffering. But that is not what we seek or need to do. We can accompany them in their grief while experiencing our own. Quiet companionship can help more than elaborate diversions. There are obviously no clear-cut rules as to what one says at these times, and one will take one's cue from what the bereaved person or family appear to want. Often, for example, they will be rehearsing the loss, and may want to recall good memories of the person and the relationship that is ended. You may be able to join in such a sharing of recollections; often you will be most helpful by simply listening. Try not to bring up your own problems and losses. Sometimes one hears the visitors swapping gory experiences in some sort of macabre Lowlier-Than-Thou contest, like veterans showing off their scars. Remarks like "I've been through it all myself, dear, I know what it's like" and "Poor Mrs. Rederring had a much worse time of it, you know" aren't very helpful. If the deceased was very old and handicapped or had suffered severely during a long illness, death might seem to you to have been a merciful release. In time, his family may be able to share that point of view, too. But in the early stages of bereavement it's not necessarily of much assistance to bring out all the hoary clichés about how "It was all for the best, wasn't it?" or "It was God's merciful will." Maybe it was, but it doesn't always feel like that.

Try also to avoid offering trite and overconfident advice. "You're so young—why, you have a whole life ahead of you!" (So did he, once, she thinks.) "There'll be plenty of time for you to remarry; to have other children." "In time, you'll forget." (But I don't want to forget! he protests silently.)

However much you may want to help, this may be made more difficult by your own response to the death and the echoes which another's grief may arouse among your own past experiences. By all means, share your grief with the bereaved person, and share your tears, too, if appropriate. If, however, your own distress is really severe and you have difficulty keeping it under some sort of control, perhaps it's best not to visit until you are calmer. A widow may have enough worries without having to devote herself to consoling you.

Generally, you needn't stay long. Ten or fifteen minutes are likely to be sufficient at first. Be ready to stay longer if necessary, however, if the person genuinely seems reluctant to be alone and wants you to stay. Be ready to just be *with* the bereaved person. Be prepared to leave if and when he wants you to, without feeling or looking hurt. As at all other times when we decide to help others, we must take our cues from them, and respond to their needs and wishes, though using our own knowledge and skills to decide how best to meet those needs. It is no kindness to impose our own conditions and wishes on others, or to seek to persuade them that they really need what we feel like giving them. That is self-indulgence—and, when dealing with a vulnerable person, exploitation.

Don't say: "If there's anything I can do to help, just let me know." Be more definite; make some practical suggestions. You may be able to help by breaking the news to others. Perhaps you can take the telephone calls; deal with other visitors; provide food; notify relatives at a distance by telephone, telegram, or letter.

The bereaved may express a good deal of anger and resentment, both openly and in more oblique and indirect ways. This may be directed at God, the world in general, the doctors or hospital, or at you—for being well and for not being bereaved. Though the emotion is understandable, its expression may be quite irrational. Certainly one is unlikely to be able to argue it away logically, and suggesting that it is not entirely rational will just be offensive. Listen, share, and express understanding: "Yes, that must be frustrating. I'd be angry too."

The big question is often "Why?" "Why me? Why did it happen to us?" Don't try to explain; there's no explanation. Besides, the "Why?" is largely a rhetorical question, an eloquent expression of outrage, not really expecting a reasoned response. Why me? Why *not* me? One of my patients prepared a collage, across which ran an inscription: "WHY ME? 'CAUSE IT'S MY TURN."

Death is not teleologically explicable in any emotionally satisfying terms. The best response one can usually offer is a compassion that doesn't need elaborate words, and can be effectively communicated in silence.

COPING WITH YOUR OWN BEREAVEMENT

No matter how long the dying has been, no matter how clearly expected or however well rehearsed, the reality of death comes as a shock. This time it's final. It's irrevocable and unchangeable. It's happened. You may be glad the suffering has ended. But there is still the grisly, malignant chorus of the "if only's": "If only we had . . ." "If only I hadn't . . ." "If only we had had a few more weeks . . . or days . . . or even hours. We could have done and said so much more." But unless your relationship has become quite redundant, there will always, no matter how much time you had, be yet more things you could have said or done. So long as you have done as much as you could, you can expect no more of yourself. There is nothing to be gained by living in the past. Whereas the good things that have happened to you are immutably preserved in the past, the bad things, the problems, are still amenable to improvement.

You are not responsible for everything that has happened to you; you are responsible for what you feel about it, for the meaning and significance you attach to it. That exists in the present, and is now, or at least potentially, under your control. You can define many of the unfortunate things that have happened to you in life as unmitigated failures; you may define yourself as unchangeably crippled by them. If you choose to make these definitions, they will be true. You will be thus crippled. But this is not necessary. You can concentrate on what you can learn from the situation and what opportunities it may contain. An opportunity is often little more than a misfortune looked at from a different angle.

"I cannot go on living without him." Having spent, perhaps, many years living together, it is very hard to envisage how you could live without him, but you will find a way. So often, one attempts to face the whole future at once: "How can I face twenty years without him?" But you will not live that period all at once, only day by day. Don't try to face twenty years alone. Face today. When that has been achieved, face tomorrow. You will find more and more ways in which you can cope. The Chinese have a saying that the journey of a thousand miles starts with a single step. There is no way you can take the fifteenth, or the two hundred seventh step, before you have taken the first. Looking too far ahead or too far behind can give you vertigo and make you unsteady, however surefooted you may be.

"It's not fair; we had worked so hard to enjoy this retirement together." "It's not fair: I need her now to help me bring up the children." Even: "It's not fair: everyone's been worrying about him and his needs—nobody's bothered about me." Let's not bother about arguing that one out. Sure, it's not fair at all. There is no good reason why you deserved this sadness. But this didn't happen because you deserved it, or because the deceased deserved it. It happened. What you can influence is not whether or not death will occur at some time (for it always will), but what you will do with it when it does happen. In the words of the collective wisdom of several religions and beliefs: Let us have the courage to change what we can and the wisdom to accept what we cannot change.

Loss is always difficult to accept, and it takes a while for our bodily and emotional systems to adjust to it. People who have a limb amputated often continue to feel the limb that isn't there any more for quite a time. Similarly, when a person has been amputated from your life, there will be a finite period before you can function fully without him.

There may be times, especially in the first six months of a

bereavement, when you have some odd experiences that you may hesitate to tell anyone about for fear of being thought peculiar. You may experience hallucinations. You may hear the voice of the person who is dead, often merely calling your name. Especially in a part of the house you associate with him, you may see him for a time, quite clearly, before you realize that this cannot be so, and the image fades. A man of 82 told me about how this affected him after his wife's death. "I go into the kitchen," he said, "and there she is, sitting at the kitchen table, like she always was when I got home. I stand there and look at her, and then I remember that she's dead, and it sort of fades away. I was scared to tell my daughter, in case she thought I was mad. But it's a comfort to me, and I'm glad she comes to me." A boy told me how, as he fell asleep, he felt his mother stroke his hair, though she'd died several years before. It's important to realize that these are entirely normal experiences, and quite common, though you seldom hear about them because people are hesitant to talk about them.

In the early stages, there are many decisions to be made, concerning the funeral and other arrangements. You may not welcome these responsibilities, but on the whole they're probably helpful. It is useful to have something to do. Go ahead with these small decisions, but try to skip the bigger ones until you are more steady and more sure of what you really want.

If you have not been accustomed to handling the financial affairs in your family, it would be advisable to find someone within the family, or at your bank, who can serve you as a financial adviser. There will be many other people quite eager to take advantage of your naïveté with shaky financial propositions. Don't rush into any commitments without good, unbiased advice. A widow may have difficulties dealing with matters like insurance, or coping with the family car; a widower may find it hard to shop effectively for groceries—both should freely seek guidance from friends and family. Don't be too proud to admit that there are some things you don't know about. Besides, people usually enjoy finding out that they know more about something than you do; they enjoy being experts.

In describing how they come to terms with their grief, most

people seem to fall back on phrases like "working through it," and it is undeniably hard work, though rewarding. Friends often try to help, and one comes to realize that it is often more difficult to learn how to accept help gracefully than it is to give help, because one needs to come to terms with how much one may need other people. Some people, stunned by the sudden loss of someone on whom they were very dependent, seem to resolve to avoid dependency in the future and seek to become quite unrealistically self-sufficient. It is as if they were saying: "If that's what can happen if you depend on/love somebody, I'll never do it again!"

As you meet each new person who has not yet heard about the death, you may come to repeat the story of the events many times. This, too, may serve a useful function. After several mechanical repetitions of the facts of the death, you may begin to believe them yourself. Don't be ashamed of the fact that your grieving is usually, basically, for yourself and for your loss, rather than truly for the one who has died. This is perfectly natural. Our own outrage and deprivation looms large, and it is indeed we, the survivors, who are the true and continuing victims of a death.

Sexual feelings may cause some problems. While some people find sexual activity a great comfort, many find their feelings blunted for quite a time afterward. Sometimes, people may offer you opportunities for sexual involvement at the most unexpected times and in quite uninviting circumstances. Try not to be greatly offended. Often it is well-meant even if clumsy; at other times someone may indeed be trying to exploit your situation. But getting deeply disturbed about it is likely to leave you feeling far worse than the unwelcome offer. No one will make you an offer you can't refuse. Usually, a simple, direct, and open "No, thanks" will suffice. Women are particularly likely to be the recipients of such clumsy and bumbling overtures.

Later, your sexual drive will return, often with a poignancy that startles you. The decision as to how to order your life so as to meet these straightforward human needs, either by direct sexual activity, or by sublimation in other activities, will need to be made, and no one can make the decision for you.

The widow with young children will face special problems.

She will need, at least for a time, to try to function as both mother and father. How will she support the family? Do insurance policies and investments take care of her financially, or will she need to go to work, perhaps for the first time in her life, or at least for the first time in years? Can other family members function as babysitters? Or are there day-care facilities in the neighborhood or at work?

Maintaining discipline with the children often becomes difficult, for several reasons. Some of the children's anxieties related to the death and their changing circumstances may show up in school problems or errant behavior. In the past, it may have been advantageous for one parent to function as the hard-nosed disciplinarian, the other as the softer, sympathetic partner. It is more difficult, as the single parent, to function as the legislator, prosecutor, judge, jury, defending counsel, and court of appeal!

There is a natural tendency for you (or one of the many others who will feel themselves qualified to comment) to turn to the (oldest) son, of whatever age, and say, "Well, you're the man of the house now!" This can be an awfully heavy responsibility to place on the child. Indeed, he may feel that he has to carry the main burden of coping with affairs to protect you, and may be left with little opportunity to deal with his own needs.

Grown children may be concerned about taking care of you, both physically and financially, and may worry about how much of an imposition this might be. Differing reactions are seen. In some families, the children withdraw and the surviving parent seems to undertake not to reveal any needs lest they all feel guilty. In other families, the children may insist on taking over the parent's perfectly viable independence, absorb him or her into one of their own families, and treat the parent as if he or she were incapable of functioning alone.

The young widow or widower may have difficulties with parents and in-laws. Potentially, they can be invaluable sources of support. Perhaps the in-laws, however illogically, blame you in some way for the death—as if, somehow, it wouldn't have happened if your spouse had stayed with his own family. They may be especially jealous of the memory of their child, and may feel that you should dedicate the rest of your life purely to that memory and resent any other relationships you may later form. While they can provide you with great help in raising your children, any differences of opinion about childrearing may be exaggerated.

One weakness of some of the popular books on widowhood is that, pretty uniformly, they have been written by rather untypical women—highly independent and articulate professional women, with many more resources to draw on than the average woman.

After the funeral comes what is the hardest time for many. All those people who were around to help and comfort have gone back to leading their own lives. They've had their time of grieving and can leave it behind more readily than you can. Now is the quiet time, when the real work of grieving needs to be done. Gradually you must achieve a degree of emotional separation, breaking the ties that bind you to the person you have lost. You must regain the capacity for forming other ties and interests so that you can get involved with life again. It is often very difficult, and you tend to believe that it will be impossible, but it will happen. At first the memories flood back into your mind, welcome yet painful.

Gradually you may notice that for short periods the sense of hurt is not so great. As you come to accept emotionally what has happened, these episodes of peace increase in quality and in frequency, until they finally coalesce. It is not a question of forgetting, but of regaining the capacity to remember peacefully. Move at your own natural pace, and take up your regular activities as and when you feel ready to do so. Yet don't make loneliness and solitude a way of life, for this can get to be an unwholesome habit. Make expeditions into the outside world, and gradually lengthen the amount of time you spend with others, when you have to pay some attention to something outside yourself and your own feelings. You may dread returning to work, but it could make things easier for you. You may find it best to return part-time at first. Work will help you to escape from your intense introspection and add variety to your days. It will also tire you—and thus help you sleep better.

At some stage, preferably not too long after the death, you will need to attend to the disposal of the belongings of the person who has died. Some special items you will, of course, want to keep, and some you will give to friends and members of the family. Much of the rest can be given to organizations which can distribute them to others who can use them, and some will be discarded. It will not become easier to do this if you put it off. On the other hand, major decisions like selling the house, moving to another town, and so on should be put off until you have recovered from your grief. There may be an impulse to travel, in the hope that a change of surroundings will make you feel better. This doesn't always work. Your sorrow is the first thing you pack, and you will carry it everywhere with you. Our capacity to cope with change is limited. Struggling to cope with the major changes in your life is not made easier when you are farther away from your home resources.

To overcome your loneliness, you must move from the extremes of self-concern to concern for others. You will receive by giving. Apart from the time you will realistically require to work on your own problems, there will be a temptation to spend much more time in circuitous, repetitious, and quite unproductive ruminations. Better to become concerned with other people's problems. You can find healing and helpful activity in many ways—for example, working with hospitals, schools, charities or your church as a volunteer.

It is often helpful to keep your mind and hands busy. Hobbies, handiwork, books, music—they may seem empty at first, or on the other hand may seem to threaten to produce too strong an emotional reaction. The interest and enjoyment in such activities will return; the excess of emotional associations will subside, and in the meantime may give you an opportunity to express and discharge your sorrow. Physical exercise can also help, and will be a healthier way of helping you sleep better than will drugs.

Even after you think you've gotten over the loss, many little things may bring back a sliver of memory and make you recall your vulnerability. Coming home from work to the empty apartment; going to work and having no one to say goodbye to. Realizing you'll have to work late tonight, grabbing the phone—and suddenly remembering you've got no one to ring, no one who'll notice that you're late. The time of evening he used to arrive back from work, and nobody comes. Seeing other happy couples (and the fierceness of your jealousy, even if short-lasting, may surprise you). The first time you revisit places, restaurants, theaters, friends you'd always visited with her.

Just catching sight in a crowd of someone who looks like her, or dressed as she used to, or glimpsing a car like the one he used to drive. Having to cope for the first time alone with a blocked drain; sewing on your first button or darning your first sock. Deciding what to do with her shoes, or with his favorite pipe. Catching yourself recalling that you've just finished the last jar of the marmalade she made for you. His fishing magazine arriving because you forgot to cancel his subscription. Tiny, trivial things—yet each one can suddenly pitch you back into the despondency and grief, so you feel you're right back at square 1, and fear you'll never get over it. But you will. It often feels as if you won't, as if all those friends who say things like "Time is the great healer" are just making empty promises and quoting trite proverbs. It is as if all the rules about how people do recover from great losses are about other people—you seem to have special exemption from them. We all know that our love was special, and somehow greater than anyone else's has ever been. (There may be little modesty in grief.) But, of course, making competitive comparisons with other people's suffering is always a pointless exercise. Your problems are the worst you have, your grief is the most severe you have, and the dimensions of other people's problems are simply not relevant, because you don't have them. Naturally you feel most sorry for yourself: who else understands you so well as to be able to feel appropriately sorry for you?

A widow may sometimes feel that her children are insensitive or readily forgetful of their dead father because she does not see them grieving as much as she expects, or in the way she expects. Grief has many styles, however, and some children may wish to grieve in privacy. Families are at times uncomfortable about agreeing on common rules and understandings for managing their grief. "They don't seem to mention him now—I must try not to speak of him any more," the widow thinks, while the children may be thinking that since their mother seems to get upset when they mention Dad, they'd better avoid doing so. Unless the family can periodically check out what each member's needs and wishes are, and how they can best be met, there is an increasing likelihood that the worst balance, rather than the best, will be achieved. At all stages of life, families tend to tie themselves into knots as each member unwittingly assumes that he knows what the others want and what they are thinking, and act on those very tenuous assumptions. So air your feelings and share them with the rest of the family; make it quite clear to them what you expect of them and what you hope you can do for them. Some of your requests may meet argument or even refusal. Good. Better an open and understood, clearly agreed disagreement than a silent and smouldering resentment. Let the others help in some way. The gap between being sensibly brave and an obsessively self-denying martyr is not very wide.

If your children are still young, the decision about remarriage is entirely up to you. When they are a little older, from 6 or 7 into the teenage years, they will more necessarily play a part in your decision. They will remember their dead parent well, and they will remain members of the new family for several years. You will want to insure that they can meet your potential spouse in a variety of different circumstances. The help of a qualified counselor may also be helpful. Teenagers often feel strongly on the subject, either in favor of or against remarriage, and can be especially critical of a prospective new parent, particularly one of the same sex. Discussing their ambivalent feelings with them starting at a comparatively early stage will be more beneficial than trying to present them with a *fait accompli.*

It can be difficult to face going out again and resuming your regular activities. It can take more courage to face the little things than the big things in life. Going out shopping for the groceries alone for the first time can become an ordeal. Making the change more complete could help. Try a different store, a different day or time, and go with a friend. When it seems very hard to decide what to do first, maybe it's not very important where you start, so long as you start. Choose a simple task and get started. Once you've begun, it will be far easier to see your priorities, and you will have gained in confidence for having already achieved something.

It has been useful to learn about grief. But some care-givers, clergy, family, and doctors, can depend too heavily on a timetable of grief and recovery, telling the bereaved when they "should" be showing signs of improvement, and when they "should" be "as good as new," or warning them not to grieve "too long."

The social response to widowhood was especially well described by my friend Grace:

> Widows are a stigmatized group in society, primarily because we don't fit the "couple" format, though society doesn't hesitate to load onto us all the responsibilities that normally fall to the couple. Society would like the widow to raise her children (without much support from the community, naturally); to be a law-abiding, well-educated, healthy conspicuous consumer, doing her share of keeping the individual debt level high—and then die off, since by this time she is no longer sexually attractive, and as a housewife she has no marketable skills, and there's no real use for middle-aged or elderly females.
>
> In different ways, people seem to see widows as fair game. My next door neighbor died of cancer. He was a printer and she a bookkeeper. I was horrified when I saw the bills that were presented to her for payment after his death. A dozen portraits were delivered, with a bill—he had supposedly ordered them. Expensive fishing gear was delivered—again with the pretense that he had ordered it shortly before his death. Yet they were a couple who told each other about anything they were buying, and he had been far too ill for many months to have ordered anything. They were very insistent about getting paid for these things. She was so used to being the passive female that she did pay for them.
>
> As a result of this, I was ready for the same sort of thing when my husband died. I got the usual copies of his obituaries encased in plastic, and that sort of thing, but less of the "previously ordered" goods. Instead, the pitch had a more subtle and more expensive theme. A man called and was most insistent that he had to see me. He wanted to include a write-up of my husband in something he touted as a *Who's Who of Scientists*. The printed text alone would cost me $500, and if his picture was to be printed on the opposite page, it would be $750. The next time he called, I agreed to meet him, giving him an address that was the waiting room of my attorney. When he realized where I'd met him, I've never seen such a

furious man. I'm sure he would have paid more than the $750 for the privilege of throttling me! But I had no more trouble with him.

So many women are not aware that they should have an attorney, or feel they can't afford one (the point is, they can't afford not to have one). Even a widow in modest financial circumstances should be able to get some help from Legal Aid.

Social workers and others who have tried to include widowers in their programs for widows seem to find them nonresponsive or even rejecting. They seem to see any contact as the beginning of the "casserole" or "chicken soup" brigade. I've been afraid that I would set off their "rape complex," so I avoid them. So many unmarried men seem to have the feeling that any unmarried woman who makes any kind of approach to them is simply trying to marry them, to get a meal ticket. It's just as illogical as the attitude of the woman who feels that any man who approaches her is merely trying to set her up for sexual exploitation.

In some ways I envy the widowers. They do not experience the great loss of income that so many women do. Also, the fact that they still usually have a work situation that is unchanged gives them a place in their life where they can still be the same as they were before. Their work is the same, the people around them are the same, and more important, at work their identity is not influenced by whether they have a wife or not. Men also do not meet the "five o'clock curtain"; when they leave work, they are welcome in social activities. An extra man at dinner is a plus; an extra woman is a "problem." An unattached man is always eligible. A widow, especially one with dependent children, is viewed as severely socially handicapped. Widows find that they are invited to lunch, or maybe a matinee, but when the man of the house comes home, they are no longer welcome.

The widower is really the forgotten person. The bereaved have always been unsettling, for they remind us of things we would rather not remember; and we have, as a society, ignored them whenever we could get away with it. Recently, the widows have at last made a concerted bid for our attention, and have earned it. The widower, somewhat rarer and even quieter as a species, has very often been ignored. There is a tendency to assume that he must be getting on all right, because we don't hear much from him or about him. That may be so, but it is what used to be assumed about widows, and that proved to be a false assumption. Both groups suffer problems related to the common sexual stereotypes. The macho image of male self-sufficiency can make it especially difficult for the widower to admit to problems or to seek help.

Associations and Groups

One way in which increasing numbers of bereaved people are dealing with the problems inherent in reordering their social lives is through one of the many clubs or groups that have been formed to allow them to share their experiences and help one another, and where they can feel sure of finding people who can accept them and understand their experiences. Studies suggest that widows typically don't seek out formal social service agencies for help unless they were involved with them before being widowed. A range of widow-to-widow programs have been established; the major ones are listed in the Appendix.

Returning to Life

Trying to readjust to a way of life as a single person again will be hard. It is commonplace for the bereaved to complain that life no longer has any meaning. This is temporarily true, for most meanings the individual has invested in life have included the deceased, and a transition is necessary to allow a revision of all these definitions of what makes life purposeful and important. The widow has to begin to separate her purposes and plans from the husband who had been a central part of them. She may gradually proceed from imagining his presence to considering what his wishes would have been, to trusting her own judgments with some reference to his preferences and wishes, until she relies purely on her own resources. One of the marks of lack of effective liberation of the woman in many marriages is the extent to which the widow has difficulty in adjusting to a more independent role.

Good Grief

In good grieving the aim is not the obliteration of memories of the one you have lost. On the contrary, he or she will be tenderly remembered, but without enslaving the living to those memories to the extent that they are prevented from developing further relationships. The widow does not need to forget her husband, but the time comes when she can spend days and even weeks without thinking of him—and when she does, it can be with pleasure and not with pain. One does not stop caring for the dead, but one distills what was essentially important in the relationship and reinterprets it so as to meet the new future. You give up the person— without giving up what he or she meant to you.

Grief is closely related to love. Only a person incapable of loving anyone or anything is likely to be able to avoid grief. Love renders one vulnerable to loss, yet finally it is what enables us to cope with loss.

REFERENCES

BEQUAERT, L. H., *Single Women: Alone and Together*. Boston: Beacon Press, 1976.

PARKES, C. M., *Bereavement*. New York: International Universities Press, 1972.

REES, W. D., and S. G. LUTKINS, "Mortality of Bereavement," *British Medical Journal*, 4 (1976), 13.

YOUNG, M., B. BENJAMIN, and C. WALLIS, "Mortality of Widowers," *Lancet*, 2 (1963), 454.

12

Life
and Living

Whoever teaches people how to die, teaches them how to live.
Montaigne
Death is the greatest kick of all—that's why they save it till last.
Graffito, San Jose State University

Throughout this book we have examined many aspects of the facts of death and how they affect your life today. The trends emerging from the recent rediscovery of the realities of mortality are likely to be of continuing interest.

The first such trend is the development of what has become known as Death Education. Properly, this term refers to the educational recognition of death as one of the dimensions of life, and its reintroduction as a subject worthy of study from the point of view of most of the subjects and disciplines into which the study of life is arbitrarily divided. It is entering a more stable and responsible stage of growth following the pioneering efforts of the 1950s and 1960s and the exhibitionistic excesses and gimmicks of the shallow folk who jumped on the bandwagon in the late 1960s and early 1970s. There is now an organization, the Forum for Death Education, and a journal, coordinating the effects of competent educators in the field (see Appendix). It is clear that teachers dealing with these subjects must be capable of dealing with the emotions and problems that may be aroused or revealed during such teaching, and that they should have a competent consultation service to back them up. Although a great deal still remains to be achieved, there has been a steady improvement in the training of doctors, nurses, and other health professionals, guiding them into the skills necessary for providing better terminal care.

Another development has been the increasing interest in alternative ways of providing terminal care, including home care, hospices, and better liaison care in hospitals. The concept of the *hospice* (Latin, whence the modern term *hospital*) has gained strong, almost excessive support and popularity. The most publicized hospice is Saint Christopher's in London.

Too many people seem to think Saint Christopher's is the only one. Actually, in the Middle Ages, the hospice was a place that welcomed passing pilgrims who were weary and hungry, and perhaps ill. Today, in France, the term has long been used to describe institutions for the elderly, foundling children, and the incurably ill. In Ireland, Mother Mary Aikenhead, who founded the Irish Sisters of Charity, also set up a hospice in Dublin, at Harold's Cross, which had a particular interest in caring for the dying. Saint Joseph's Hospice in Hackney, London, was founded in 1905; its sisters were providing home care even earlier. Other early hospices included the Hostel of God, Saint Luke's, and St. Columba's of England, and the House of Calvary and the Homes of the Dominican Sisters of Saint Rose of Lima in the United States. There are now functioning more than thirty hospices and similar centers of care, and there are over twenty more in various stages of planning and building. The international Work Group on Death, Dying and Bereavement (see Appendix) has formed to link clinicians with educators and researchers in this important area.

St. Christopher's is therefore part of a long tradition in caring for the sick and dying. It is a fine and inspiring institution, though real enough to deserve neither the excessive praise it often receives (as if the visitors, too, received the euphoria-producing elixirs that benefit the patients) nor the air of smug arrogance some hospice workers present elsewhere. The earthy realism of the Saint Christopher's staff and most others involved in terminal care in other settings is very different from the sanctimonious self-satisfaction of the few.

It is clear that hospice care is generally of high quality, and it has taught more orthodox hospitals a great deal about how they could improve their standards. Several studies comparing hospice care with ordinary hospital care have shown that hospice patients remain more mobile, suffering less severe pain and anxiety, and that their families show less anxiety and fewer physical symptoms and are able to spend more time with the patient and far more time talking to staff, other patients, and other visitors. Patients' families are more likely to be able to help care for the patient and to get to know the doctors involved.

There is much we can learn from the hospices, but they will not and should not become the predominant way in which we care for the dying. Such care is never likely to become available for all patients, and the rest would not be much helped if hospital staff and general practitioners were able to opt out of their duty to provide good terminal care for all, wherever they are, by simply leaving it to the "death doctors" who work in the special "death hospitals." Death belongs to all of us, and the care of the dying is a responsibility that is not limited to a few special people or places. There is room, certainly, for those of us who have made a special study of the subject, who have come to be *clinical thanatologists*, to advise on the management of special difficulties. There is still a function to fulfill in aiding the general return toward a more natural management of death, a terminal equivalent of natural childbirth, with a reciprocal function to that of a midwife, as *accoucheurs de mort*.

Alternative ways of providing care are still being explored and developed. Home care teams have been operating in New Haven, Connecticut, and in association with Saint Christopher's Hospice and Saint Joseph's Hospice in Britain. At Saint Luke's Hospital in New York and the Royal Free Hospital in London, groups of hospital staff function as multidisciplinary symptom-control teams which can also deal with psychosocial problems and serve as resources within the general teaching hospital.

This book has raised a great many questions and answered some of them. This is in the nature of living, and in the nature of philosophy. It is valuable to be able to discern the questions, even if we cannot find clear answers to all of them. We certainly should not pretend that there are definite and specific answers for all the questions; anyone who offers you such glib answers is exceeding his mandate and deceiving you, or himself, or both. Perhaps you have been able to find more personal answers, valid and true for you, to some of the questions. In this attempt, through considering the End, we may have been seeking some facts of life and the nature of reality—both universal and personal reality. The lack of answers need not frustrate us—perhaps reality is the questions rather than the answers.

Meeting with the dying, we have much to learn: respect for one another and for the human spirit, courage, and the capacity to accept, to endure, and to love.

For everything there is a season, and a time to every purpose under heaven:
a time to be born, and a time to die;
a time to plant, and a time to pluck up what is planted;
a time to kill, and a time to heal;
a time to break down, and a time to build up;
a time to weep, and a time to laugh;
a time to mourn, and a time to dance;
a time to cast away stones, and a time to gather stones together;
a time to embrace, and a time to refrain from embracing;
a time to seek, and a time to lose;
a time to keep, and a time to cast away;
a time to rend, and a time to sew;
a time to keep silence, and a time to speak;
a time to love, and a time to hate;
a time for war, and a time for peace.

Ecclesiastes 3:1–8

Appendix

RESOURCES

Widow-to-Widow Projects

Arising from the work of Dr. Phyllis Silverman and Dr. Gerald Caplan at Harvard University in 1967, there are now many widow-to-widow projects across the United States. For example:

Connecticut Council—Widows, Widowers Associated
60 Lorraine Street
Hartford, Connecticut 06105
(Other chapters in Bridgeport, Danbury, New Haven, Norwalk, and Waterbury)

Family Service of Westchester, Inc.
(Widow and Widower Club)
470 Mamaroneck Avenue
White Plains, New York 10605

Widows' Consultation Center
136 East 57th Street
New York, New York 10022

Widow-to-Widow Program
Needham Community Council
51 Lincoln Street
Needham, Massachusetts 02192

Widowed to Widowed Program of San Diego
6655 Alvarado Road
San Diego, California 92120

Religious Groups

Fellowship of Christian Widows
1439 Almeria Drive
Hayward, California 94544

Jewish Widows and Widowers
Beth El Temple Center
2 Concord Avenue
Belmont, Massachusetts 02178

NAIM Conference
(More than thirty chapters)
109 North Dearborn Street
Chicago, Illinois 60602
Also:
2021 North 60th Street
Milwaukee, Wisconsin 53208

THEOS Foundation
(Twenty-one chapters throughout the
U.S. and Canada)
11609 Frankstown Road
Pittsburgh, Pennsylvania 15235

Widow and Widower Outreach Program
Jewish Family Service Agency
1600 Scott Street
San Francisco, California 94115

In Great Britain, the major group dealing with widowhood is:

CRUSE
Cruse House
126 Sheen Road
Richmond, Surrey TW9 1UR
United Kingdom
(Phone 01-940-4818)

Other Relevant Organizations

Big Brothers/Big Sisters of America
220 Suburban Station Building
Philadelphia, Pennsylvania 19103

(Over 235 local agencies whose volunteers can help boys who have no father or girls who have no mother)

Jewish Big Brother Association
17 Franklin Street
Boston, Massachusetts 02110
(Also in Baltimore, Cleveland,
Los Angeles, and New York)

Parents Without Partners
7910 Woodmont Avenue
Washington, D.C. 20014
(Over 600 local chapters deal with the
welfare of single parents and their
children)

*National Foundation for Sudden Infant
Death*
1501 Broadway
New York, New York 10036
(Most local chapters offer counseling
services)

*The Society of Compassionate
Friends*
Post Office Box 3247
Hialeah, Florida 33013
(An organization of bereaved parents)

Euthanasia Educational Council
250 West 57th Street
New York, New York 10019

American Cancer Society
219 East 42nd Street
New York, New York 10017
(Phone 212-867-3700)

Ars Moriendi
7301 Huron Lane
Philadelphia, Pennsylvania 19119
(An interdisciplinary group that has
pioneered in educational and practical
work relating to death and terminal
care)

Make Today Count
218 South Sixth Street
Burlington, Iowa 52601
(Phone 319-754-8977)
(A self-help group, started by Orville
Kelly, for the terminally ill and their
families, developing chapters across
the country)

American Association of Suicidology
Department of Health
2151 Berkeley Way
Berkeley, California 94704

National Save-A-Life League
20 West 43rd Street, Suite 706
New York, New York 10036

*International Association for Suicide
Prevention*
2521 West Pico Boulevard
Los Angeles, California 90006

*Continental Association of Funeral and
Memorial Societies*
1828 L Street, N.W., Suite 1100
Washington, D.C. 20036

*The National Funeral Directors
Association*
135 Wells Street
Milwaukee, Wisconsin 53203

National Selected Morticians
1616 Central Street
Evanston, Illinois 60201

American Cemetery Association
250 East Broad Street
Columbus, Ohio 43215

Associated Funeral Director's Service
7405 Manchester Boulevard
St. Louis, Missouri 63143

*National Catholic Cemetery
Conference*
710 North River Road
Des Plaines, Illinois 60016

National Association of Cemeteries
1911 North Forest Meyer Drive, Suite
409
Arlington, Virginia 22209

*National Foundation of Funeral
Services*
1600-1628 Central Street
Evanston, Illinois 60201

*National Funeral Directors and
Morticians*
734 West 79th Street
Chicago, Illinois 60620

Guild of American Funeral Directors
30112 Silver Spur Boulevard
San Juan Capistrano, California 92675

Cremation Association of America
1620 West Belmont Avenue
Fresno, California 93701

Principal Hospices

Saint Christopher's Hospice
51-53 Lawrie Park Road
Sydenham, London SE26 6DZ
United Kingdom

Saint Joseph's Hospice
Mare Street
Hackney, London E8 4SA
United Kingdom

Saint Luke's Nursing Home
Little Common Lane, off Abbey Lane
Sheffield S11 9HE
United Kingdom

HOSPICE, Inc.
765 Prospect Street
New Haven, Connecticut 06511
(Phone 203-787-5779)

Hospice of Marin
Kentfield, California 94904
(Phone 415-457-1015)

Pain Clinics
(specializing in pain control)

Pain Study Group
New York University Medical and
Dental Center
550 First Avenue
New York, New York 10016
(Phone 212-679-3200, ext. 3370)

Pain Treatment Center
Johns Hopkins School of Medicine
Baltimore, Maryland 21205
(Phone 301-955-6405)

Pain Consultation Center
Mount Sinai Medical Center
4300 Alton Road
Miami, Florida 33140
(Phone 305-674-2070)

Pain Treatment Center
Scripps Clinic and Research Foundation
La Jolla, California 92037
(Phone 714-459-2390)

Pain and Health Rehabilitation Center
Route #2
La Crosse, Wisconsin 54601
(Phone 608-784-3420)

Nerve Block and Pain Studies Center
University of Virginia

Charlottesville, Virginia 22903
(Phone 804-924-5581)

The two regional headquarters of the
International Association for the Study
of Pain are:

Eastern U.S.A. Regional Chapter
550 First Avenue
New York, New York 10016

Western U.S.A. Regional Chapter
Department of Anesthesiology, RN-10
University of Washington Medical
School
Seattle, Washington 98195

Death Education

*National Institute for the Seriously Ill
and Dying*
Henry Avenue & Abbottsford Road
Philadelphia, Pennsylvania 19129
(Phone 215-842-2300)

*Forum for Death Education and
Counseling*
Post Office Box 1226
Arlington, Virginia 22210
(A nonprofit organization formed in
1975 to promote better death education
and counseling; publishes a newsletter)

RECOMMENDED READING

Having read and reviewed over 800 books in the area of death, dying, and bereavement, I can recommend the following as the most valuable for the general reader. The many really bad books on the subject have been omitted, as have those of more specialized and professional interest.

Chapter 1   The End: An Introduction

Vital Signs: The Way We Die in America, by John Langone. Boston: Little, Brown, 1974. 363 pp.
 Expert journalism, with interviews and apt quotations from a variety of workers in the field, and a minimum of theorizing and preaching.

The Meaning of Death, ed. Herman Feifel. New York: McGraw-Hill, 1959, 350 pp.
 A classic book of studies from the point of view of philosophy, literature, religion, and art, as well as clinical and experimental studies. Includes contributions from Jung, Tillich, and Marcuse.

New Meanings of Death, ed. Herman Feifel. New York: McGraw-Hill, 1977. 365 pp.
 A collection of key essays on aspects of death in contemporary society.

Deaths of Man, by Edwin Shneidman. New York: Quadrangle Books, 1973. 240 pp.
 An eloquent and highly literate study of man's relationship to death.

Twentieth Century Book of the Dead, by Gil Elliot. Baltimore: Penguin Books, 1973. 242 pp.
 A disturbing new necrology, dealing with this century's most populous nation—the nation of the dead—the 100 million man-made deaths of the twentieth century.

Chapter 2   Death Is a Four-Letter Word

The Psychology of Death, by Robert Kastenbaum and Ruth Aisenberg. New York: Springer Publishing Co., 1972. 500 pp.
 The most thorough review of the psychology of death, covering much of the published research in a literate and interesting style.

Man's Concern with Death, by Arnold Toynbee et al. New York: McGraw-Hill, 1969. 280 pp.
 A persisting classic, including the brilliant contributions of Toynbee and Keith Mant on definitions of death.

Helplessness: On Depression, Development, and Death, by Martin Seligman. San Francisco: W. H. Freeman, 1975. 250 pp.
 The dangers of learning helplessness and hopelessness, and their part in bringing about an understanding of anxiety and depression, sudden death, and the causes and effects of fatal illnesses.

Chapter 3   What Is It Like to Die?

On Death and Dying, by Elisabeth Kübler-Ross. New York: Macmillan, 1969. 250 pp.

Probably the best-known and most influential book in the genre. Deals warmly with the experiences of the dying and those who work with them.

Passing On: The Social Organization of Dying, by David Sudnow. Englewood Cliffs, N.J.: Prentice-Hall, Inc., 1967. 176 pp.

Brilliant sociological study of how death occurs and how it is socially managed by hospital staff. Fascinating reading.

On Dying and Denying, by Avery Weisman. New York: Behavioral Publications, 1972. 250 pp.

A work of great wisdom and sophistication, concerning the complexities of denial. A valuable corrective to those who oversimplify the situation.

Chapters 4 and 5   Living Mortal; Living Your Own Death

Death and Western Thought, by Jacques Choron. New York: Collier, 1963. 320 pp.

Readable and highly competent survey of philosophical approaches to death, from pre-Socratic to present-day views.

Death and Modern Man, by Jacques Choron. New York: Collier, 164. 228 pp.

A wide-ranging view concerning fear of death, immortality, and the meaning of death.

Western Attitudes Toward Death, by Philippe Aries. Baltimore: Johns Hopkins University Press, 1974. 111 pp.

The best historical perspective on how our attitudes toward death have developed.

The Book: On the Taboo Against Knowing Who You Are, by Alan Watts. New York: Vintage Books, 1972. 146 pp.

Brilliantly lucid and witty book, offering a coherent manner of coming to terms with life and death.

Jewish Reflections on Death, ed. Jack Riemer. New York: Schocken Books, 1974. 184 pp.

An eloquent series of essays on the Jewish experience of death, suffering, and solace, traditional and modern.

Living with Cancer, by Ernest Rosenbaum. New York: Praeger, 1975. 214 pp.

A positive and humane description of living with terminal illness, based on eleven detailed case histories of very different people with cancer.

Death and Ethnicity: A Psycho-Cultural Study, by Richard Kalish and David

Reynolds. Los Angeles: University of Southern California Press, 1976. 224 pp.

The most thorough and carefully performed study of attitudes toward death among contemporary American blacks and Japanese-, Mexican-, and Anglo-Americans.

Chapter 6   Living with the Dying

A Very Easy Death, by Simone de Beauvoir. New York: Putnam's, 1966. 106 pp.
  Unforgettable account of the far-from-easy death of de Beauvoir's mother.

Awareness of Dying, by Barney Glaser and Anselm Strauss. Chicago: Aldine, 1968. 305 pp.

Time for Dying, by Barney Glaser and Anselm Strauss. Chicago: Aldine, 1968. 270 pp.
  Both of the above are detailed sociological studies of death and the way we deal with it.

Life Before Death, by Ann Cartwright, Lisbeth Hockey, and John Anderson. London: Routledge & Kegan Paul, 1973. 280 pp.
  The most thorough and competent sociological study of the last year of life. Who dies? Of what? Where? With what restrictions and symptoms? Needing and getting what help?

Chapter 7   Planning for Death

The American Way of Death, by Jessica Mitford. New York: Fawcett, 1963. 280 pp.
  A justly famous, witty, well-documented, and merciless exposure of the funeral industry. Still far too accurate for comfort.

The Loved One, by Evelyn Waugh. Boston: Little, Brown, 1948. 164 pp.
  Macabre and ferocious novel about funeral customs—also unwholesomely accurate.

Concerning Death: A Practical Guide for the Living, ed. Earl Grollman. Boston: Beacon Press, 1974. 365 pp.
  Thorough but variable in quality; useful in comparing different religious points of view in dealing with death.

The Cost of Dying and What You Can Do About It, by Raymond Arvio. New York: Harper & Row, 1974. 159 pp.
  Soundly practical book by an experienced consumer activist, proposing alternatives to the regular expensive funeral practices, with detailed guidance on forming and running a memorial society.

Chapter 8   Children and Death

By far the best books for helping you talk with your children about death are the following:

Talking About Death: A Dialogue between Parent and Child, by Earl Grollman. Boston: Beacon Press, 1976. 98 pp.
A beautifully written and illustrated discussion to read with children; includes a detailed parents' guide to explaining death and dealing with questions that arise.

Helping Your Child to Understand Death, by Anna Wolf. New York: Child Study Press, 1973. 64 pp.
A highly competent guide in the form of answers to both children's and parents' questions.

The Private Worlds of Dying Children, by Myra Bluebond-Langner. Princeton, N.J.: Princeton University Press, 1978. 250 pp.
The best study of dying children.

Care of the Child Facing Death, ed. Lindy Burton. London & Boston: Routledge & Kegan Paul, 1974. 225 pp.
A useful guide to caring for terminally ill children.

There are a number of books for children that deal with the theme of death and are useful for different age groups. For the preschool child:

The Dead Bird, by Margaret Brown. New York: Young Scott Books, 1958.
A simple and straightforward account of the death of a bird and the way children dealt with this death.

Nana Upstairs and Nana Downstairs, by Tomie de Paoloa. New York: Putnam's, 1973.
A boy's life with his great-grandmother and grandmother, who both die, but live on in his memories.

Why Did He Die? by Audrey Harris. Minneapolis: Lerner Publications, 1965.
A small boy seeks to understand his grandfather's death.

Annie and the Old One, by Miska Miles. Boston: Little, Brown, 1971.
A clear, gentle story in which an Indian girl and her dying grandmother learn the order of nature.

The Tenth Good Thing About Barney, by Judith Viorst. New York: Atheneum, 1971.
Honest and sensitive. When Barney the cat dies, a boy tries to think of ten good things to say about him at his funeral. Deals positively with the boy's feelings and how one copes with sadness.

About Death, by Sara Bonnet. New York: Stein, Walker, 1974.
> Photographs and text for the child and a parallel commentary for the adult. About the death of a pet and a grandfather, funerals and mourning.

Growing Time, by Sandol Warburg. Boston: Houghton Mifflin, 1969.
> How a boy copes with the loss of his dog.

My Grandson Lew, by Charlotte Zolotow. New York: Harper & Row, 1974.
> Lew remembers his dead grandfather, with his mother's help.

For the schoolchild in the middle grades:

Little Men, by Louisa May Alcott. New York: Macmillan, 1963.

Little Women, by Louisa May Alcott. New York: World, 1969.
> Two classic children's books which feature the death of a central character.

Death, by Mog Vall. London: Oxford University Press, 1976.
> Superbly illustrated presentation of many different aspects of death.

With Dad Alone, by Jerrold Beim. New York: Harcourt, Brace, 1954.
> A boy's mother dies, and he has to assume new duties.

Grover, by Vera and Bill Cleaver. Philadelphia: J. B. Lippincott, 1970.
> Grover's dying mother has shot and killed herself, and he is outraged. With difficulty, he begins to face life again.

Anne and the Sand Dobbies, by John Coburn. New York: Seabury Press, 1964. A boy learns the meaning of death after his sister and his dog die.

A Taste of Blackberries, by Doris Smith. New York: Thomas Y. Crowell, 1973.
> An 8-year-old boy's friend dies very suddenly and unexpectedly. The book explores the responses of everyone involved and the ways they cope.

Charlotte's Web, by E. B. White. New York: Harper & Row, 1952.
> A famous animal fantasy, in which the central character dies.

The Mother Tree, by Ruth Whitehead. New York: Seabury Press, 1971.
> A 10-year-old girl's mother dies suddenly. She has to help with the house and care for her questioning 4-year-old sister.

The Summer Before, by Patricia Windsow. New York: Harper & Row, 1973.
> An adolescent girl's reactions to her boyfriend's accidental death.

Life and Death, by H. S. Zim and Sonia Bleeker. New York: William Morrow, 1970.
> A nonfiction book about the customs and procedures regarding death in different cultures.

For the age of 12 and over:

A Death in the Family, by James Agee. New York: Avon, 1959.
> Excellent novel describing a family and a 6-year-old boy and how they respond to the father's sudden death.

I Heard the Owl Call My Name, by Margaret Craven. New York: Doubleday, 1973.

A young missionary with three years to live is sent to a Canadian Indian village.

Death Be Not Proud, by John Gunther. New York: Harper, 1949.

A famous memoir of a 17-year-old boy dying of a brain tumor.

Chapter 9   Euthanasia and the "Living Will"

Ward 402, by Ronald Glasser. New York: Braziller, 1973. 232 pp.

A novel based on the realities of a pediatric leukemia ward, dealing with the difficulties of not always doing everything we can do and the questions of when doctors are giving treatment for the patient and when for themselves.

Death By Choice, by Daniel Maguire. New York: Schocken Books, 1975. 224 pp.

Reasonably thorough review of arguments for and against euthanasia, mainly in terms of the American situation.

Death By Decision: The Medical, Moral, and Legal Dilemmas of Euthanasia, by J. B. Wilson. Philadelphia: Westminster Press, 1975. 208 pp.

Efficient survey of the problems of euthanasia, with suggested practical guidelines.

The Right to Die, by Milton Heifetz and Charles Mangel. New York: Putnam's, 1975. 234 pp.

Vigorous discussion from the point of view of the Living Will and patients' rights. Terse and unstylish, but useful for stimulating discussion.

Freedom to Die: Moral and Legal Aspects of Euthanasia, by Ruth Russell, Rev. ed. New York: Human Sciences Press, 1977. 413 pp.

Very thorough polemic by an earnest advocate of legalization of euthanasia. Good description of the major test cases. Includes a detailed bibliography (though the book is not always reliable in its use of secondary and tertiary sources).

Chapter 10   Suicide

The Bell Jar, by Sylvia Plath. New York: Bantam, 1972. 216 pp.

A highly evocative autobiographical novel of a young girl's suicide attempts.

The Savage God, by A. Alvarez. New York: Bantam, 1974. 170 pp.

A study of attitudes toward suicide throughout history and literature and of the fascination this subject has had for writers.

Suicide: The Gamble with Death, by Gene and David Lester. Englewood Cliffs, N.J.: Prentice-Hall, Inc., 1971. 176 pp.

A very readable review of studies of suicide.

Suicidology: Contemporary Developments, ed. Edwin Shneidman. New York: Grune & Stratton, 1976. 570 pp.
> The best available textbook on the subject.

Chapter 11   Grief, Loss, and Bereavement

A Grief Observed, by C. S. Lewis. Greenwich, Conn.: Seabury Press, 1961. 60 pp.
> Unique, memorable, honest observation of a widower's grief.

Bereavement, by Colin Murray Parkes. Baltimore: Penguin, 1975. 120 pp.
> A study of grief in adult life, its phenomena and consequences.

Death and the Family: The Importance of Mourning, by Lily Pincus. New York: Pantheon, 1974. 278 pp.
> Sensitive and wise account of the author's experiences in marital and family therapy with the "dying family."

Love Must Not Be Wasted, by Isabelle Taves. New York: Thomas Y. Crowell, 1974. 214 pp.

Widow, by Lynn Caine. New York: Bantam, 1975. 182 pp.
> The above are probably the best two of the recent genre of widow books, dealing with the experiences of talented and prosperous ladies who have lost their husbands.

Helping Each Other in Widowhood, ed. Phyllis Silverman, D. Mackenzie, M. Pettipas, and E. Wilson. New York: Human Sciences Publishing Co., 1975. 230 pp.
> Deals with the development of the widow-to-widow programs.

Chapter 12   Life and Living

The Death of Ivan Illych, by Leo Tolstoy. New York: New American Library, 1969. 220 pp.
> Justly famous story of the death of a bourgeois Russian judge and his transcendence.

How Could I Not Be Among You? by Ted Rosenthal. New York: Avon Books, 1975. 93 pp.
> A young poet dying of leukemia produced this very moving series of poems about his experiences.

Gramp, by Mark and Dan Jury. New York: Grossman Publishers, 1976. 152 pp.
> Superbly honest and direct account in photographs and words of a man dying of arteriosclerotic dementia, by a family who made his death an act of love.

Journals

Omega, The Journal of Death and Dying. Baywood Publishing Co., 43 Central Drive, Farmingdale, New York 11735.

Death Education, Pedagogy, Counseling, Care. Hemisphere Publishing Corporation, 1025 Vermont Avenue N.W., Washington, D.C. 20005

Essence, Issues in the Study of Aging, Dying, and Death. Atkinson College Press, 4700 Keele Street, Downsview, Ontario, Canada.

Index

Acceptance stage of dying, 43
Accidents, 10, 12
Active euthanasia, 189
Admission to hospital, 84–85
Afterlife (*see* Immortality)
Age distribution of deaths, 12–13
Aikenhead, Mary, 258
Aisenberg, R., 22, 62, 73, 74–75, 183
Aitken-Swan, J., 38, 92, 95
Aldrich, C., 74
Alsop, Stewart, 43
American Way of Death, The (Mitford), 125
Anger stages of dying, 40–41
Aries, Philippe, 122
Ars Moriendi, 7
Artificial insemination, 27
Artificial support systems, 19, 21–22, 187, 189, 193, 196, 200
Automobiles, 154–55
Autopsy, 124–25
Awareness, 102–3
Azad, Abul Kalam, 43

Bank accounts, 150
Bargaining stage of dying, 42
Becker, Ernest, 64
Being, 29
Benemortasia (*see* Euthanasia)
Bennett, A. E., 38
Bereavement, 183, 222–30
BID ("Brought In Dead"), 14–17

Bioemporiums, 26–27
Biosocial immortality, 63
Birth certificate, 153
Blacks, 71, 72–74, 139, 142
Blood transfusion, 26–27
Bluebond-Langner, Myra, 175–76, 183–84
Body, getting rid of, 48–49
Body donation, 117–22, 142
Bowlby, John, 177
Brain death, 18–22, 24
Burial:
    premature, 17–18
    (*see also* Funerals)

California Natural Death Act, 195–98
Camus, Albert, 203
Cancer, 11–12, 13, 37–39, 43, 74–75, 82–83, 92–93, 115
"Cardiac Arrest," 14–15, 17–20, 21, 32, 35
Cartwright, Ann, 45–46
Caskets, 132–33
Cassem, Ned, 115
Causes of death, 10–12, 74–76, 124–25
Cemeteries, 134–35
Children:
    death and, 170–83
    dying, 175–76, 183–85, 239–40
    visits to dying, 110–11
"Christian Affirmation of Life," 198–99
Civil service benefits, 154
Cleveland, S. E., 35

Closed awareness, 102
Cocteau, Jean, 76
Codicil, 147
Coffins, 132–33
Colostomy, 81, 82–83
"Committee of the person," 190–92
Concealment trolley, 48–49
Continuance, 65–66
Control, 79–80
Corneal transplants, 117–20
Coroners, 124–25
Counseling, suicide and, 213, 215–16
Creative immortality, 63
Cremation, 135–37, 139
Crooks, 155
Crying, 96–97, 111–12
Cryonics, 22–27
Cultural phenomenon of death, 5–8
Cure, 79–80
Curtesy, right of, 147

Death agony, 47
Death certificates, 140–41, 152, 153
Death education, 257, 264
Death fantasies, 22–27
Death rates, 12–14, 74–75
Death taxes, 143–44, 147
Definitions of death, 17–22, 32–35
    brain death, 18–22, 24
    ethics, 22
    Lazarus syndrome, 32–35
    metabolism, 18
    molecular death, 18–20
    rigor mortis, 17, 18
    somatic death, 18–19
Delusions, 34–35, 246
Denial stage of dying, 31, 36–40, 62
Depression:
    stage of dying, 42–43
    suicide and, 210–14
Dickinson, Emily, 75–76
Diggory, J. C., 61
Disasters, 3, 240
Diseases, 10–12
Dlin, B. M., 74
DOA ("Dead On Arrival"), 14–17
Documents limiting treatment, 192–201
Dower, right of, 147
"Drew Criterion," 192
Drugs, 21, 46–47, 85–86
Druss, R. C., 35

Easson, E. C., 38, 92, 95
Ego, 65, 66
Embalming, 123, 129–31, 132, 139
Engel, George, 75
Estate tax, 148–49
Ethics, 22
Ethnic influences on death, 71–74

Euripides, 55
Euthanasia, 70, 186–201
    active, 189
    California Natural Death Act, 195–98
    "Christian Affirmation of Life," 198–99
    "Committee of the Person," 190–92
    documents for, 192–201
    informed dissent and, 198–201
    law and, 188–90
    "Living Will," 194–201
    passive, 189
    therapeutic frenzy, 186–87, 201
Executors, 144, 145, 148
Experiential transcendence, 63–65

Family Information Register and Planning
    Guide, 155–69
Fantasies, 22–27
Fear of death, 57, 58–62, 64–65, 69–71, 73,
    174, 176–77
Feldman, F., 112–13
Financial preplanning for death, 141–69
    automobiles, 154–55
    bank accounts, 150
    civil service benefits, 154
    estate tax, 148–49
    executors, 148
    Family Information Register and
        Planning Guide, 155–69
    life insurance, 149–50
    safe-deposit boxes, 151
    Social Security benefits, 151–52
    swindlers and crooks, 155
    trusts, 149
    veterans' benefits, 152–54
    wills, 142–48
Fischer, H. K., 74
Franco, Francisco, 16
Frankl, Viktor, 58
Frederick, L. C., 130
Freud, Sigmund, 28–29
Friesen, S. R., 92, 95
Funerals, 122–40
    caskets, 132–33
    cemeteries, 134–35
    children and, 181
    coroners, 124–25
    cremation, 135–37, 139
    embalming, 123, 129–31, 132, 139
    preplanning, 138–40
    vaults, 134
    viewing, 131–32
Furman, E., 183

Gaylin, Willard, 26, 27
Gilbertsen, V. A., 92
Glaser, Barney, 102
Goldscheider, Calvin, 13

Gordon, D. C., 66
Gould, M., 85
Grief, 177, 180, 181–82, 222–56
Ground burial (*see* Funerals)
Guilt, 43, 178–79

Hallucinations, 34–35, 246
Harter, C. L., 73
Hartman, Alby, 188
Heart disease, 11–15, 17–20, 21, 32, 35,
    49–53, 81, 83
Hedonism, 55
Hegel, Georg, 7
Heim, A., 33
Hinton, J. M., 45, 92, 113
Hope, 75–76, 110
Hospices, 258–59, 263
Hospital admission, 84–85

Iker, H. P., 75
Ileostomy, 82–83
Immortality, 22–27, 29, 55–76
    attitudes toward, 62–65
    biosocial, 63
    continuance, 65–66
    creative, 63
    ethnic influences, 71–74
    experiential transcendence, 63–65
    fear of death, 58–62, 64–65, 69–71
    life, meanings of, 57–58
    little death, 68–69
    natural, 63
    political functions of, 57
    psychological factors, 74–76
    religious, 63
    time, 66–68
Infant mortality, 13
Informed dissent, 198–201
Insurance, 149–50
Intestate, 142–43, 147
In the Matter of Karen Quinlan (1976),
    191–96

Japanese-Americans, 71, 139, 142
Johnson, D. C., 35
Jones, E., 29
Jung, C. G., 33

Kalish, R., 71, 73, 91–92, 139, 142
Kansas, definition of death in, 19
Kastenbaum, R., 22, 73, 74–75, 171, 183
Kelly, W. H., 92, 95
Kidney transplants, 120
Kline, N. S., 92, 95
Koller, R., 83
Kornfield, D. S., 35
Kübler-Ross, E., 35–44

La Rochefoucauld, François de, 9
Lazarus syndrome, 32–35
Lerner, Monroe, 17
Lester, D., 204
Lester, G., 204
Lewis, C. S., 230–33
Lief, H. I., 83
Life, meanings of, 57–58
Life expectancy, 9–10, 12
Life insurance, 149–50
Listening, 103–4
Little death, 68–69
"Living Will," 194–201
Longevity, 9–10
Luttans, S. G., 234

McIntosh, J., 39
Maguire, Daniel C., 12
Margolis, O. S., 131
Marriage certificates, 152, 153
Maryland, definition of death in, 19
Mass death, 2, 3
Mastectomy, 81, 82
Mausoleums, 135
Means, M. H., 62
Media, 3
Megadeath, 2, 3
Mendloff, E., 74
Menninger, K., 207
Mercy killing, 188
Metabolism, 18
Mexican-Americans, 71, 139, 142
Mitford, J., 123, 125
Molecular death, 18–20
Mortality rates, 12–14, 74–75
Morticians, 129–33
Mount, B. M., 93
Mourning, 176–77, 181–82, 234–37
Mutual pretense, 102–3

Nagy, Maria, 173–75
Natural immortality, 63
Neale, Robert, 29–30
Necrophobia, 6
Negative euthanasia, 189
Neomorts, 26
Nietzsche, Friedrich, 58
Nkoane, S. K., 72
Non-being, 29
Nuclear weapons, 3, 63–64

Oden, T. C., 192
Oken, D., 93
Open awareness, 103
Organ donation, 22, 27, 117–22, 142
Organ transplants, 22, 26–27
Orgasm, 65, 68–69
Ostomy clubs, 83

Pain clinics, 264
Parents, death of, 172–73, 179–80, 182
Parkes, C. M., 233
Pascal, Blaise, 62–63
Passive euthanasia, 189
Pathological grief, 237–39
"Patient's Bill of Rights, A," 87–89
Patients' rights, 86–91
Peak experiences, 68
Pessimism, 55
Pets, death of, 171, 180
Piaget, J., 171
Pius XII, Pope, 189
Place of death, 17–22
Pneumonia, 10–11, 13
Political functions of immortality, 57
Pollution, 12
Post, Emily, 236
Post-mortem examination, 124
Premature burial, 17–18
Probate, 146
Psychological factors and death, 74–76

Radiotherapy, 37
Raether, H. C., 131, 139
Rank, Otto, 170
Rees, W. D., 45, 234
Reich, Wilhelm, 68
Reincarnation, 56
Religious beliefs, 63, 113–14, 262
Resuscitation, 14–17, 19, 32–35, 187, 192
Reynolds, David, 71, 73, 139, 142
Right to die, 192–93
Rigor mortis, 17, 18
Rilke, Rainer Maria, 45
Ritual (see Mourning)
Rothman, D. Z., 61

Safe-deposit boxes, 151
Schmale, A. H., 75
Self-deliveration (see Euthanasia)
Self-image, 206, 208
Seligman, M., 75, 183
Seneca, 59
Sex, 4–5, 80–84, 247
Shneidman, E. S., 9, 13, 17, 98, 203–6, 219
Simpson, M. A., 45
Slater, R. C., 131
Social class, 13–16
Social Security benefits, 151–52
Society, death-denying, 5, 7
Somatic death, 18–19

Stages of dying, 35–45
Strauss, Anselm, 102, 149
Strubb, C. G., 130
Sudnow, David, 14
Suicide, 58, 175, 179, 202–20
    depression, 210–14
    help for, 208–10, 214–19
    statistics, 202–8
    survivor-victims, 219–20
Support systems, artificial, 19, 21–22, 187,
    189, 193, 196, 200
Suspected awareness, 102
"Suspended Respiration," 14, 17–20
Swanson, W. C., 73
Swindlers, 155

Taboos, 4
Terminal illness, 35–40, 45–53, 70, 73
Thanatology, 5–6, 114–15
Therapy, 37–38, 99
Thomas, Lewis, 12
Tillich, Paul, 66
Time, 66–68
Treatment, responsibility for, 85–86
Trombley, Lauren, 97
Trumble, G. Y., 83
Trusts, 149
Truth telling, 91–99, 108–10

Unamuno, Miguel de, 57
Undertakers, 122–23
Untreated symptoms, 45–47

Vaults, 134
Veterans' benefits, 152–54
Viewing, 131–32
Voluntary Euthanasia Bill, 190

Waldrop, W., 85
Wangensteen, O. H., 92
Warfare, 2–3
War Orphans' and Widows' Educational
    Assistance Act, 153
Watts, Alan, 65–66
Weeping, 96–97, 111–12
Weisman, A., 37, 43, 98, 102
Widow-to-widow projects, 261
Wills, 142–48

Young, M., 234